POP HITS
FOR CLASSICAL GUITAR

Arranged by Jeff Jacobson, except "Game of Thrones" arranged by Pete Billmann
Recorded by Doug Boduch

To access audio visit:
www.halleonard.com/mylibrary

Enter Code
7787-5516-3067-9083

ISBN 978-1-5400-6291-8

Visit Hal Leonard Online at
www.halleonard.com

Contact us:
Hal Leonard
7777 West Bluemound Road
Milwaukee, WI 53213
Email: info@halleonard.com

In Europe, contact:
Hal Leonard Europe Limited
42 Wigmore Street
Marylebone, London, W1U 2RN
Email: info@halleonardeurope.com

In Australia, contact:
Hal Leonard Australia Pty. Ltd.
4 Lentara Court
Cheltenham, Victoria, 3192 Australia
Email: info@halleonard.com.au

All About That Bass

Words and Music by Kevin Kadish and Meghan Trainor

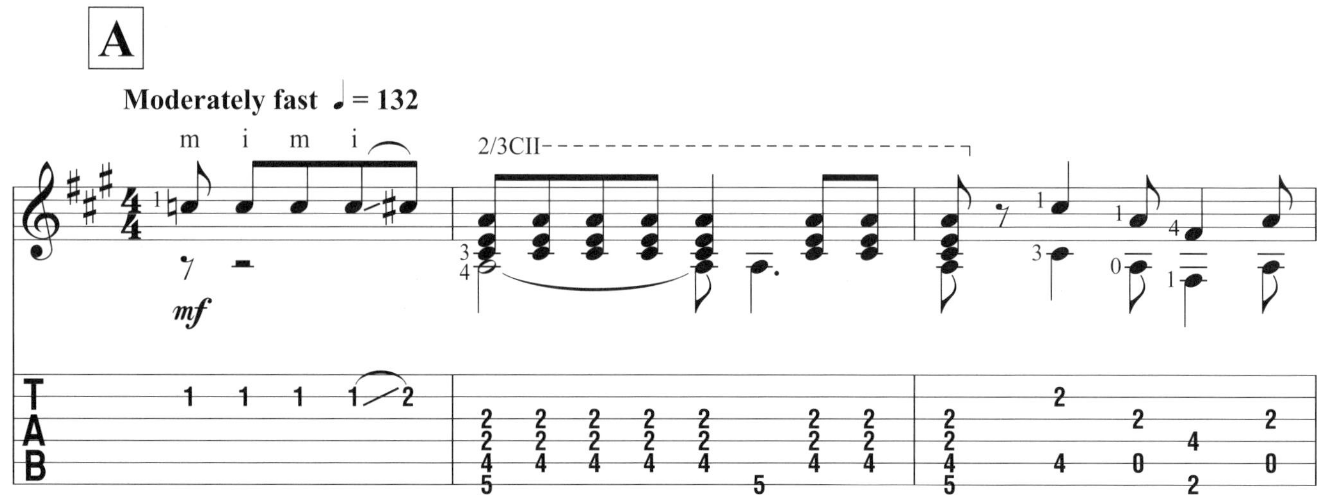

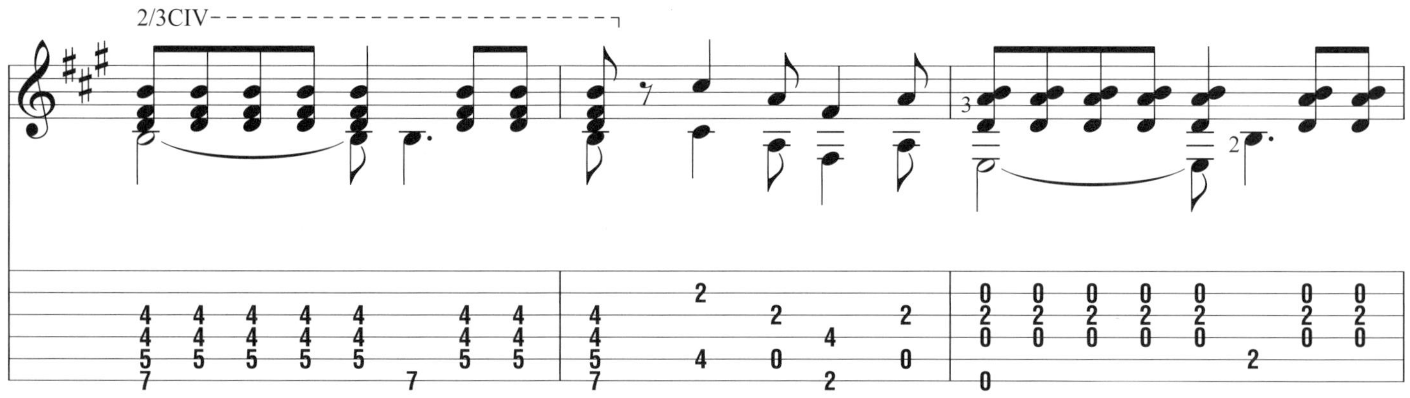

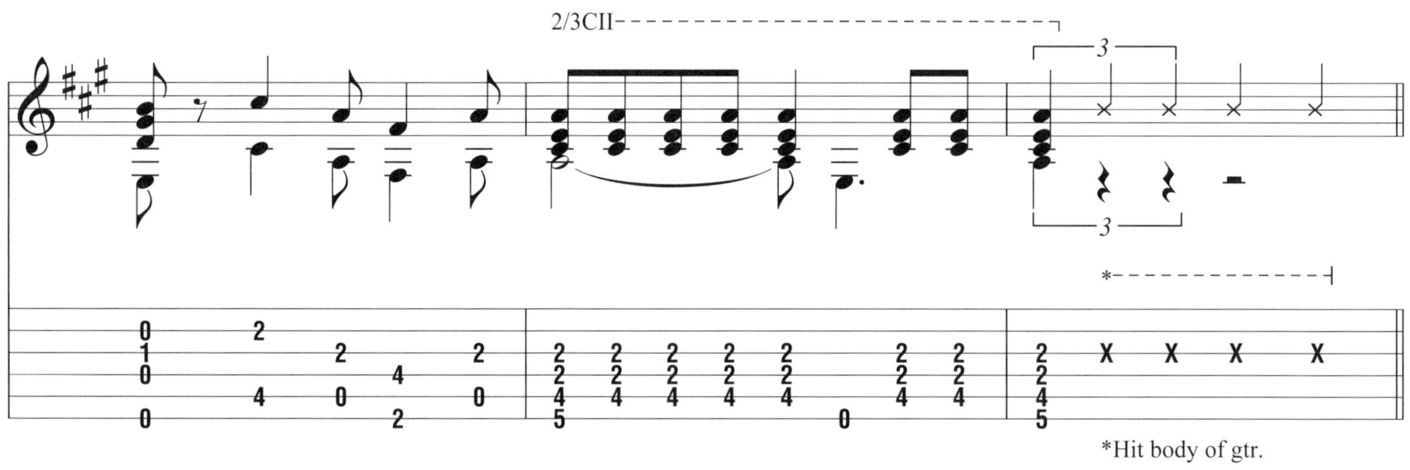

B

2/3CII

2/3CIV

C

1/2CII

1/2CII

2/3CII

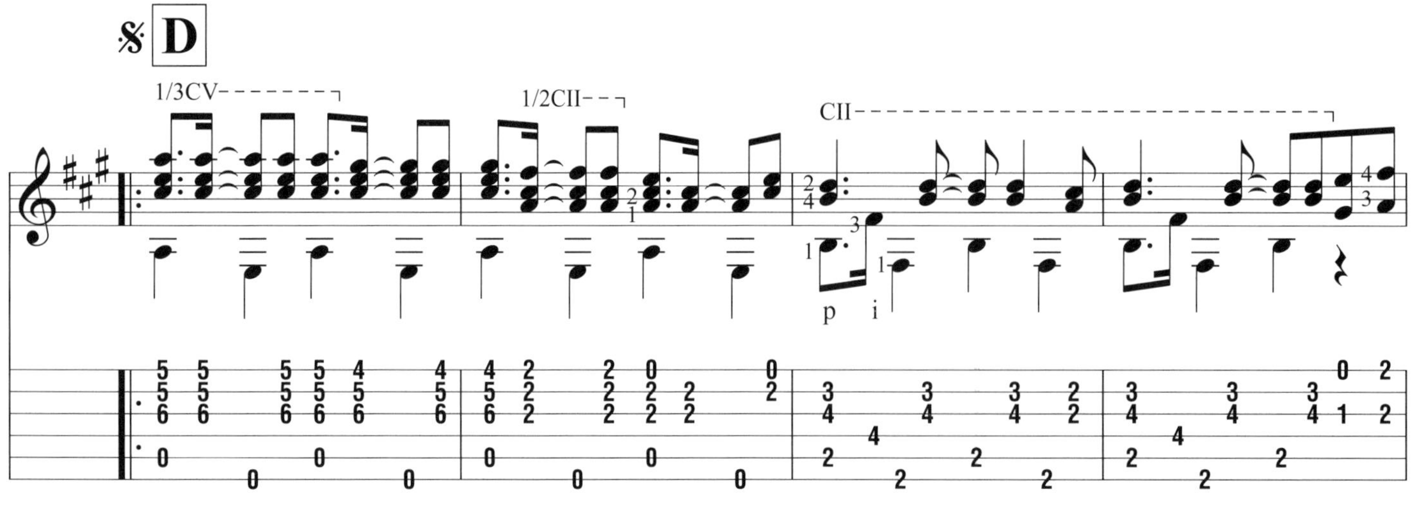
D
1/3CV
1/2CII
CII
p
i

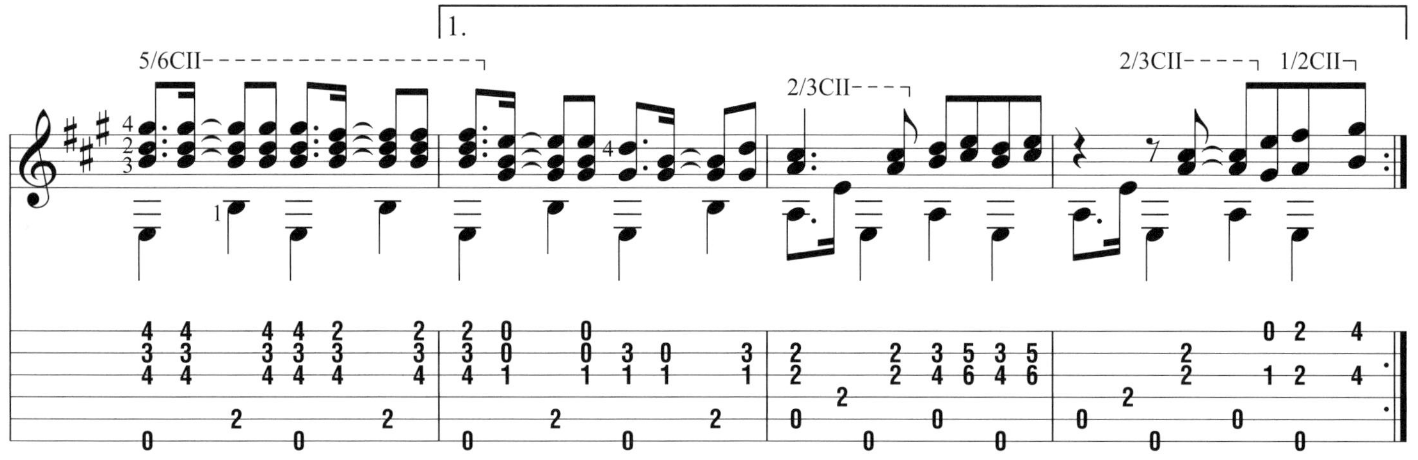
1.
5/6CII
2/3CII
2/3CII
1/2CII

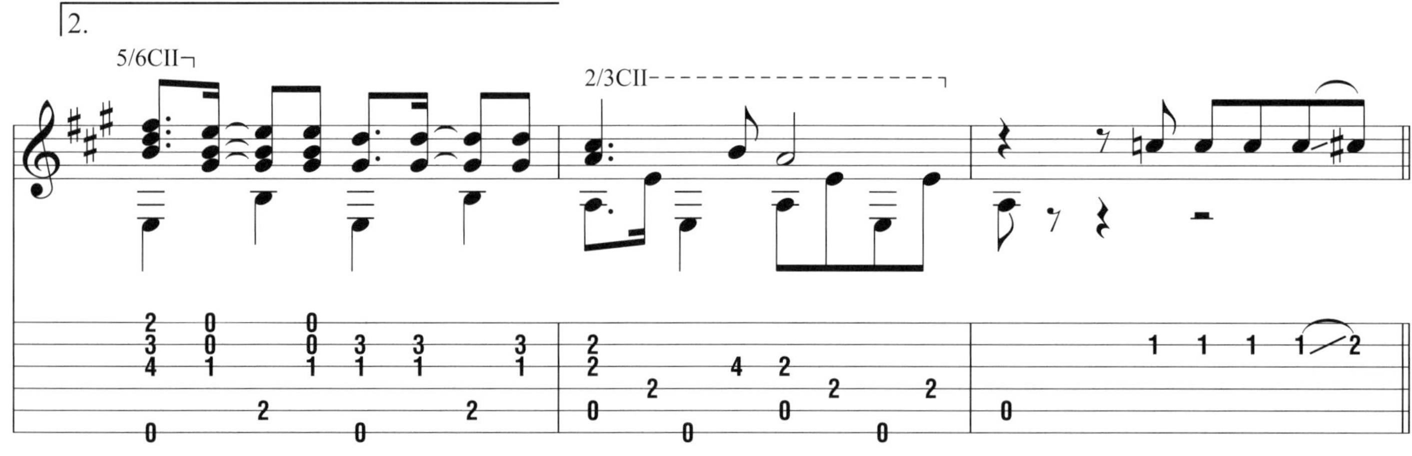
2.
5/6CII
2/3CII

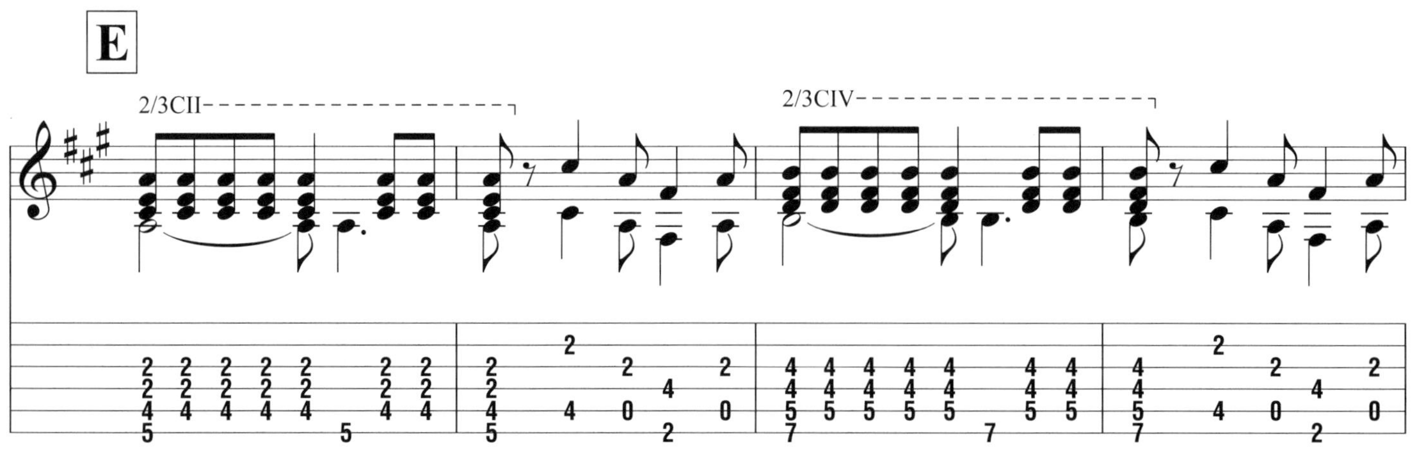
E
2/3CII
2/3CIV

To Coda

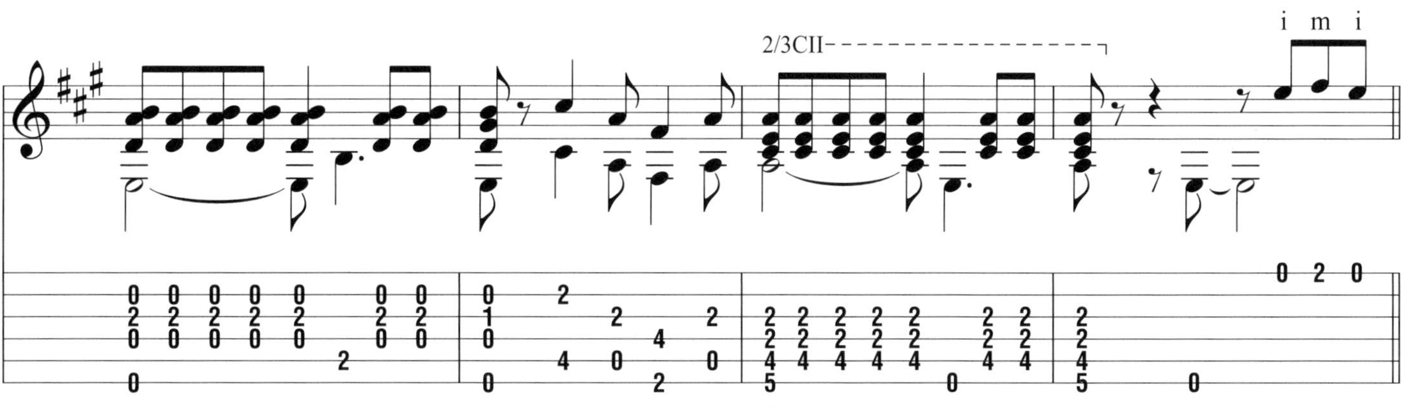
2/3CII
i m i

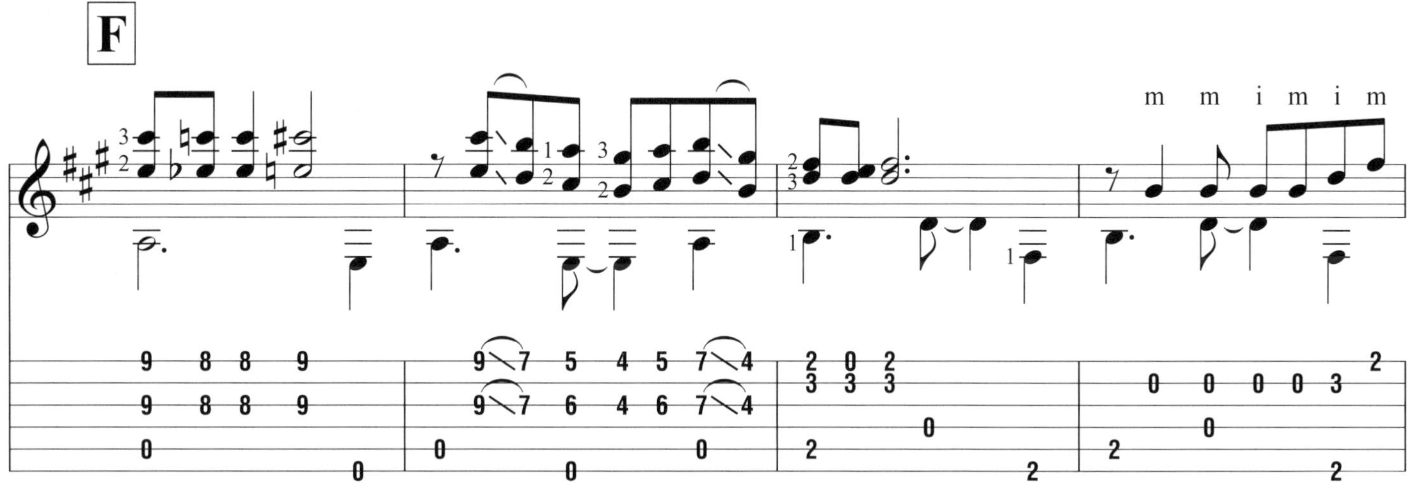
F
m m i m i m

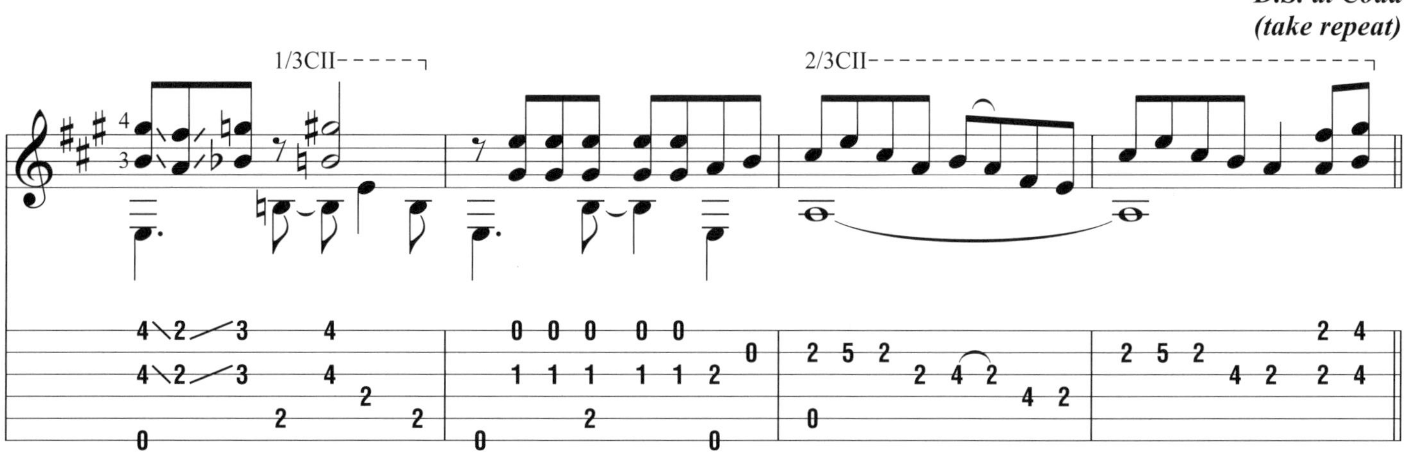
D.S. al Coda
(take repeat)
1/3CII
2/3CII

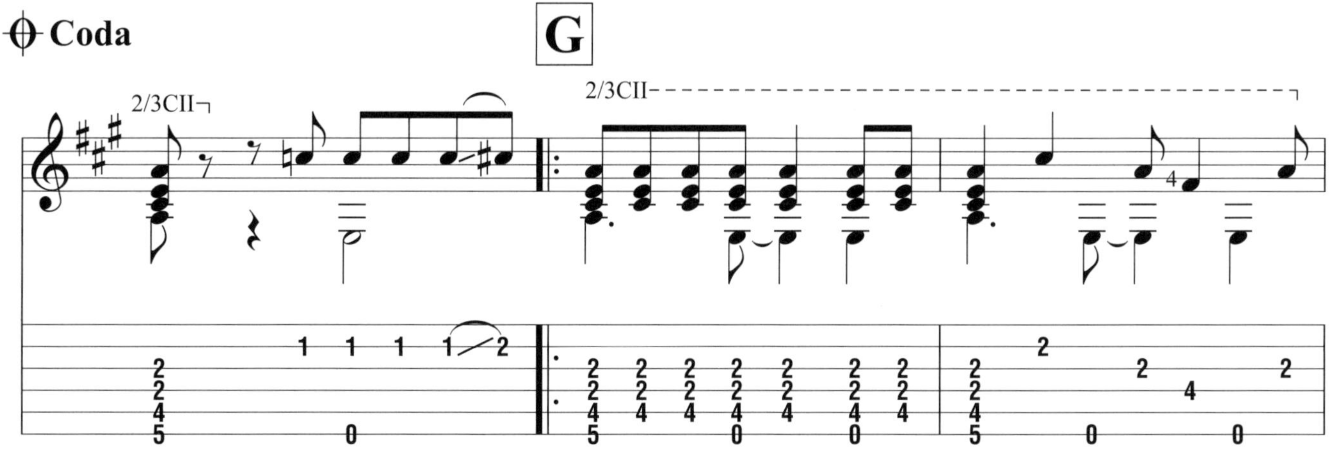
Coda
G
2/3CII
2/3CII

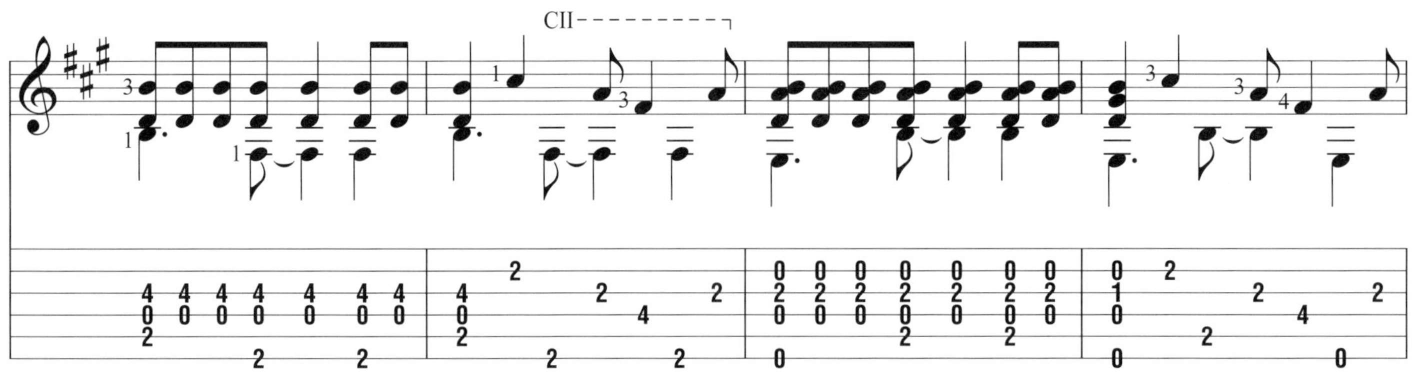

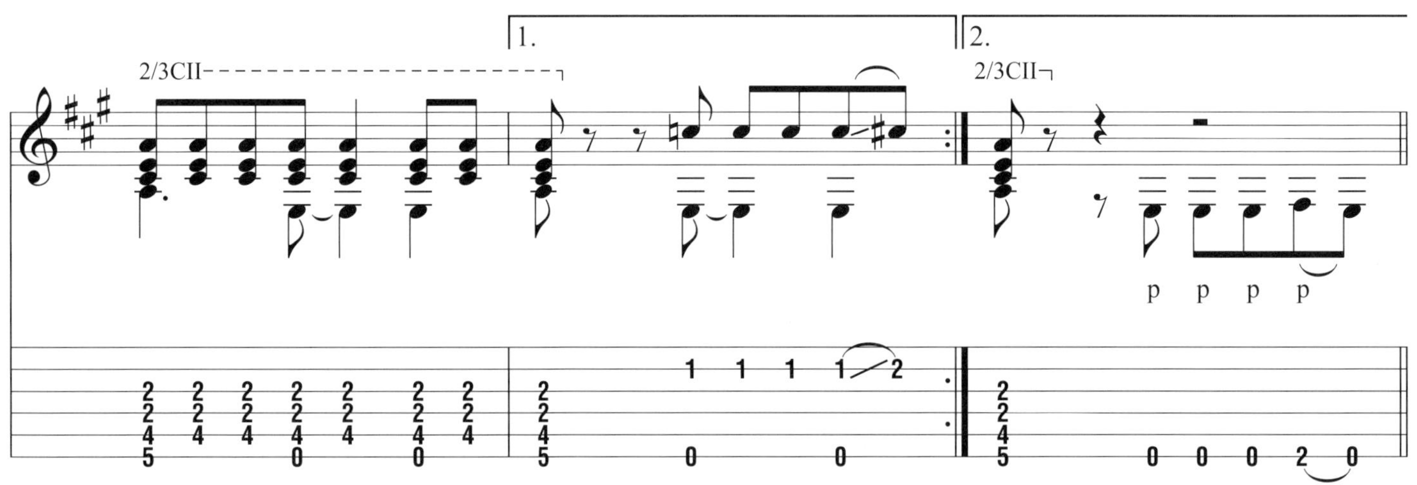

H

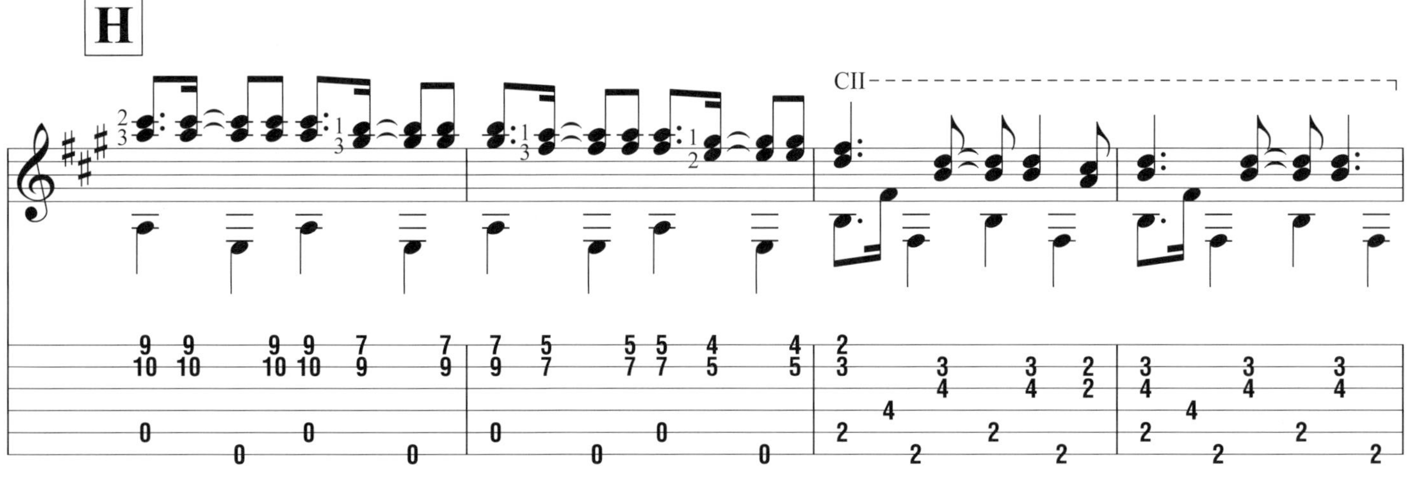

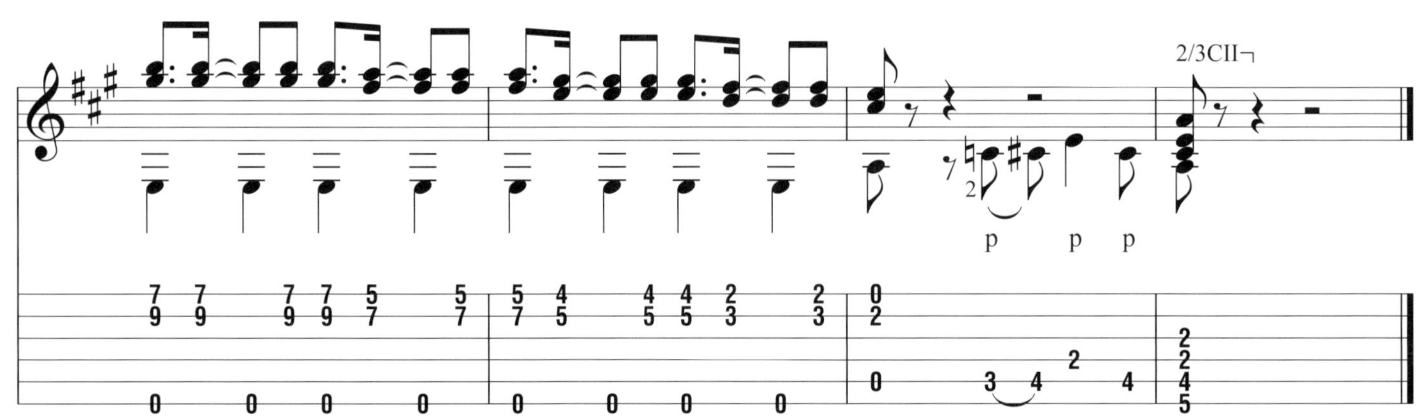

All of Me

Words and Music by John Stephens and Toby Gad

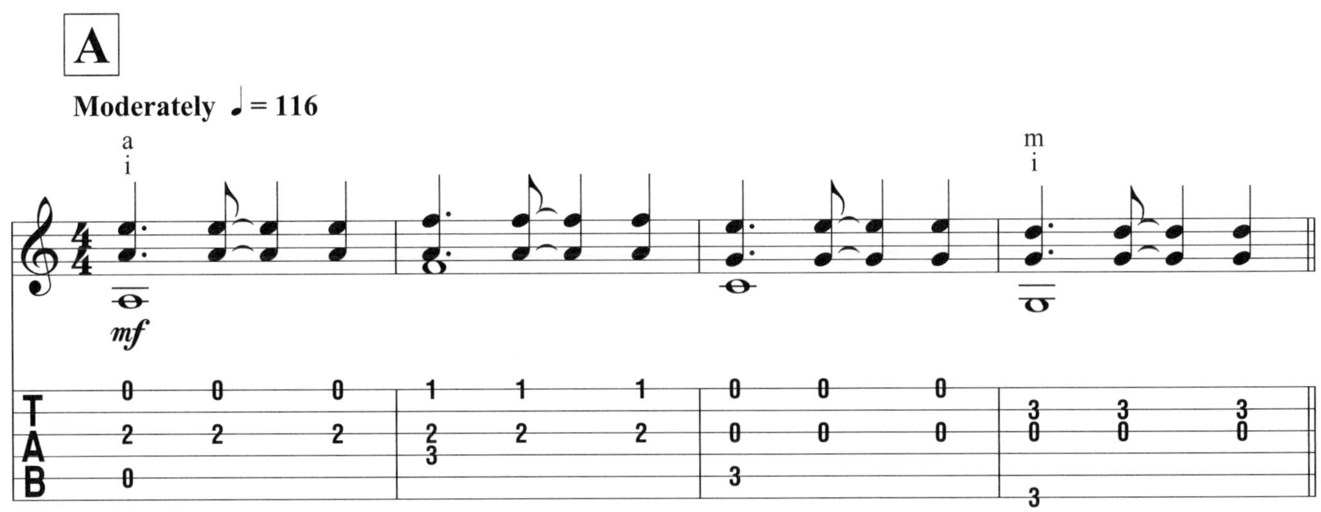

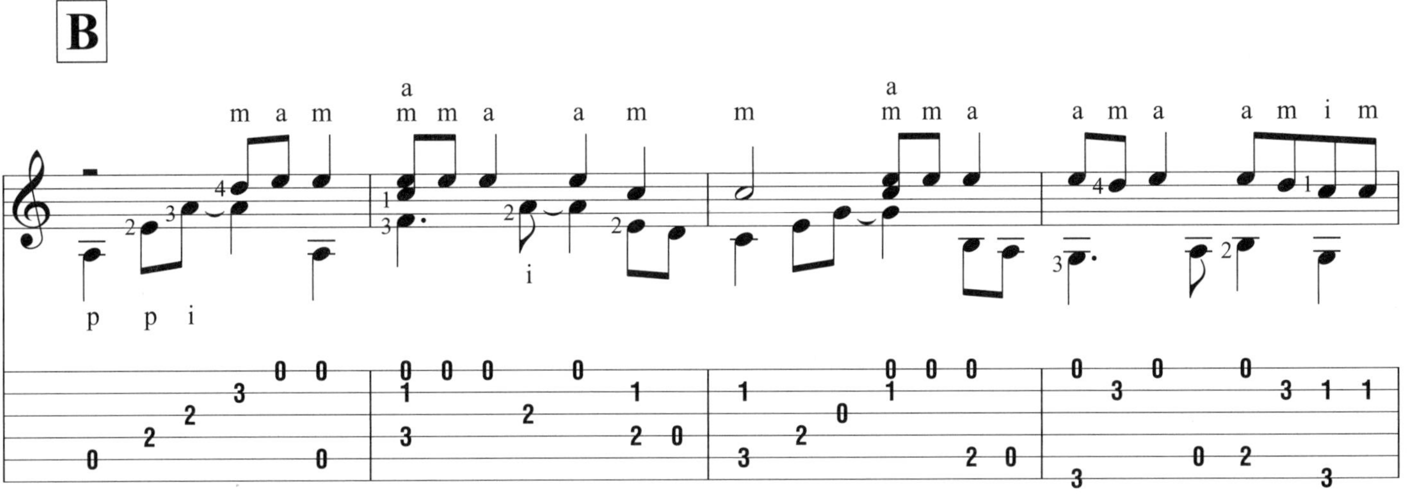

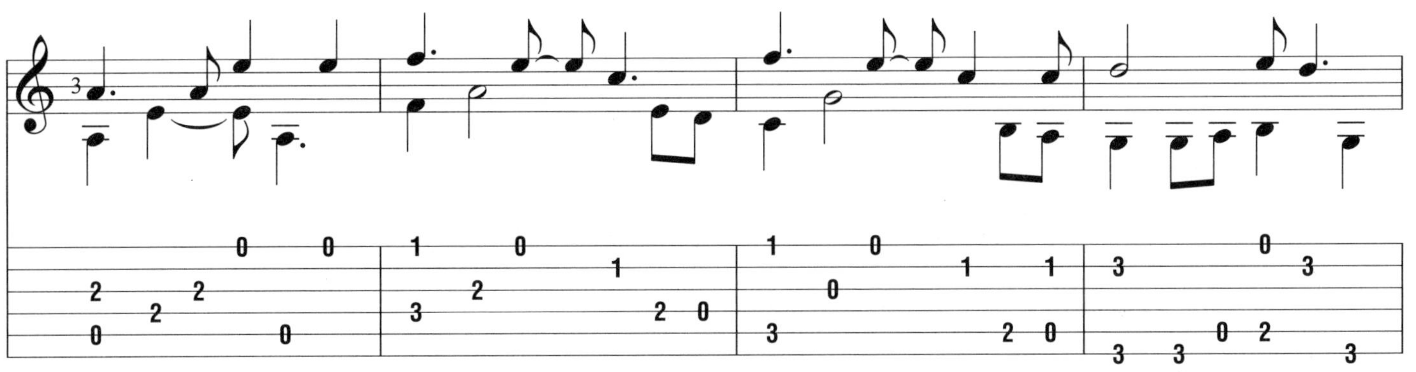

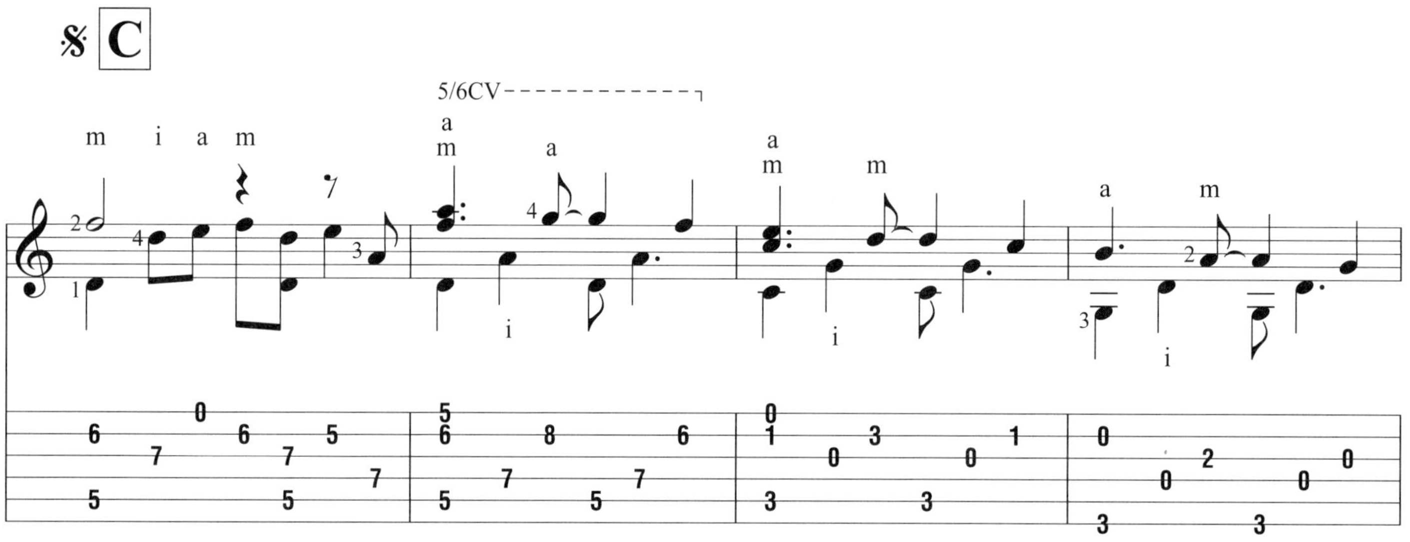
C
5/6CV

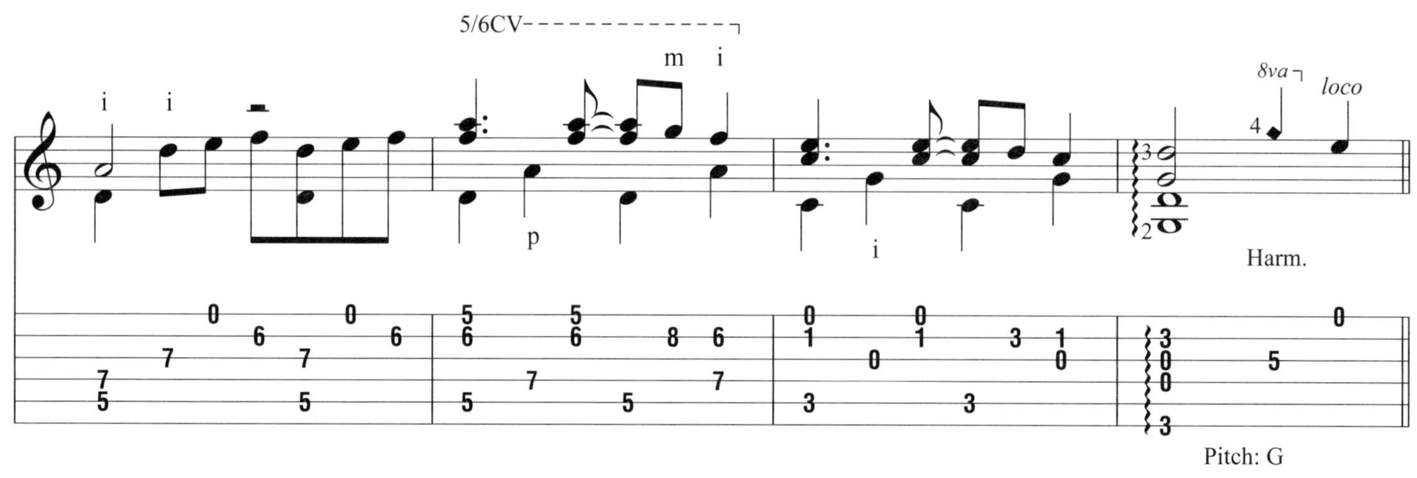
5/6CV
8va
loco
Harm.
Pitch: G

D

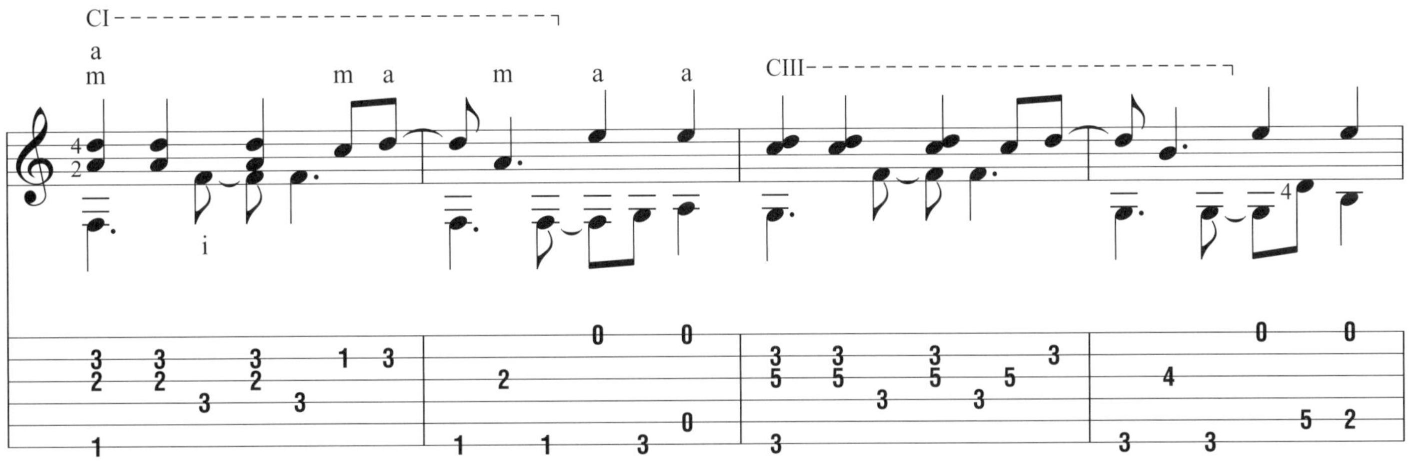

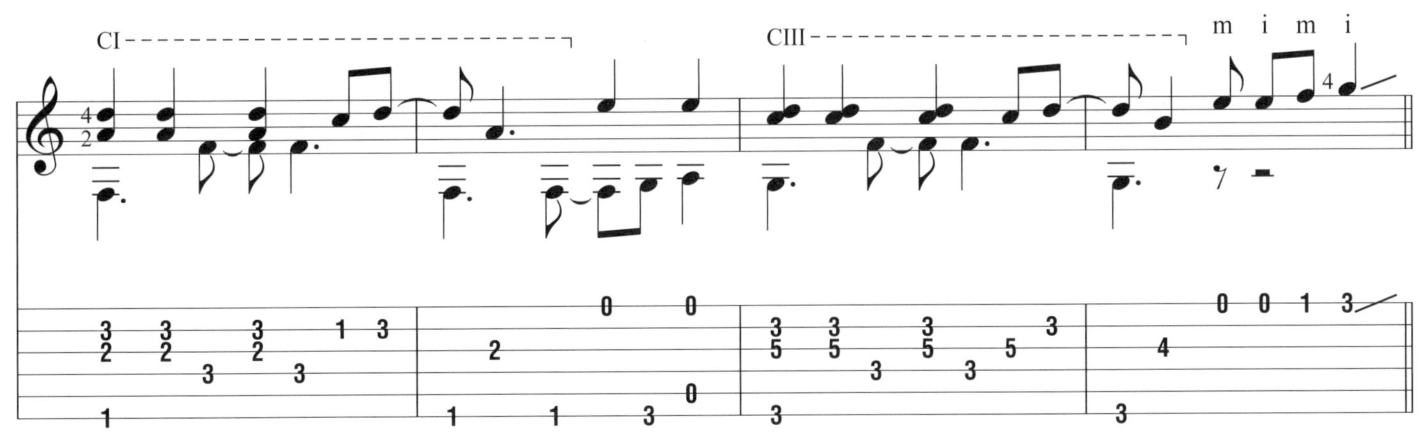

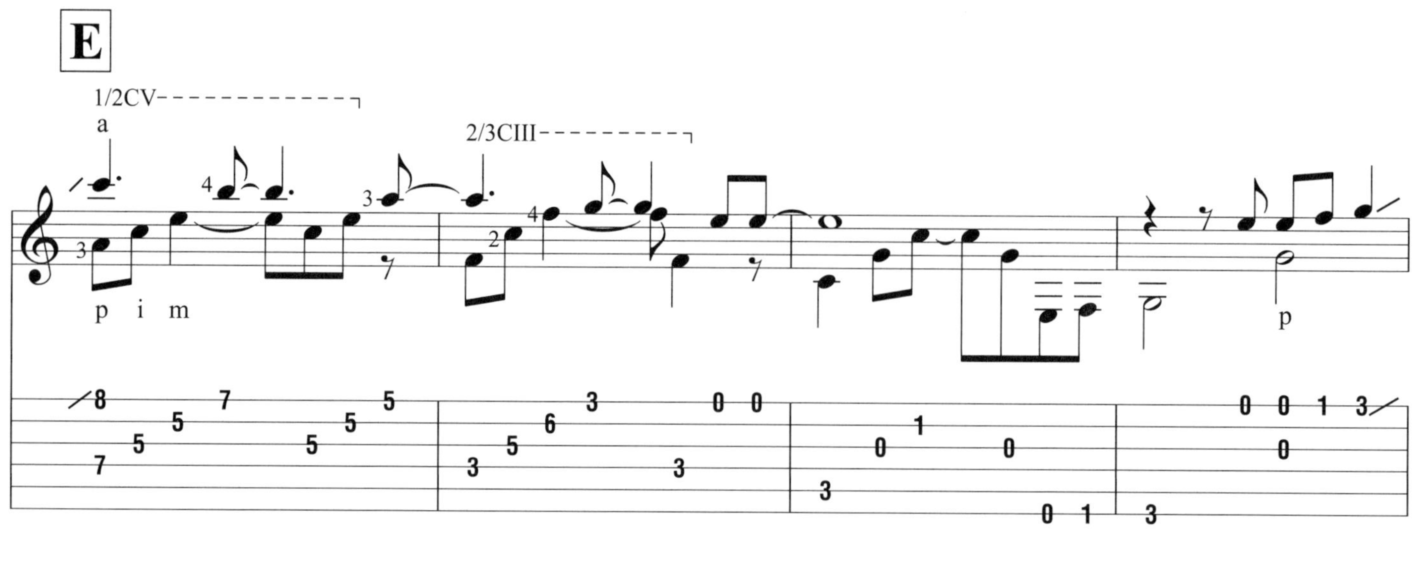
E
1/2CV
2/3CIII
a
p i m
p

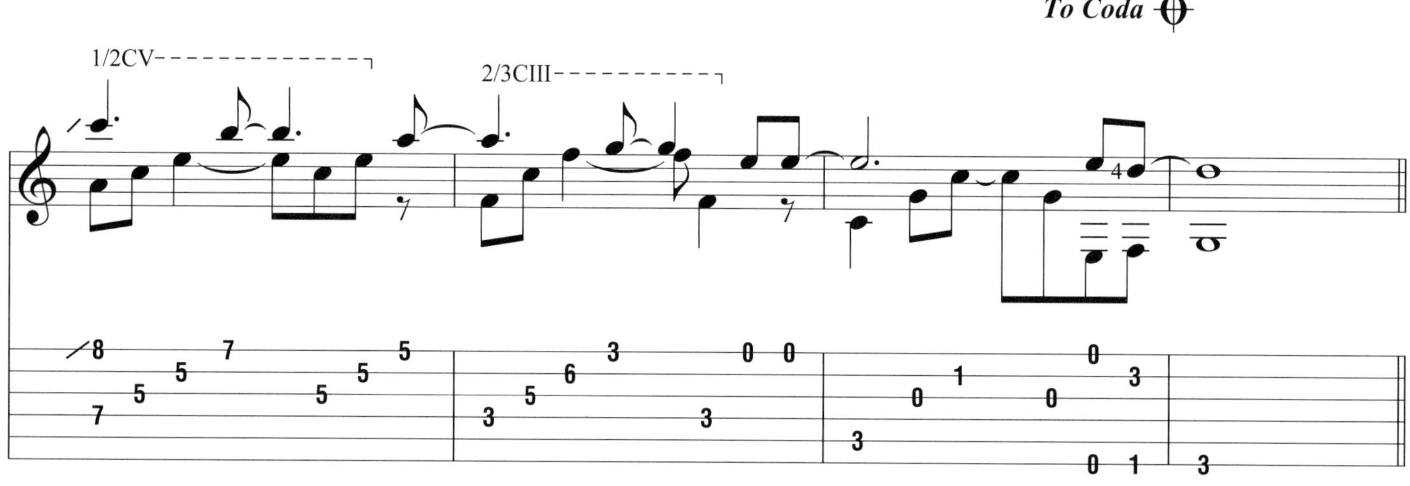
To Coda
1/2CV
2/3CIII

F

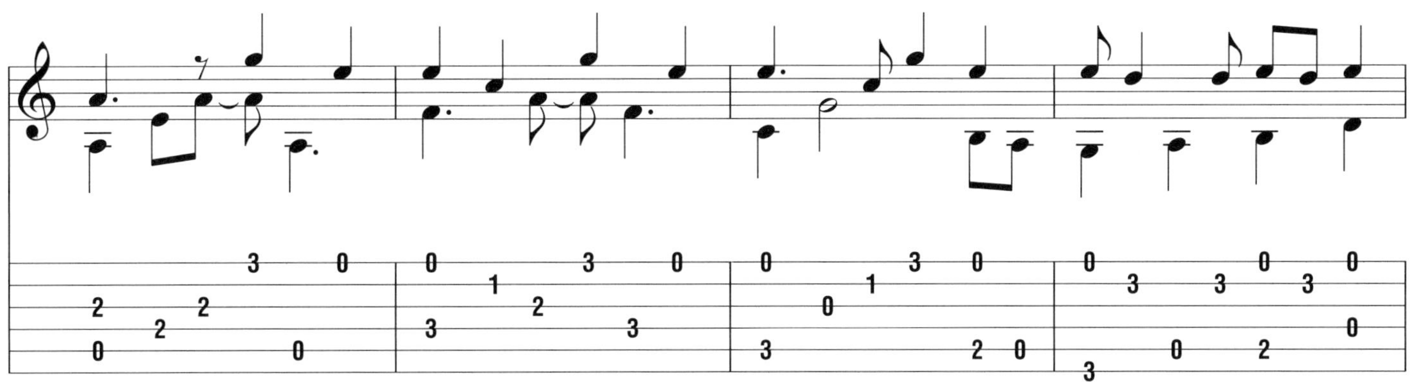

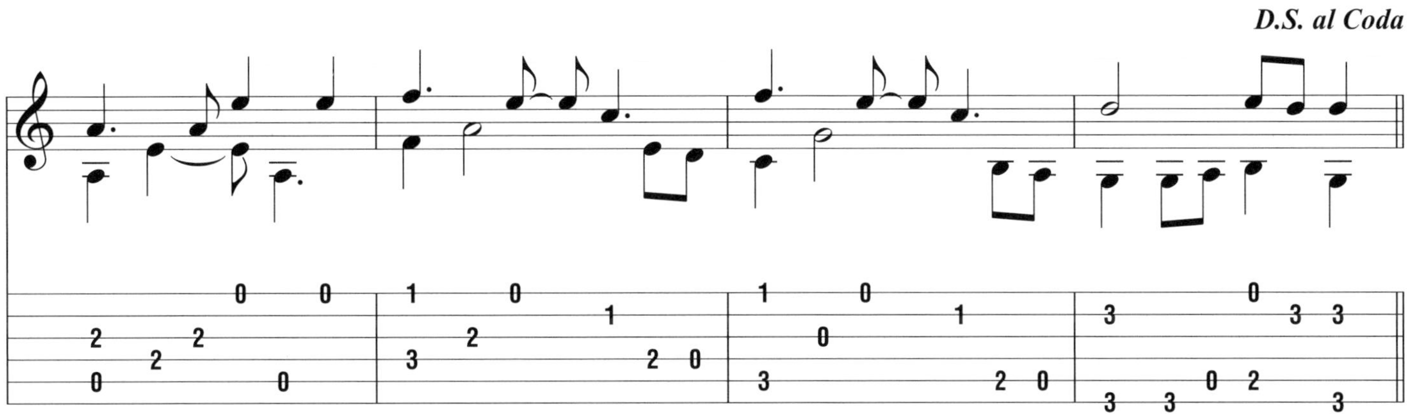
D.S. al Coda

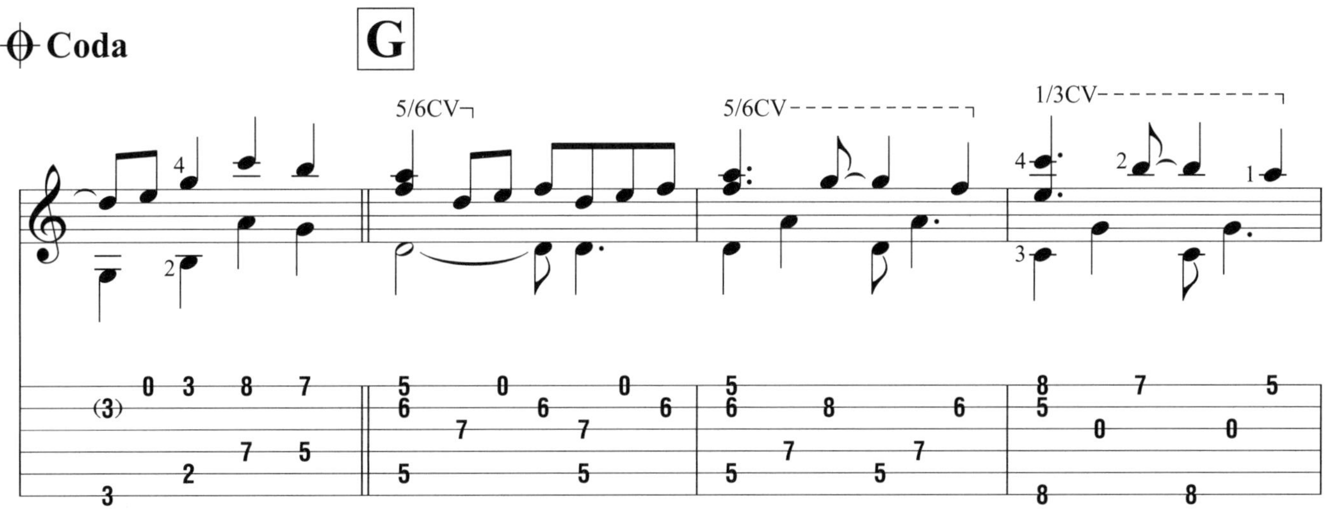
Coda
G
5/6CV
5/6CV
1/3CV

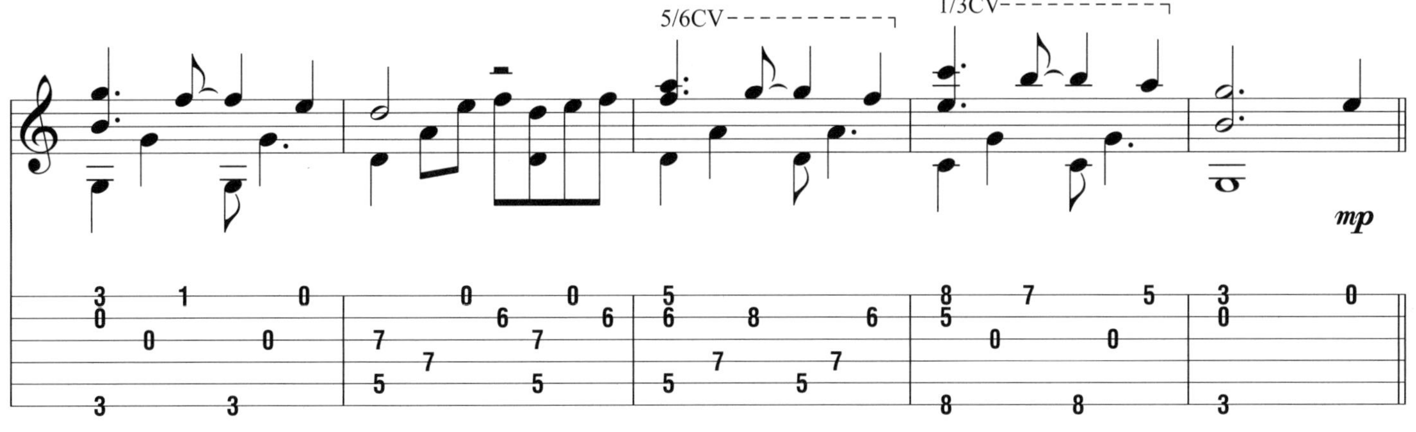
5/6CV
1/3CV
mp

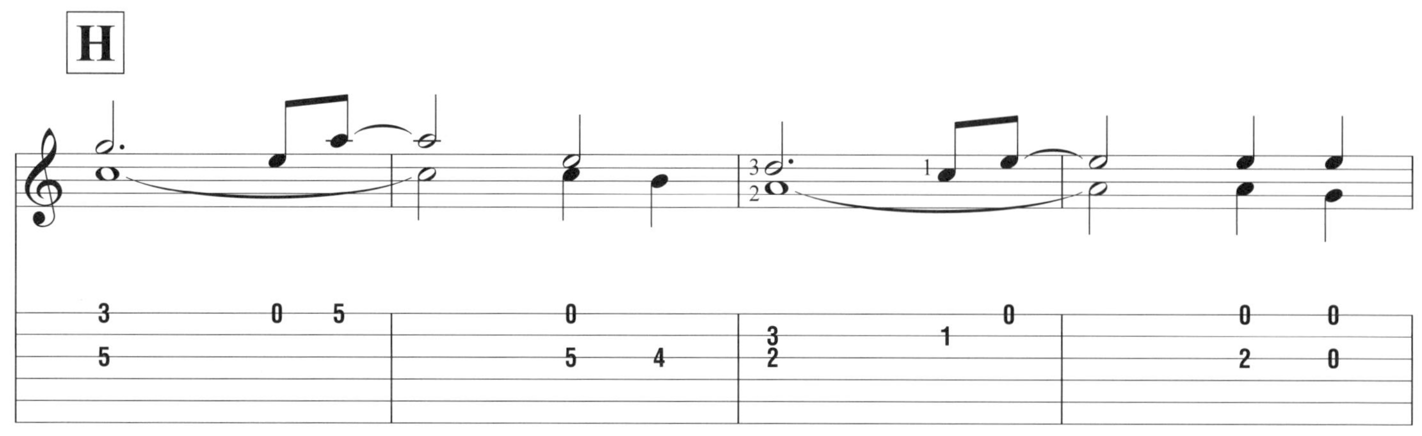
H

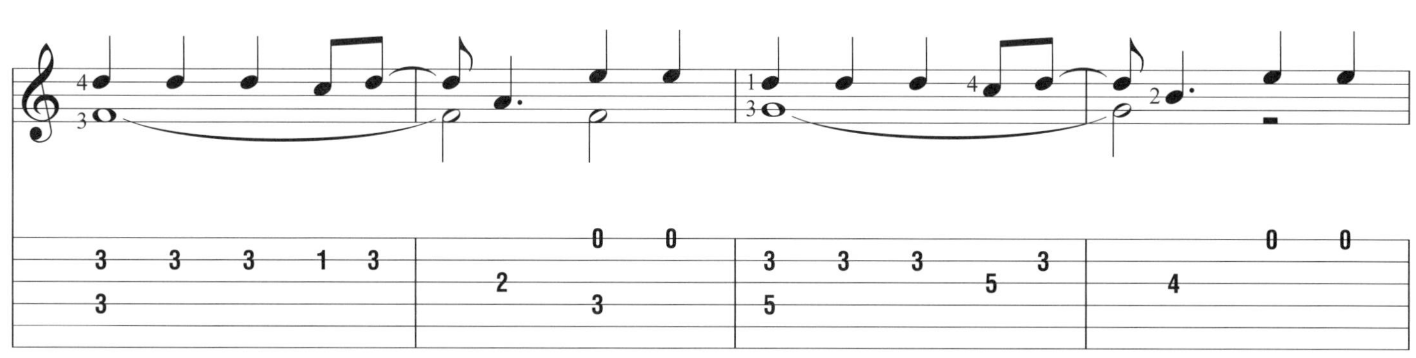

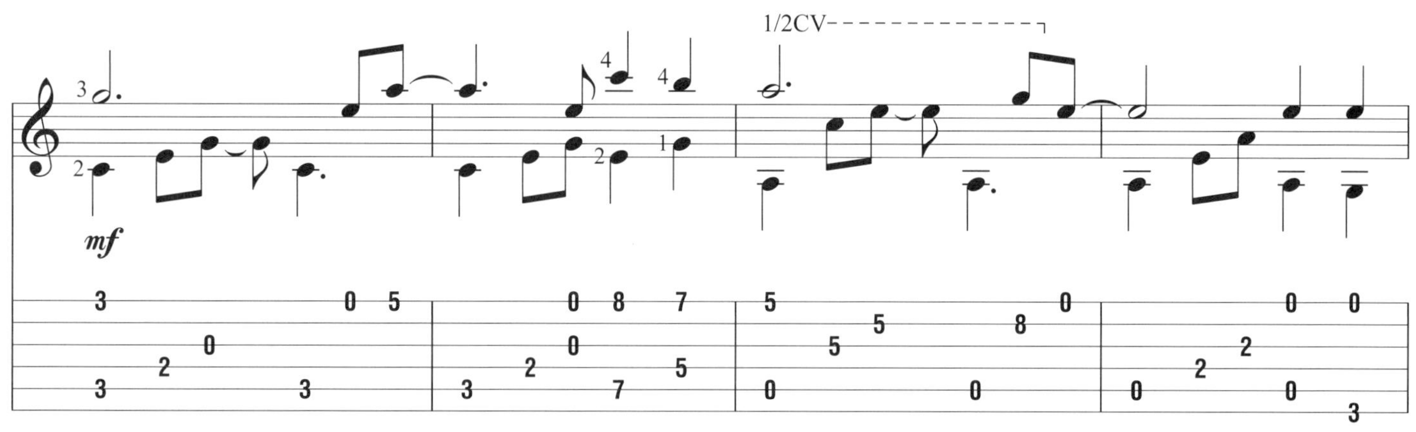
1/2CV
mf

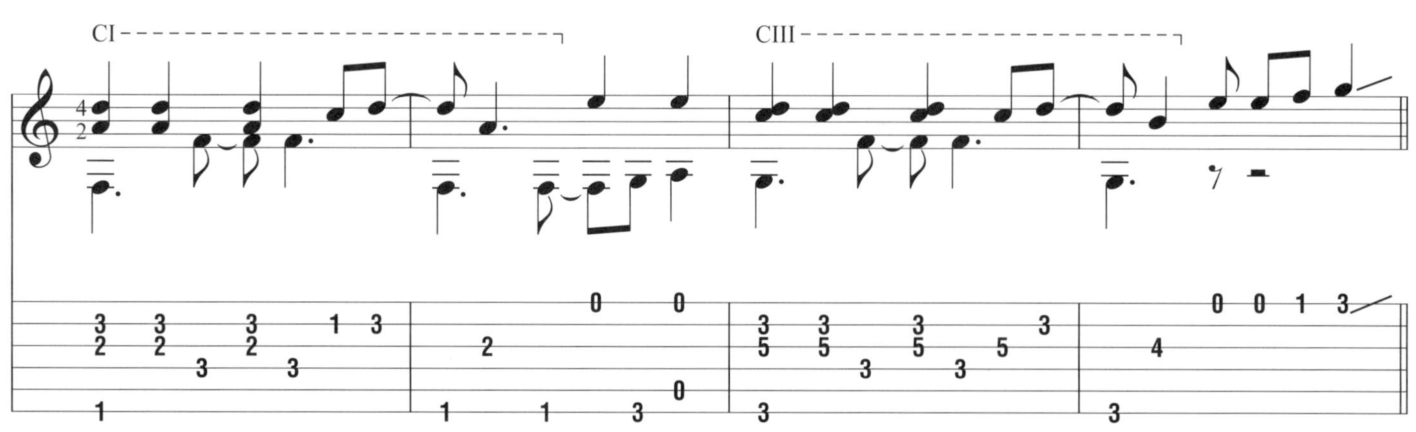
CI
CIII

I
1/2CV
2/3CIII
1/2CV
2/3CIII
1/2CV
2/3CIII
1/2CV
2/3CIII
rit.

City of Stars

from LA LA LAND

Music by Justin Hurwitz
Lyrics by Benj Pasek & Justin Paul

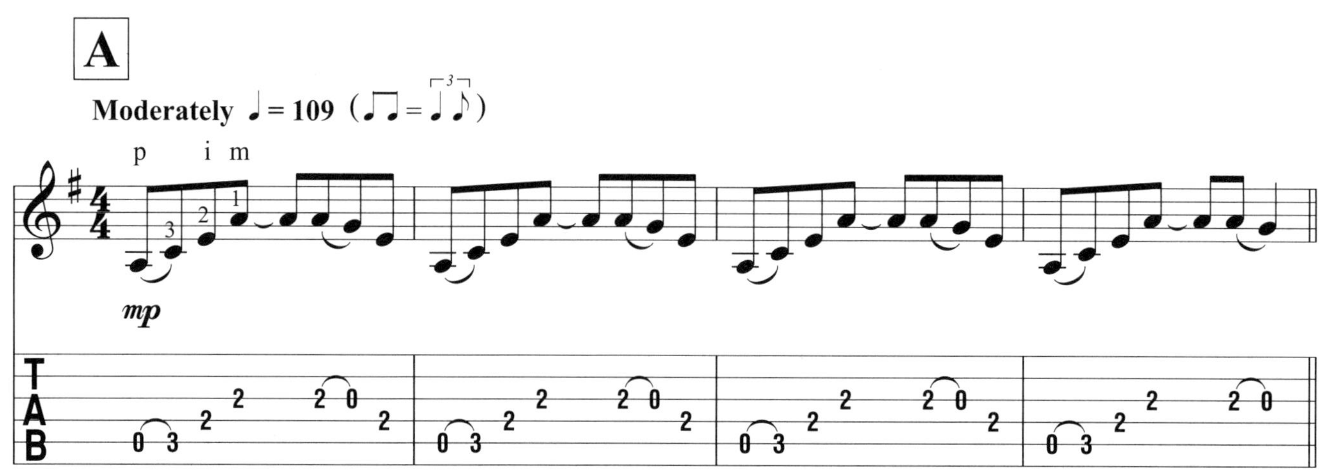

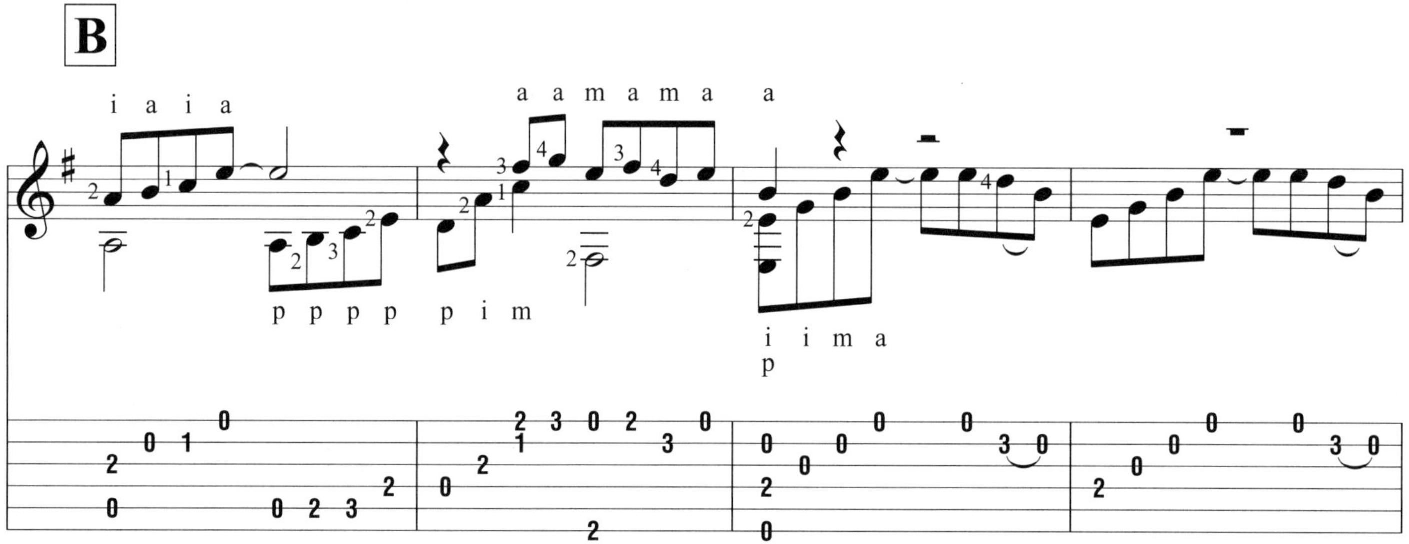

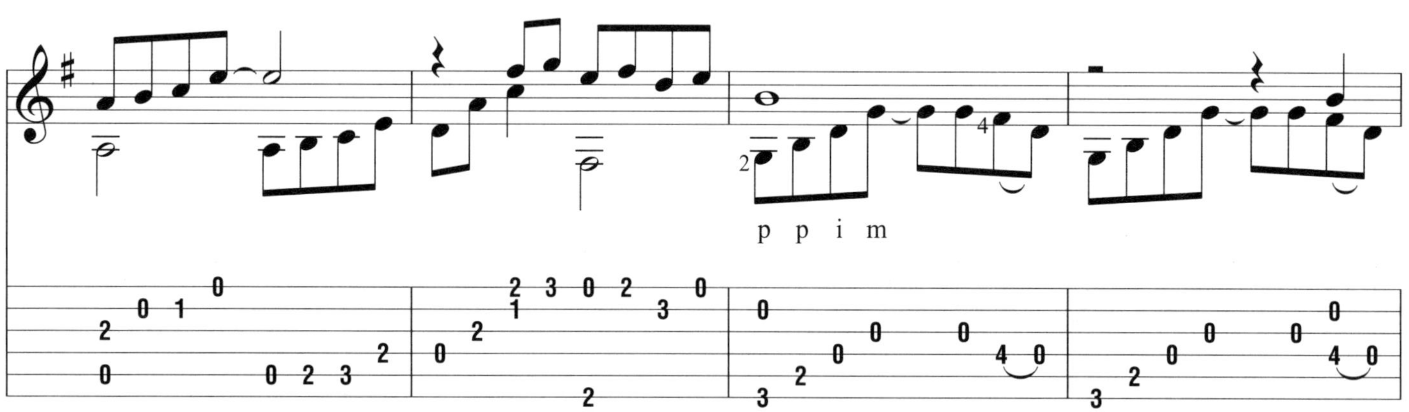

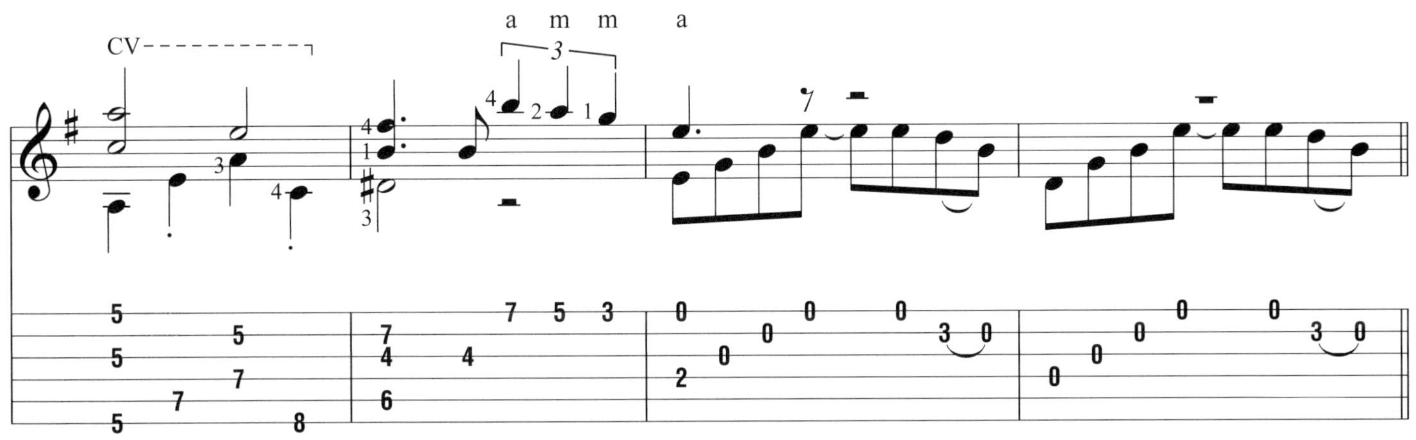

C

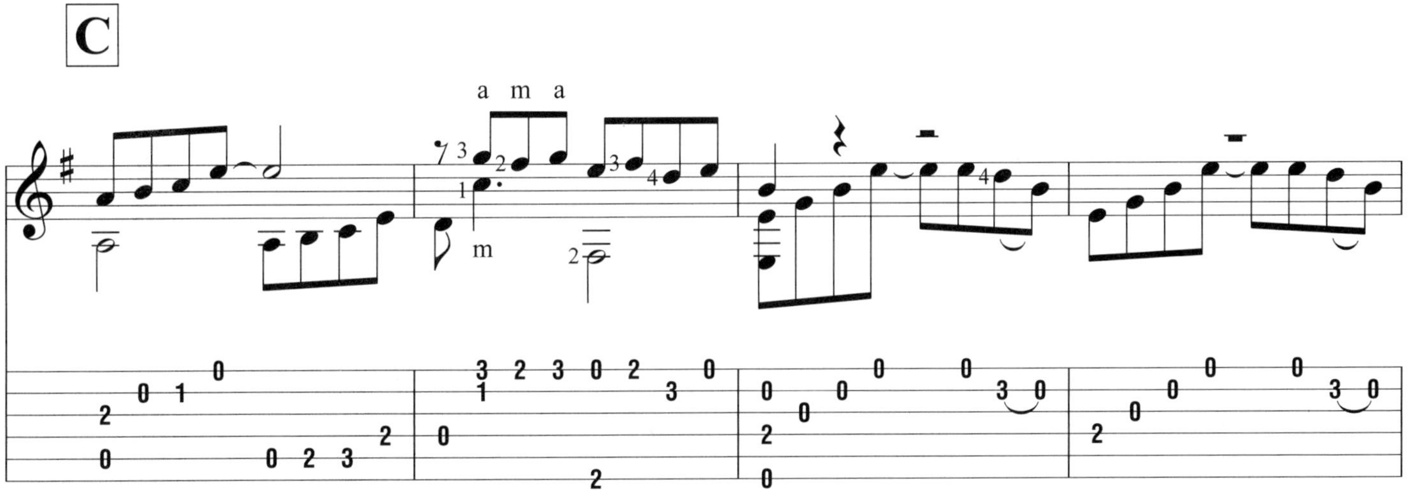

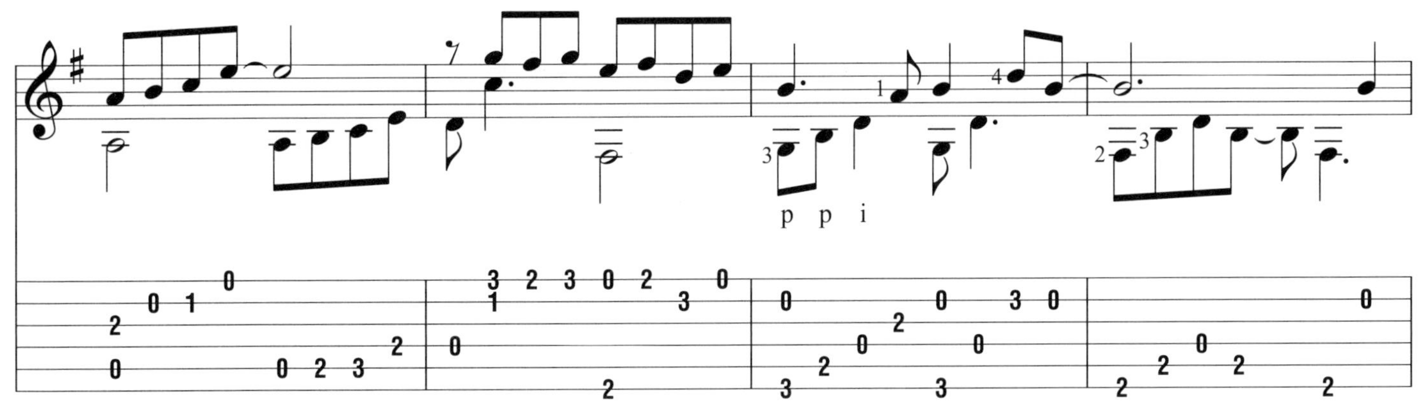

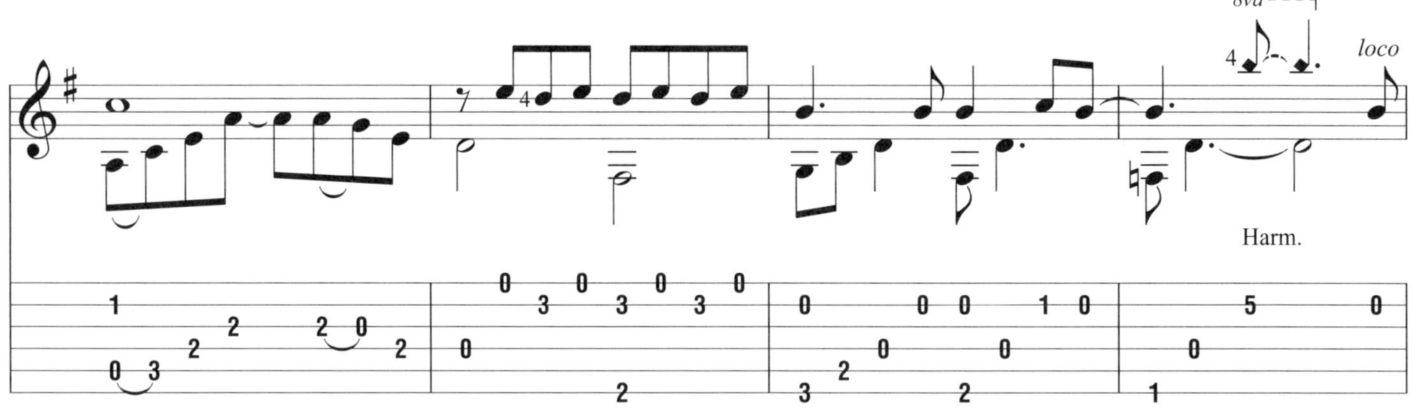
8va
loco
Harm.

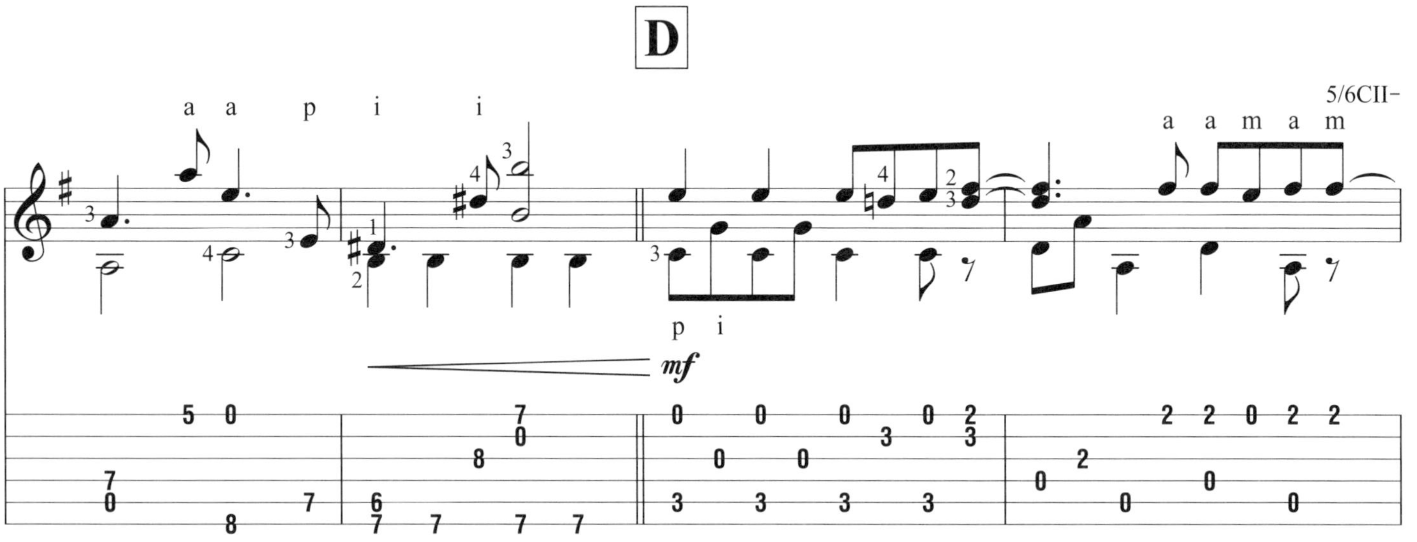
D
a a p i i
5/6CII
a a m a m
p i
mf

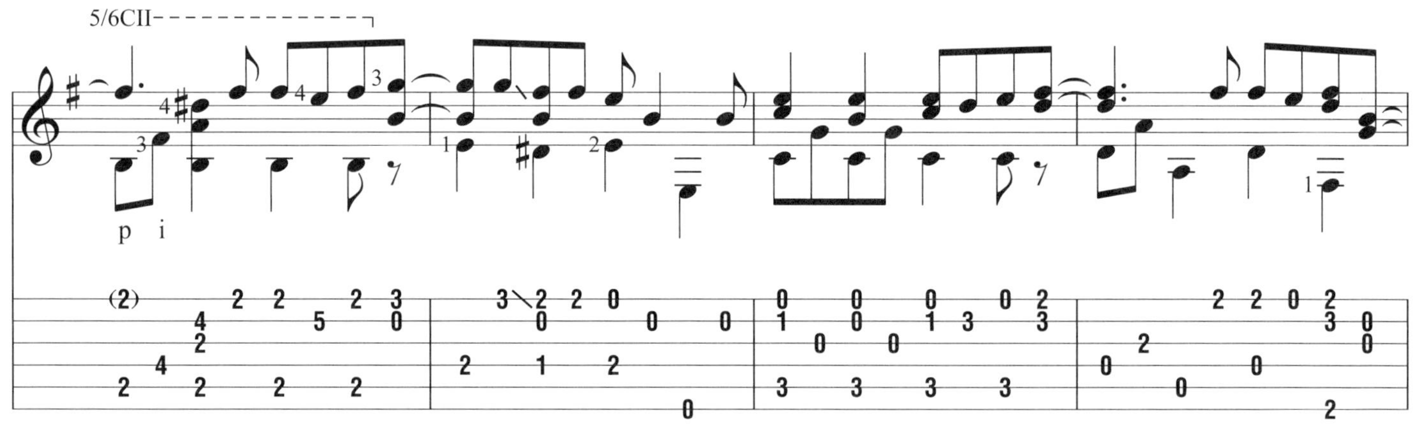
5/6CII
p i

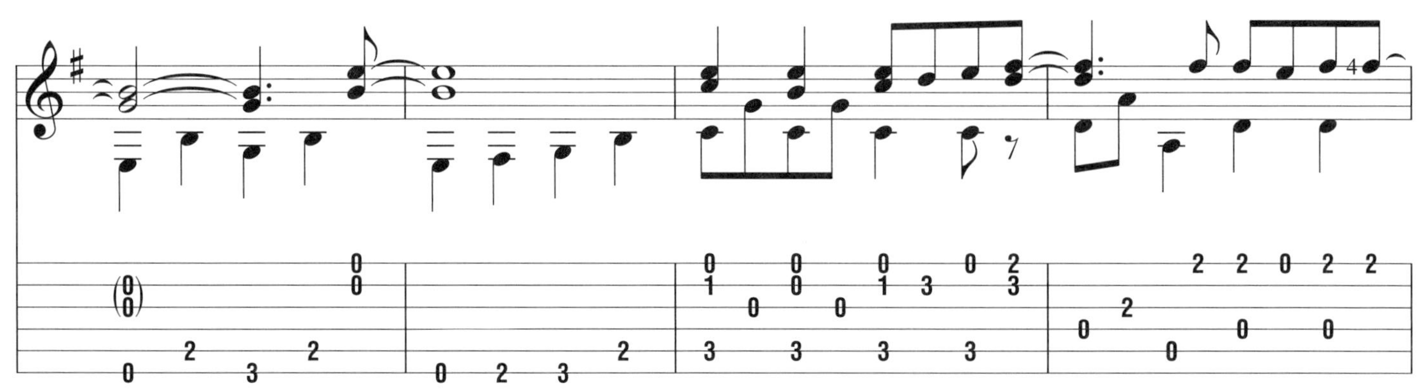

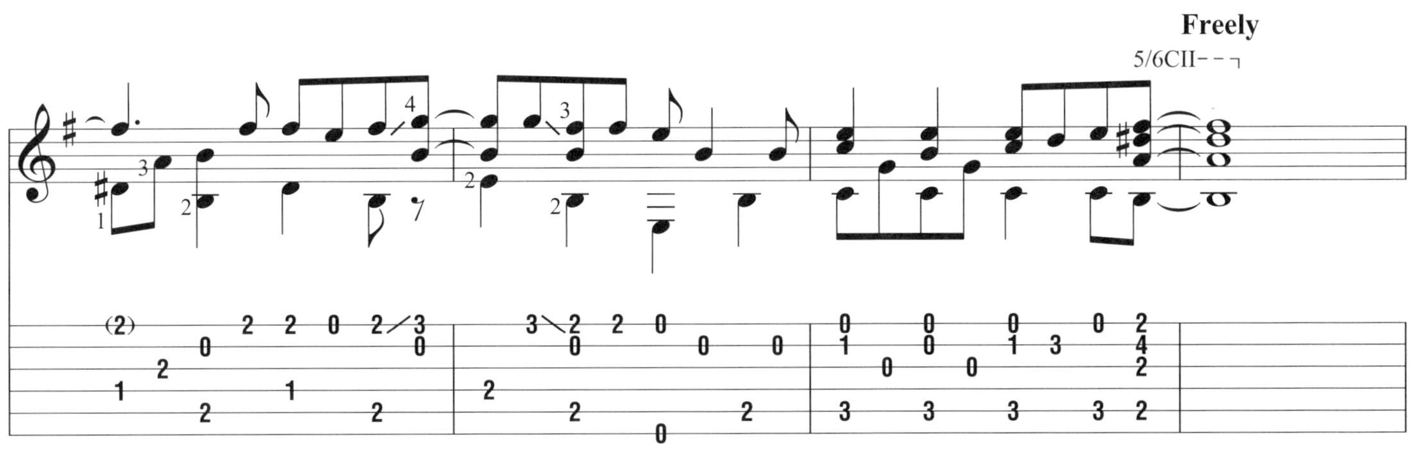
Freely
5/6CII

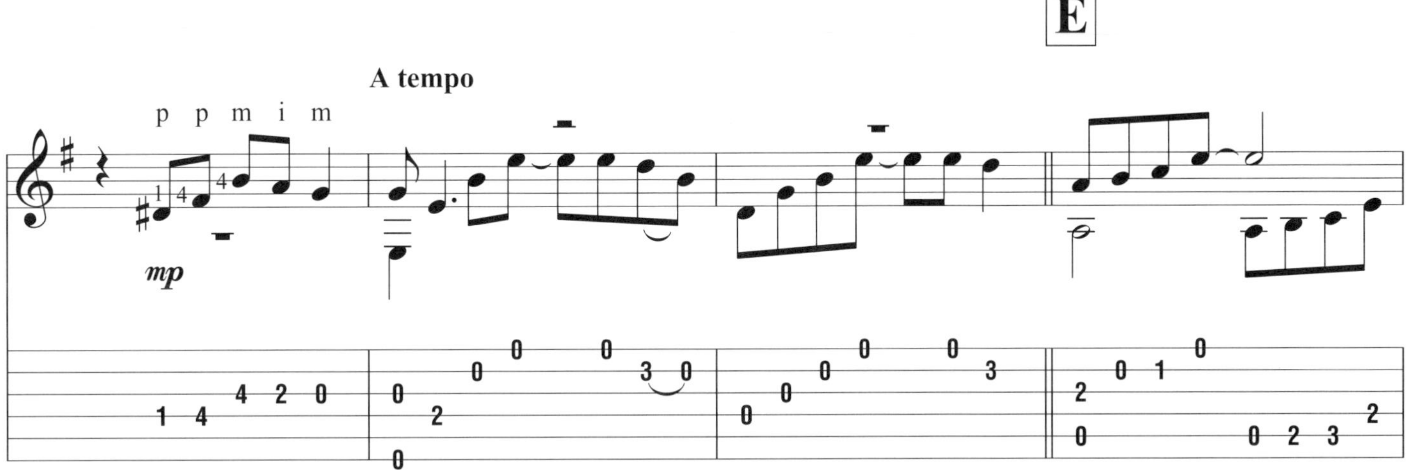
E
A tempo
p p m i m
mp

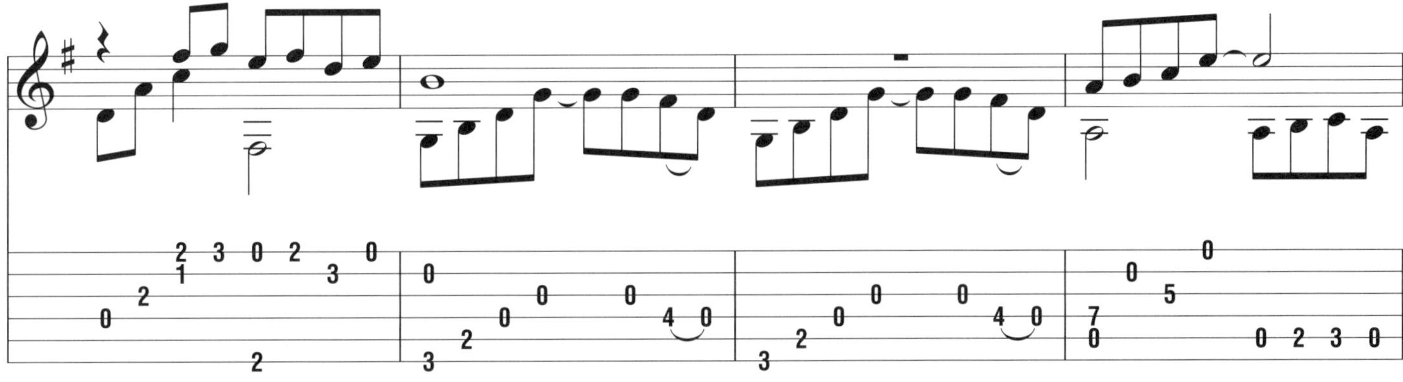

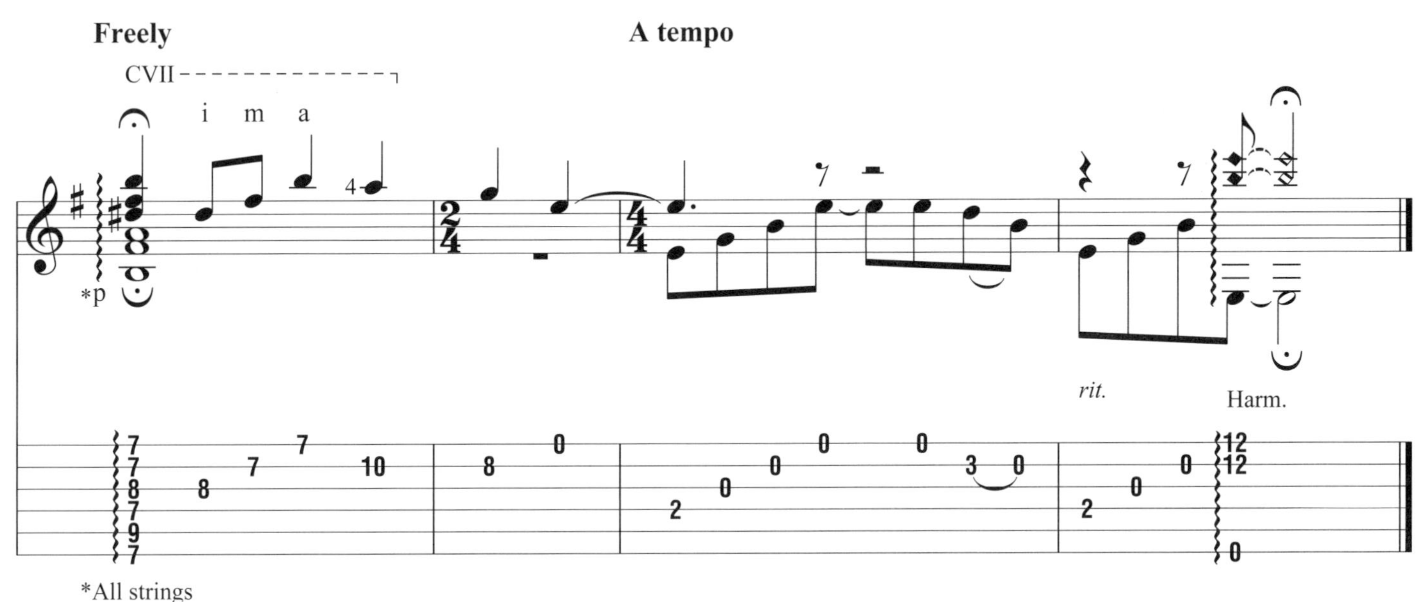
Freely
A tempo
CVII
i m a
*p
rit.
Harm.

*All strings

Despacito

Words and Music by Luis Fonsi, Erika Ender, Justin Bieber, Jason Boyd, Marty James Garton and Ramon Ayala

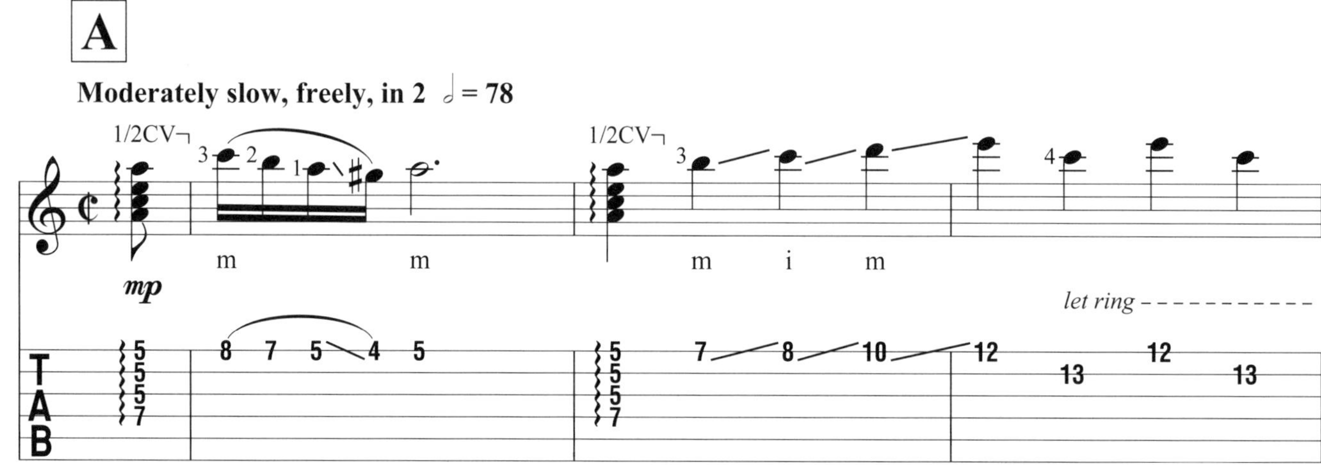

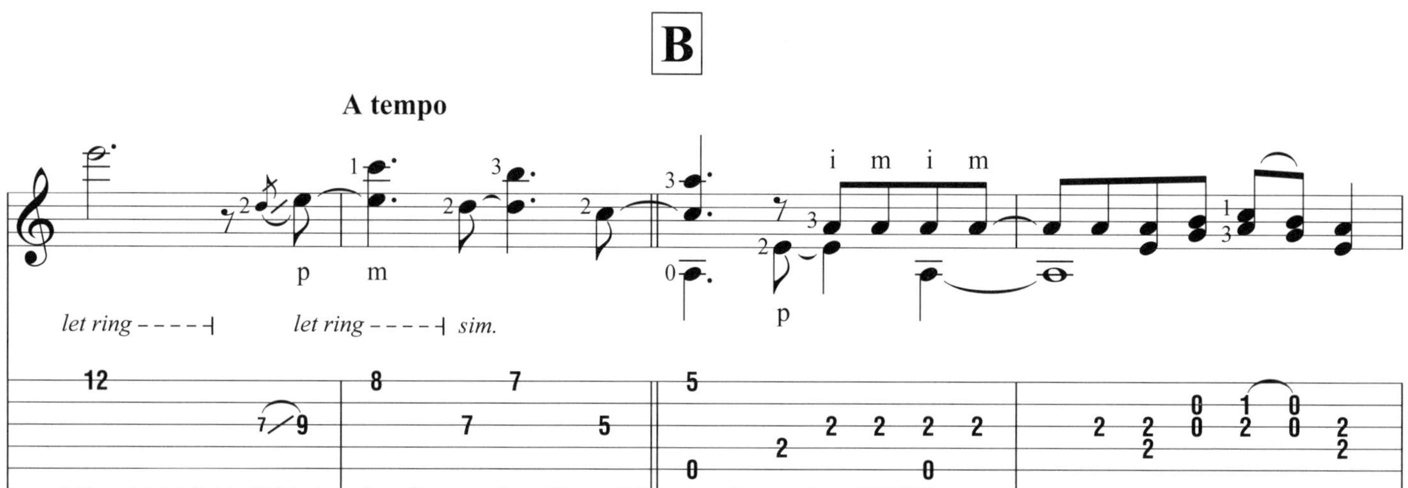

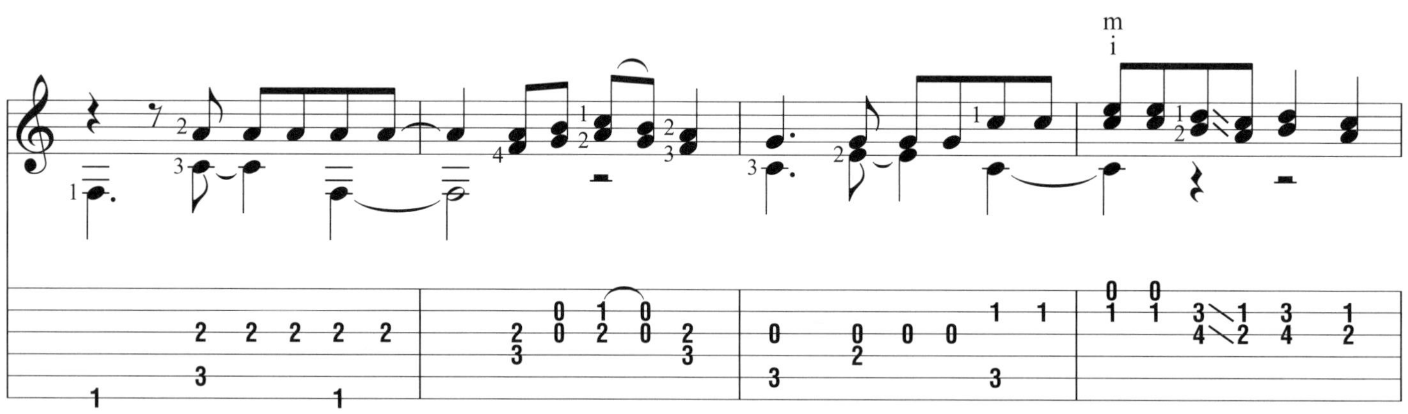

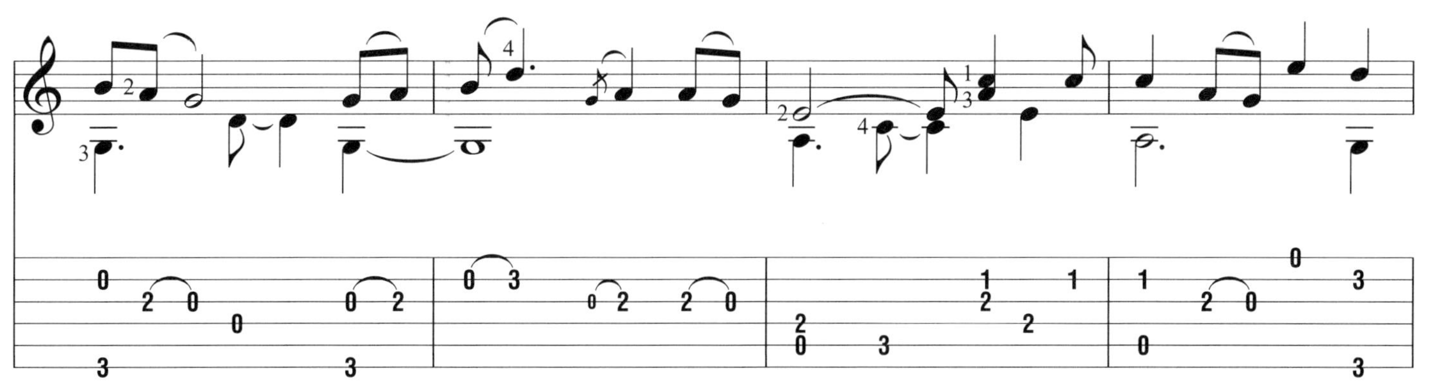

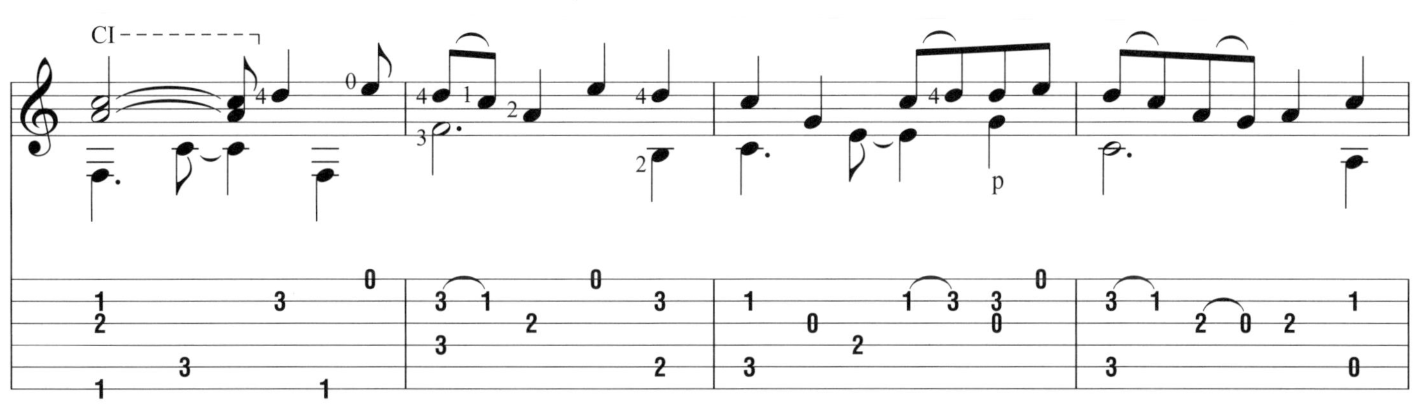
CI

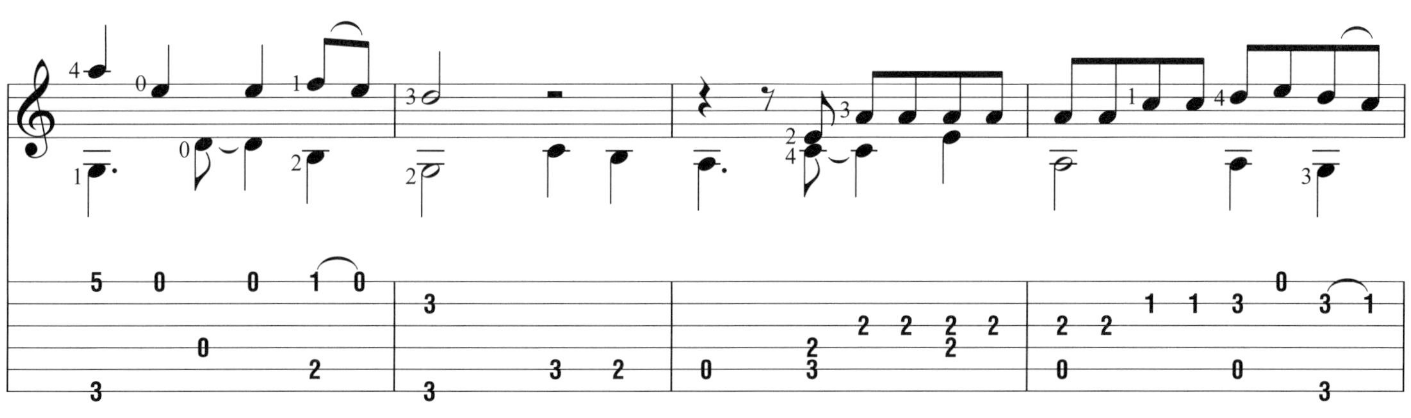

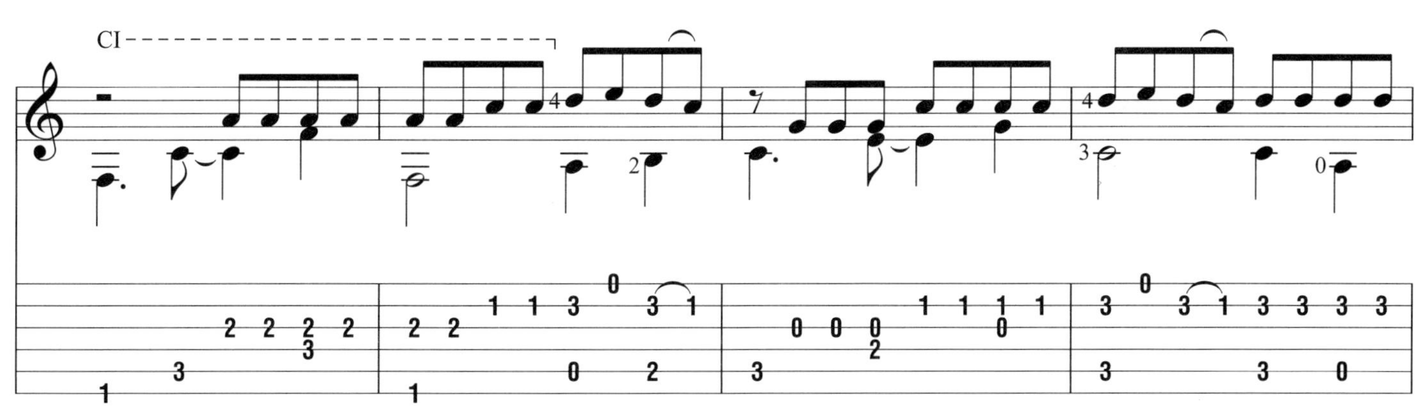
CI

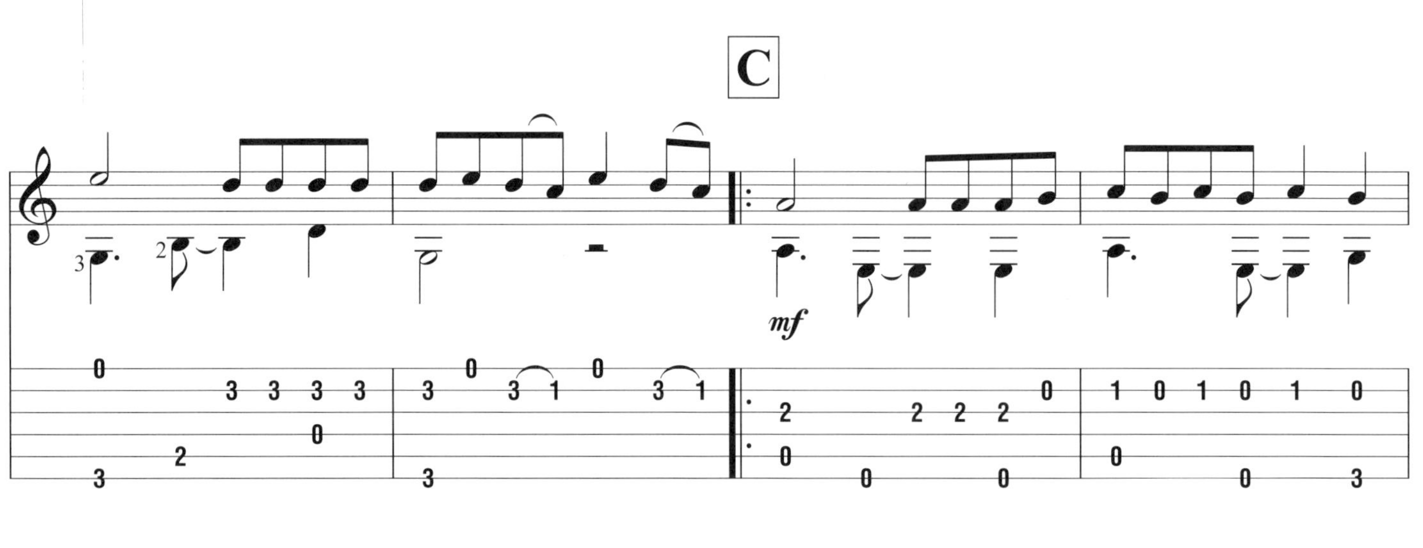
C
mf

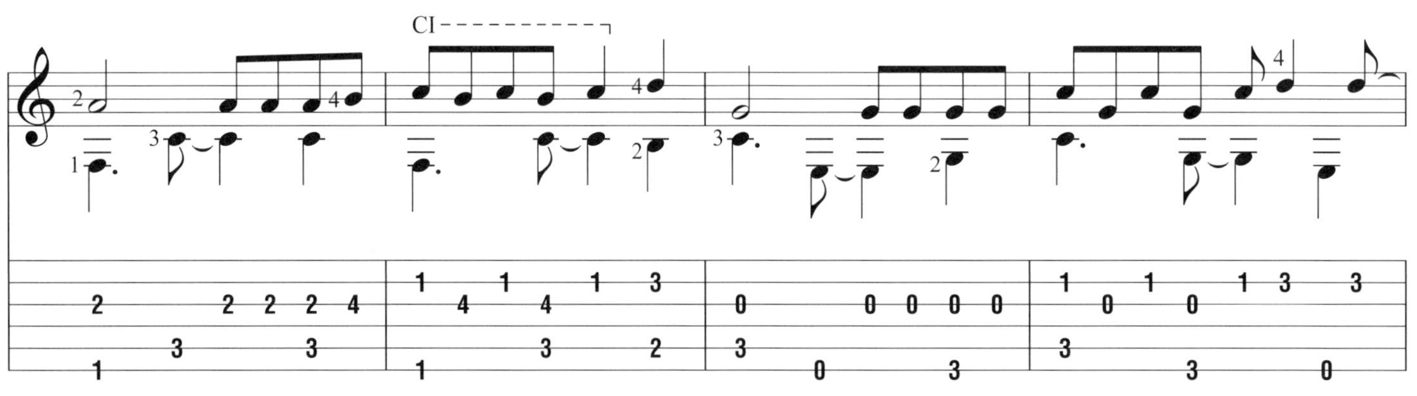
CI

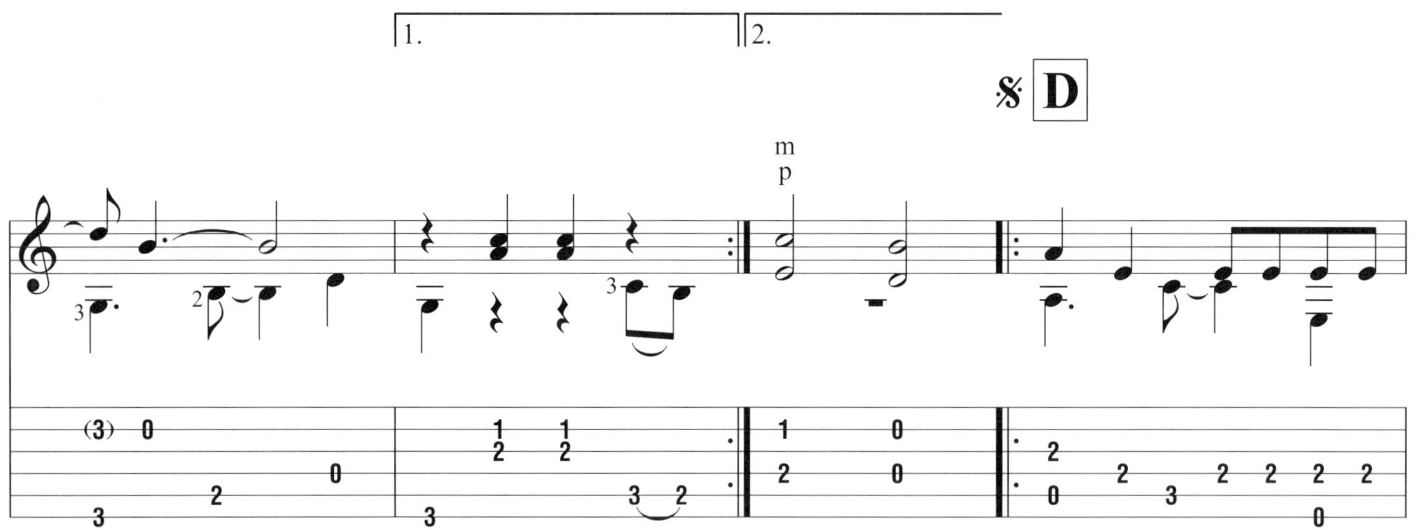
1.
2.
D
m
p

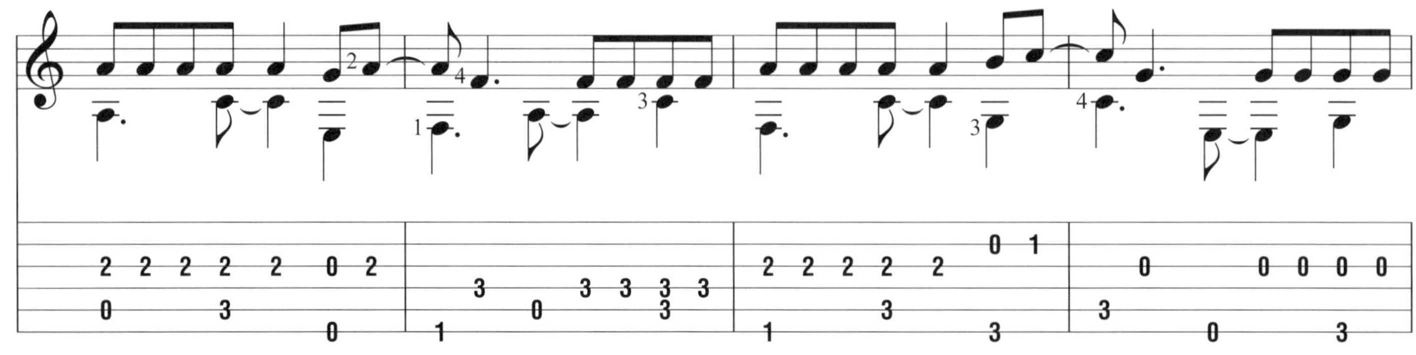

1.
2.

E
CI
f
p
*Fret w/ lower part of index finger.

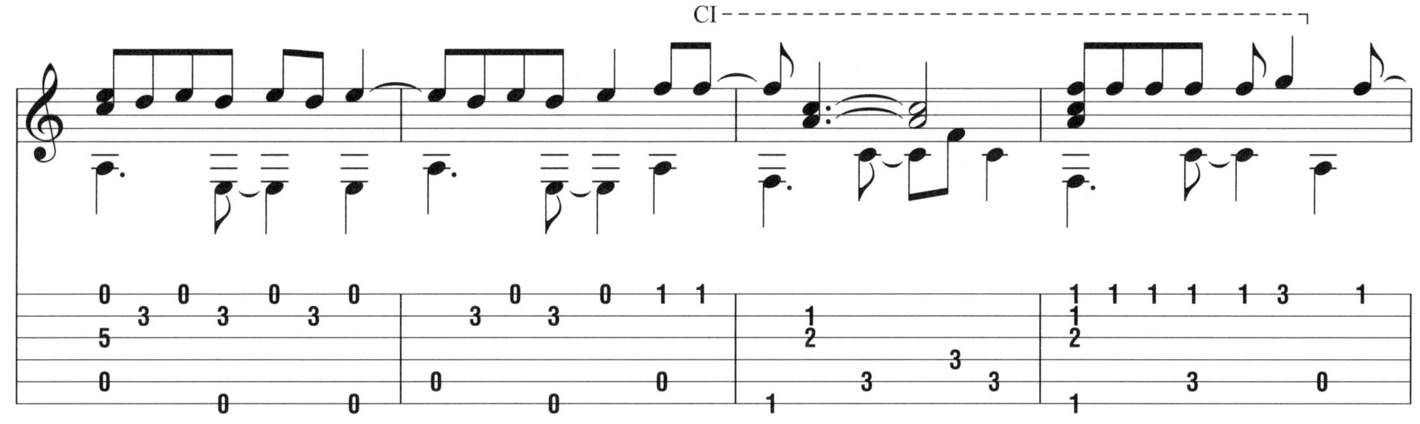
CI

To Coda 𝄌

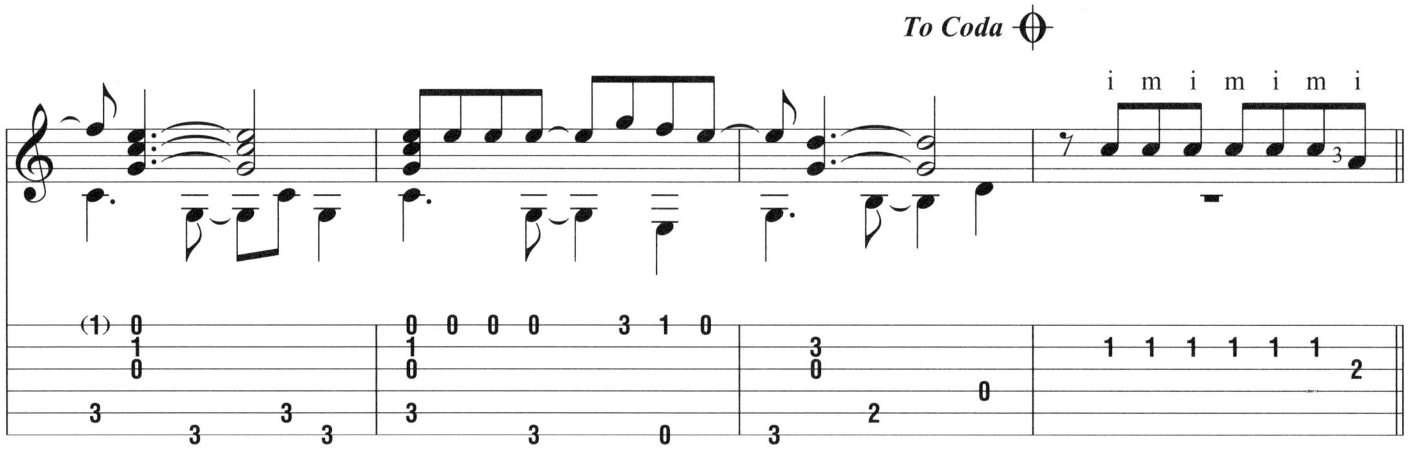

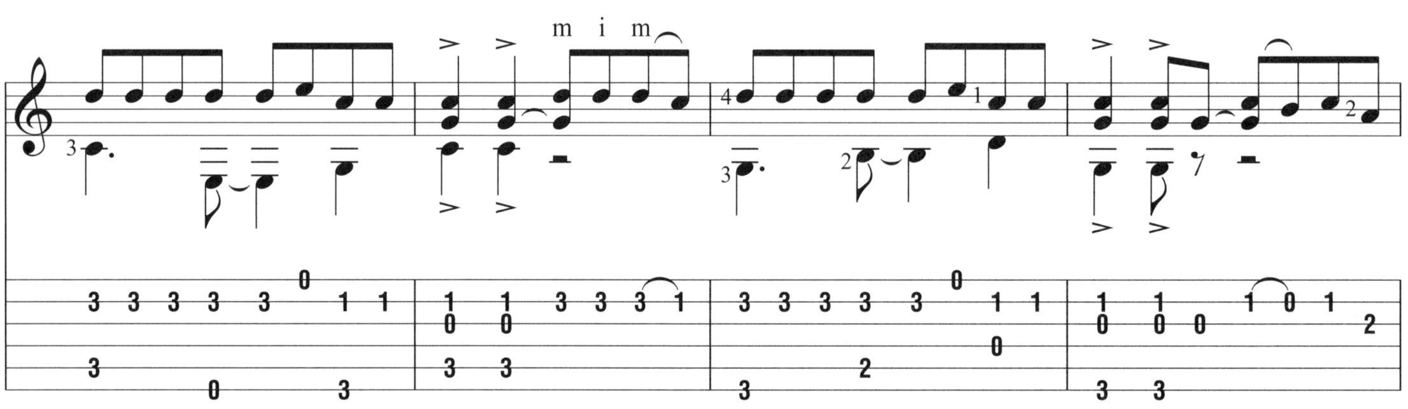

G

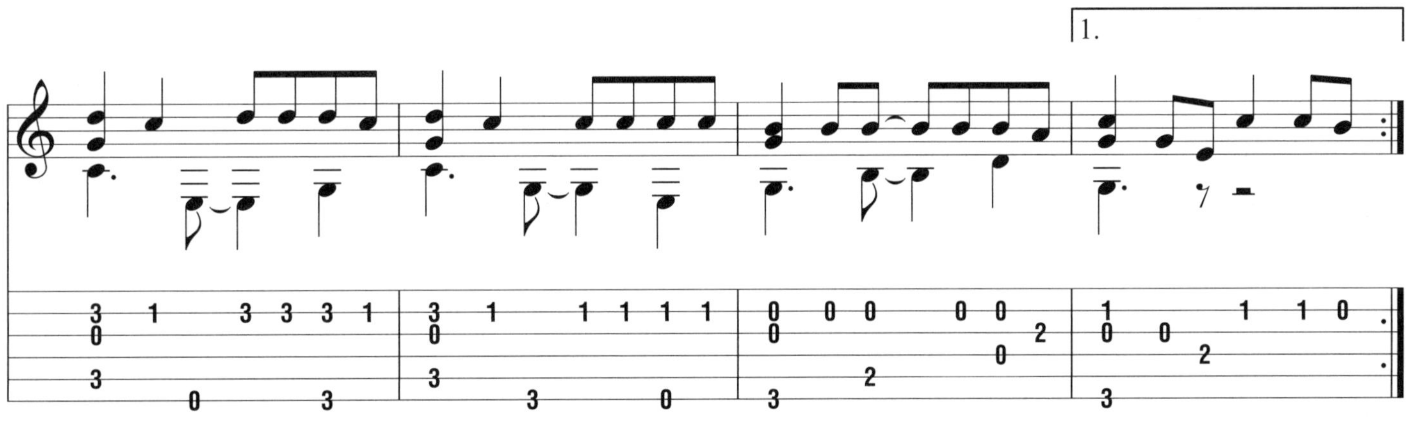

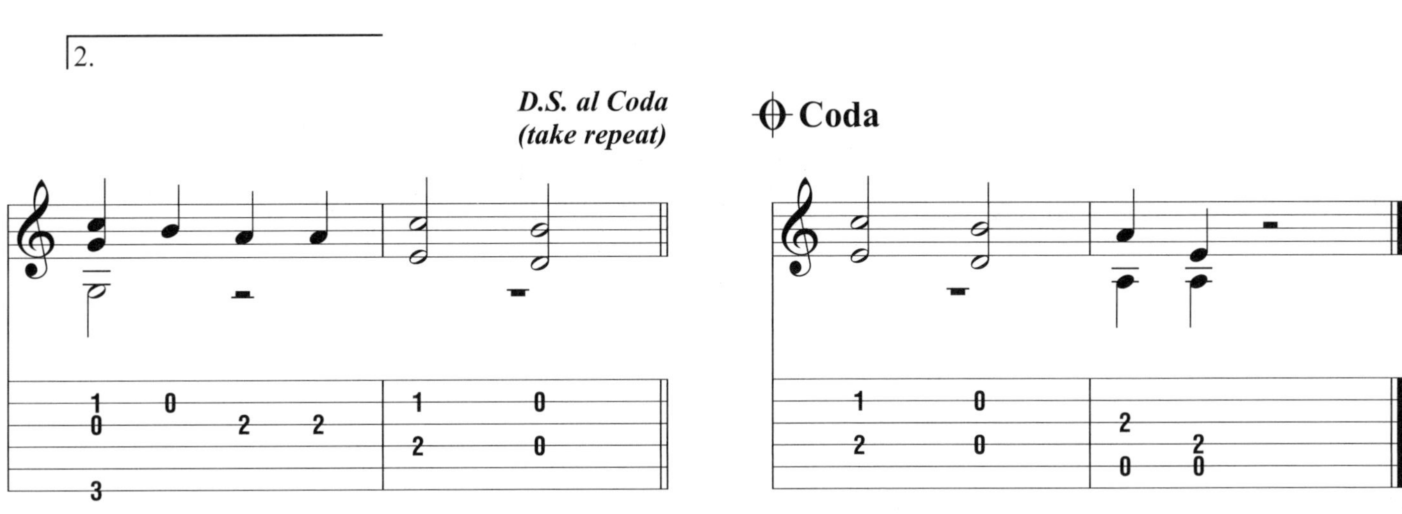

Game of Thrones

Theme from the HBO Series GAME OF THRONES

By Ramin Djawadi

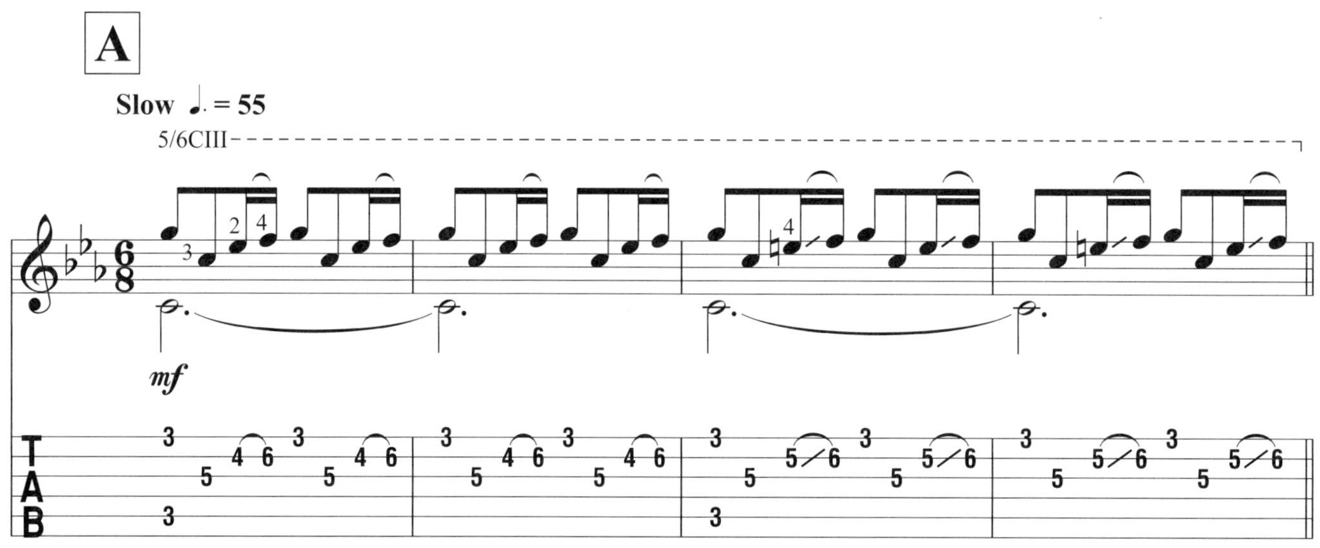

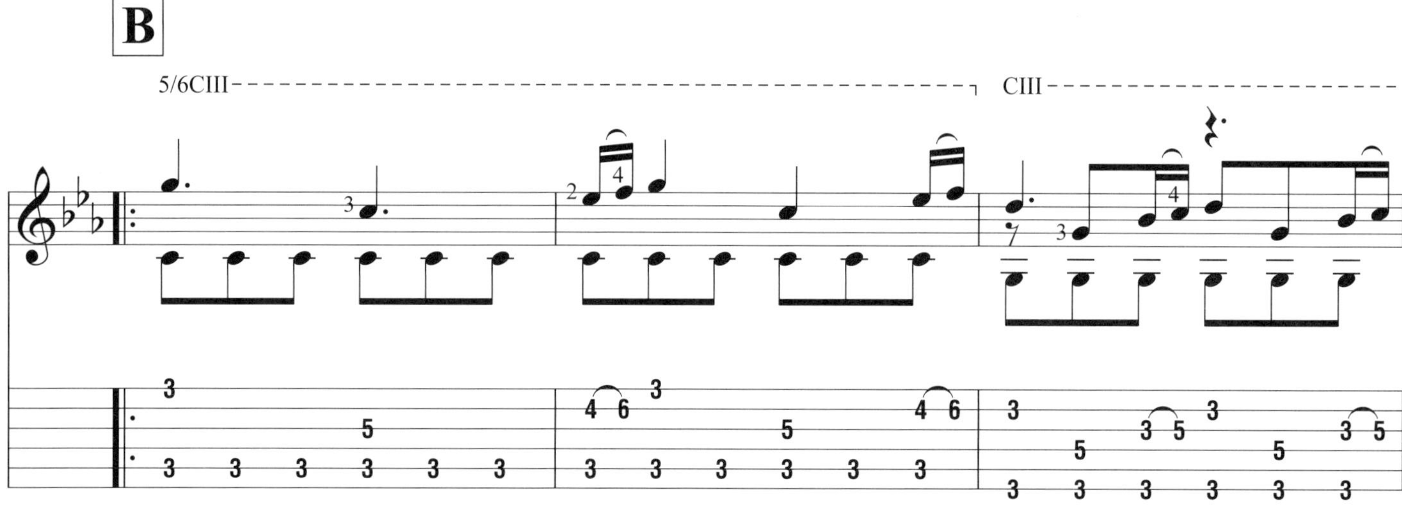

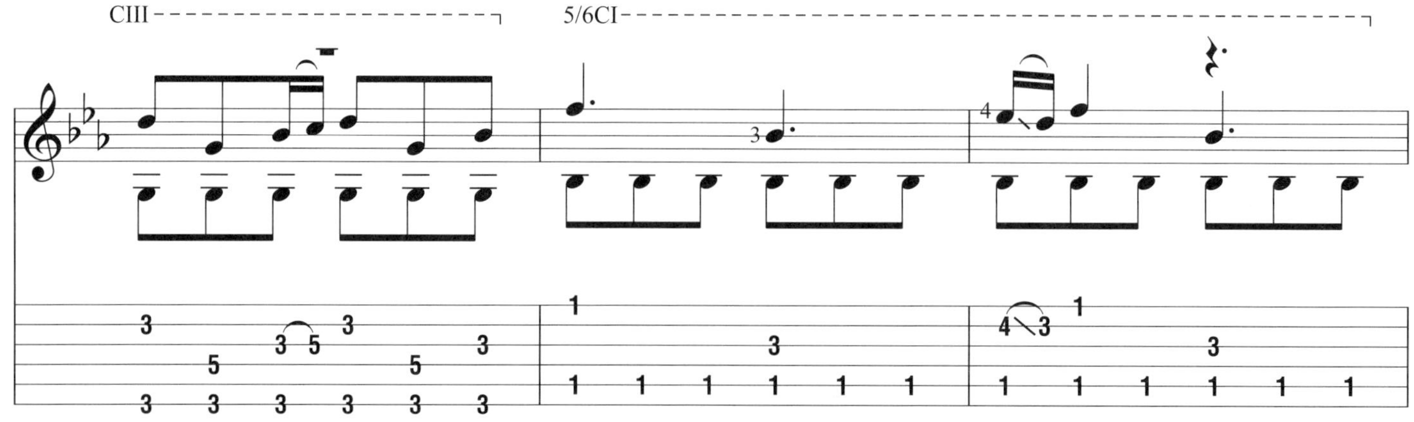

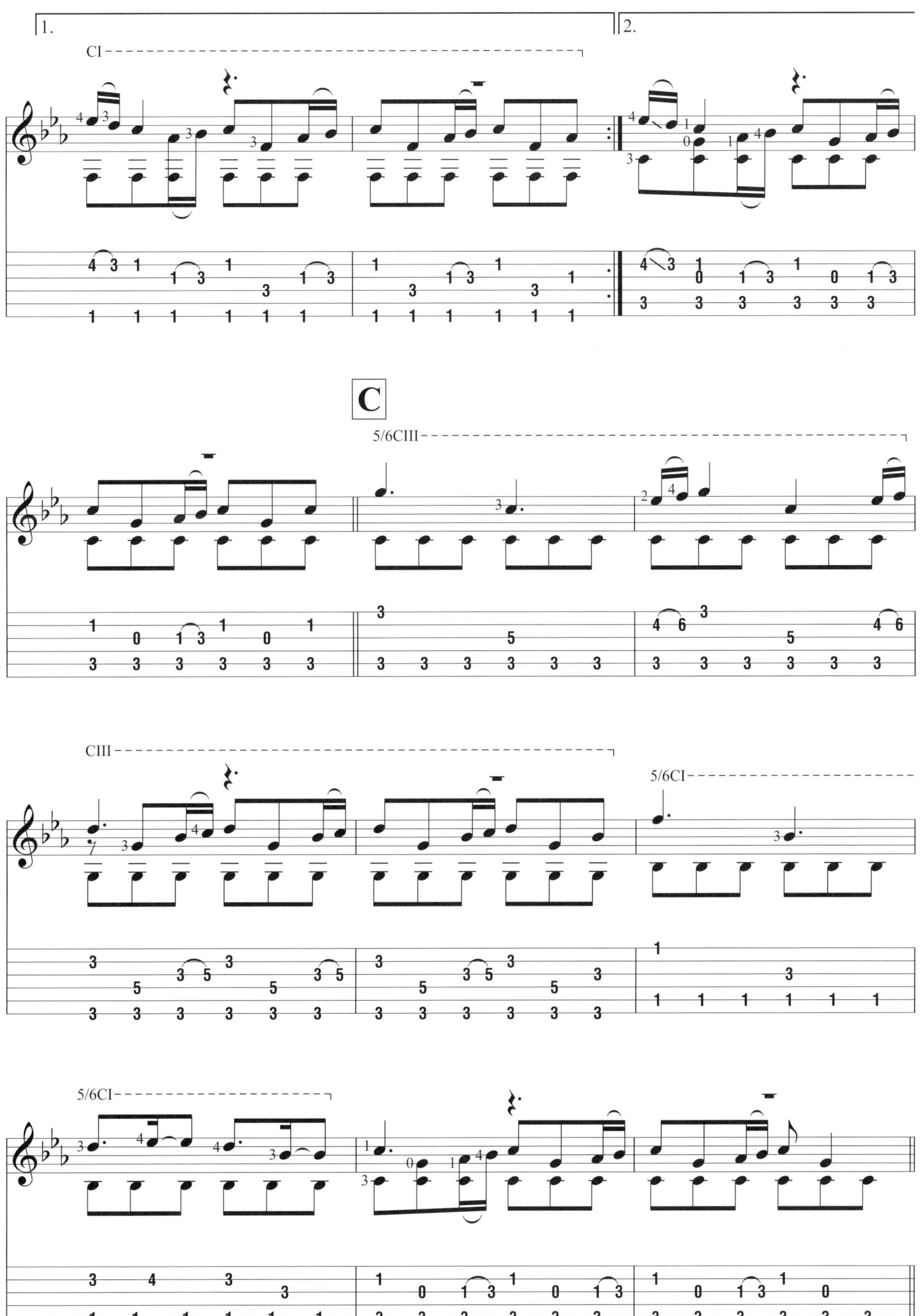

1.
2.
CI
C
5/6CIII
CIII
5/6CI
5/6CI

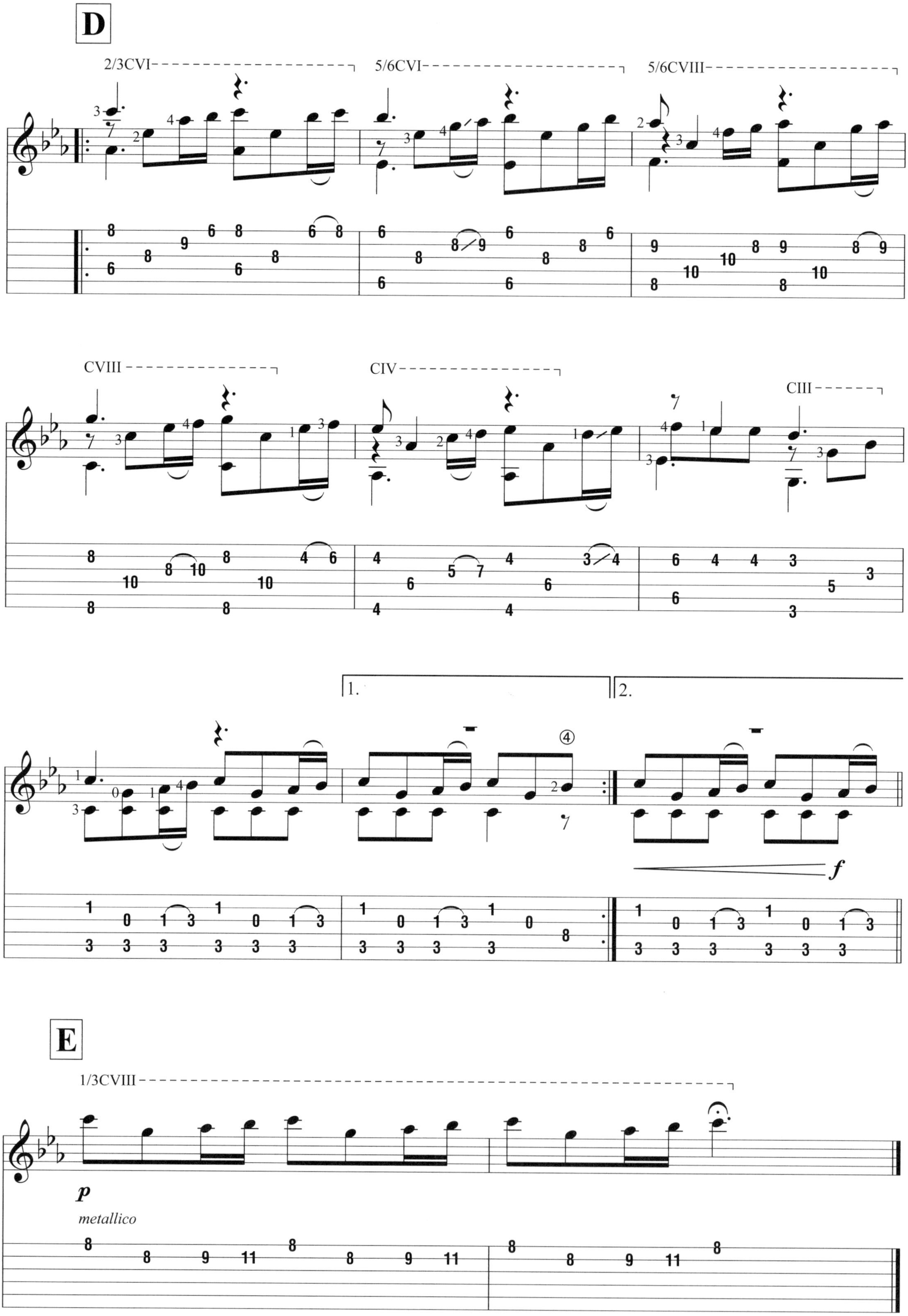

D

2/3CVI 5/6CVI 5/6CVIII

CVIII CIV CIII

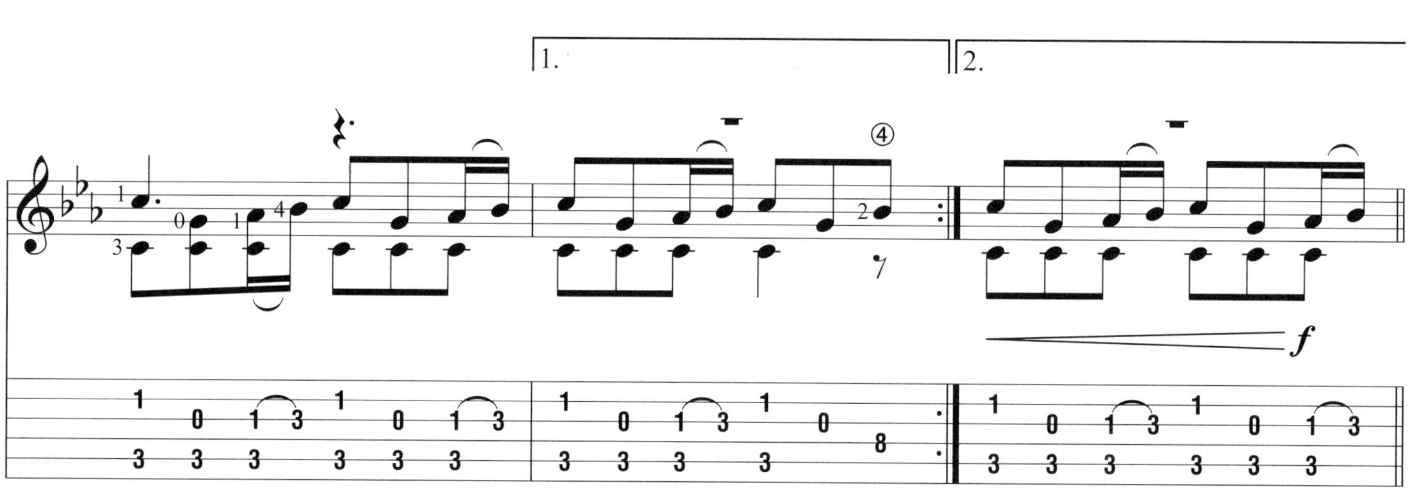

E

Let It Go

Words and Music by James Bay and Paul Barry

Drop D tuning:
(low to high) D-A-D-G-B-E

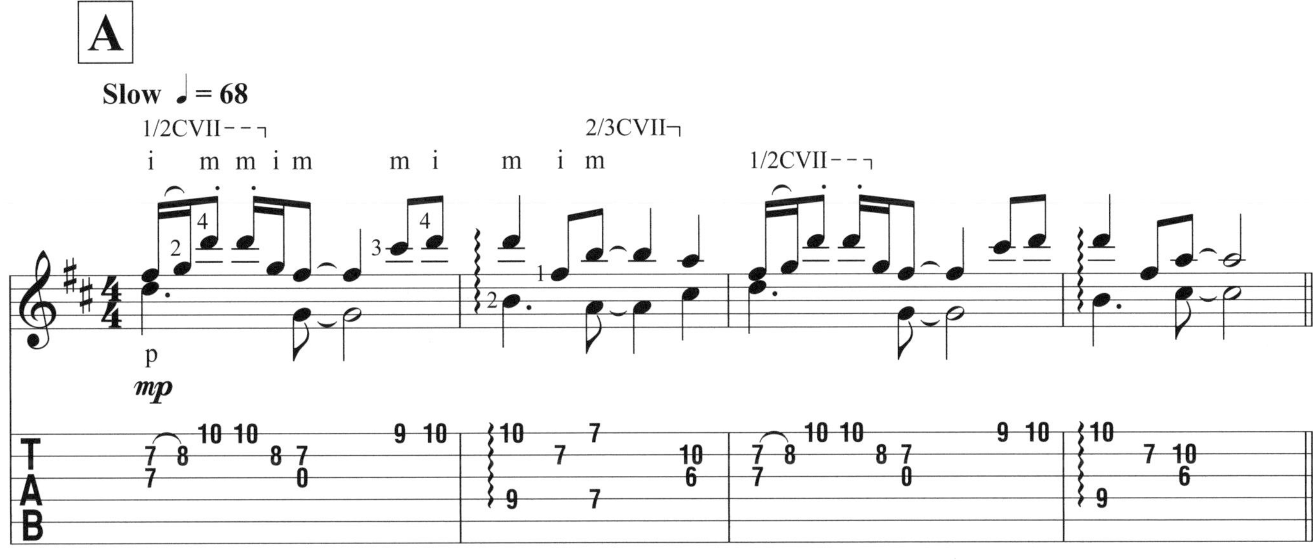

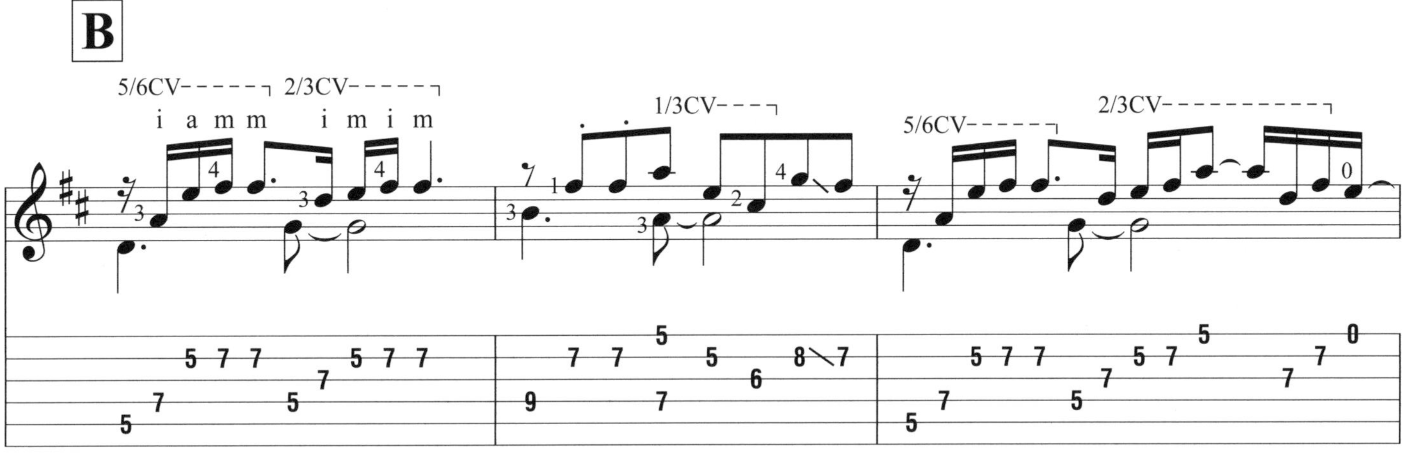

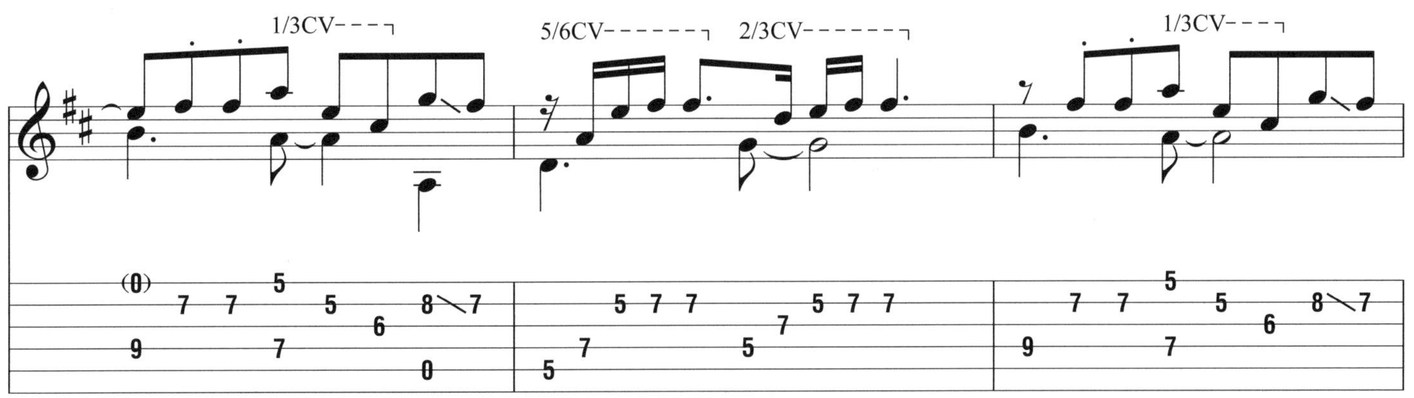

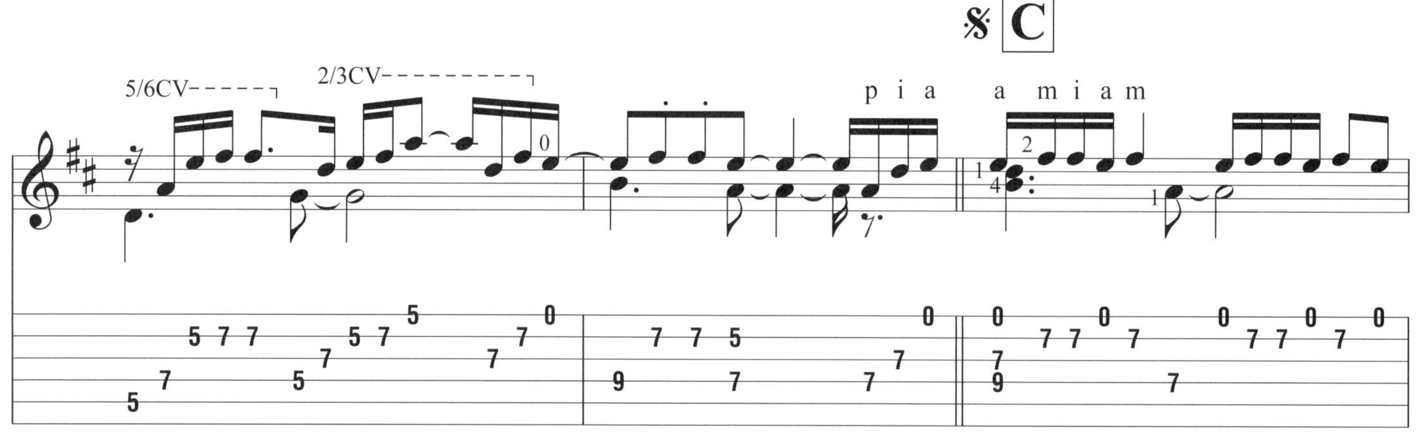
C
5/6CV
2/3CV
p i a a m i a m

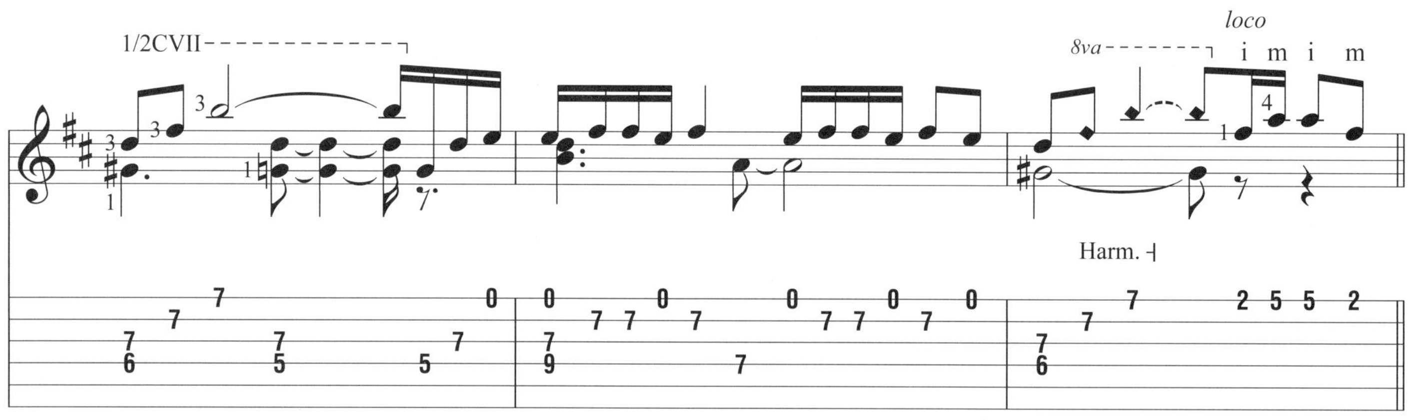
1/2CVII
loco
8va
i m i m
Harm.

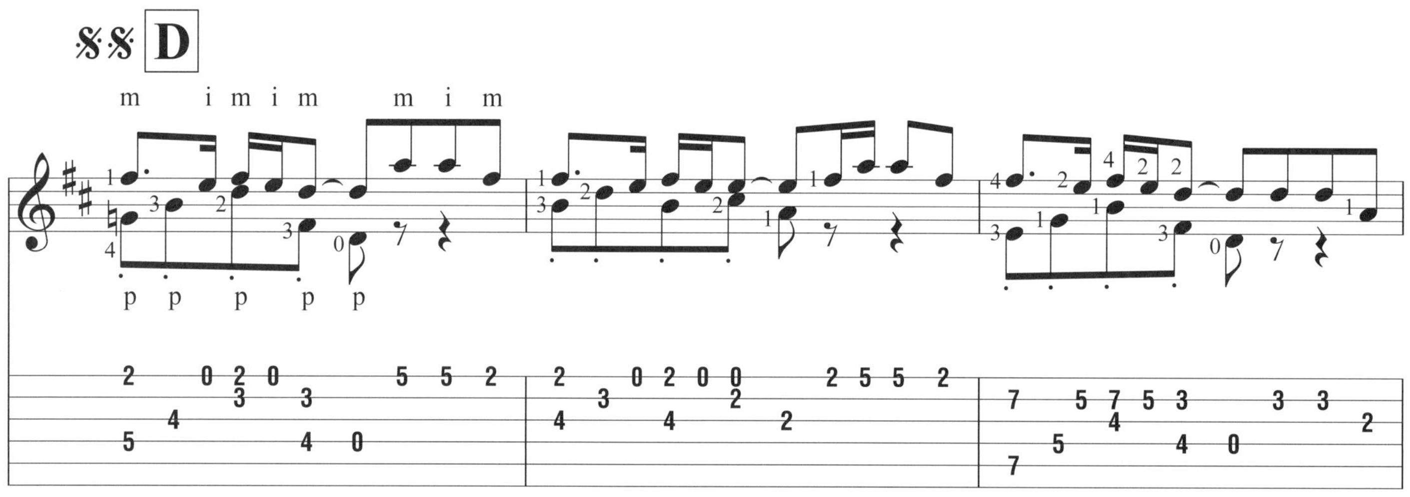
D
m i m i m m i m
p p p p p

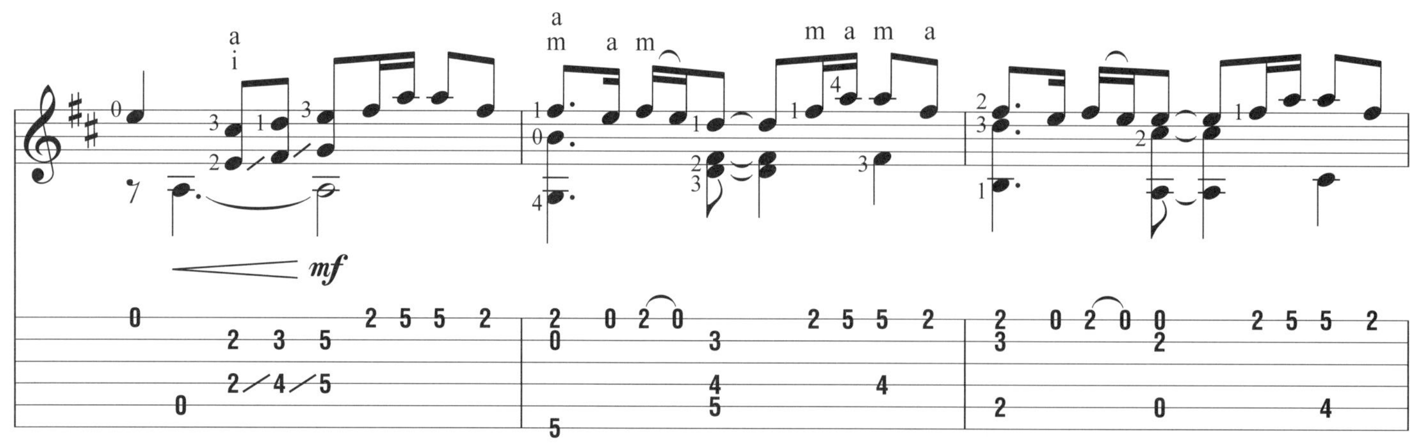
a
i
a
m a m
m a m a
mf

To Coda 2
E
mp
To Coda 1
F
5/6CV
CV
1/2CVII
1/3CV

D.S. al Coda 1
Coda 1

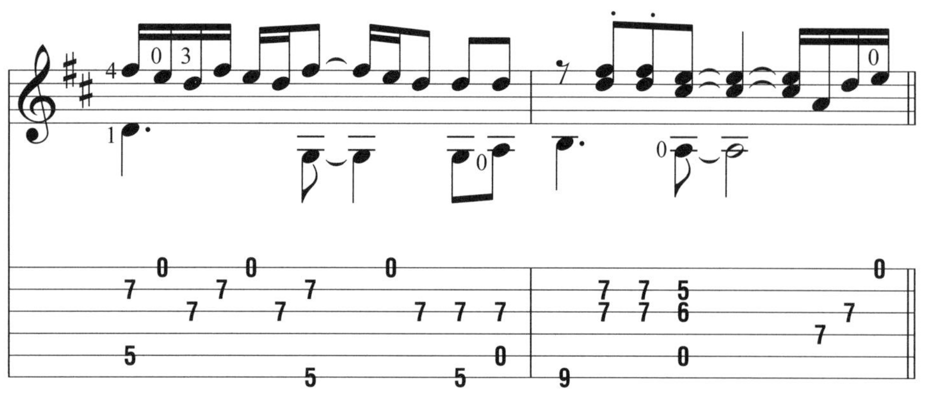

G

2/3CII
5/6CII

D.S.S. al Coda 2
i m i m i
2/3CII

Coda 2

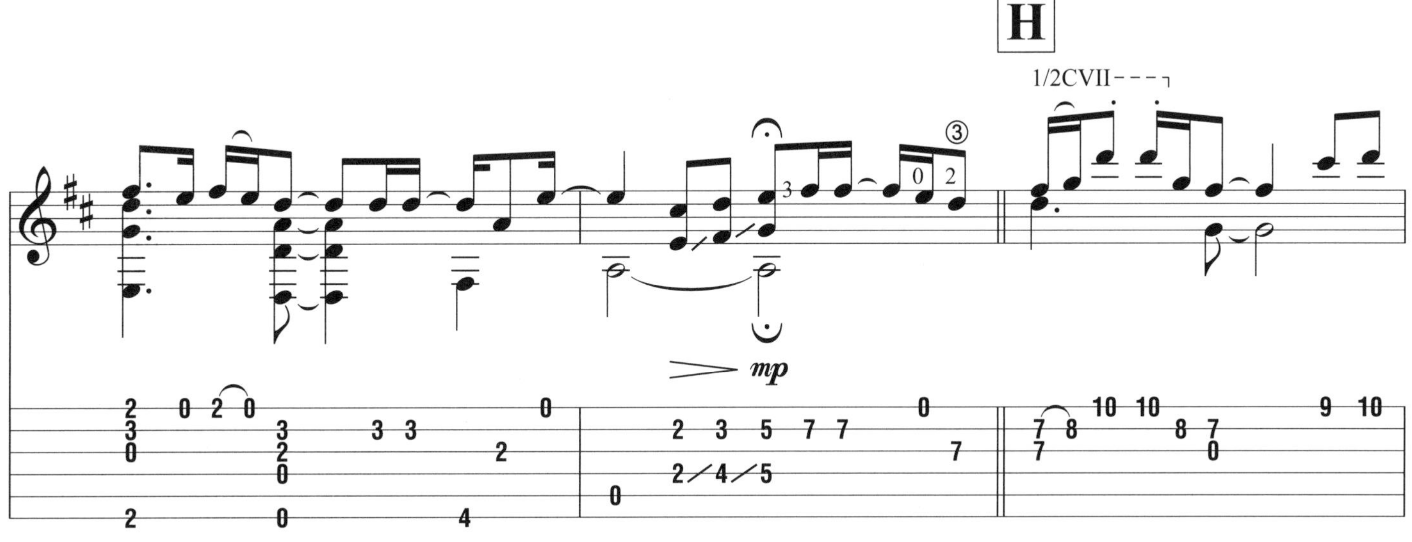
H
1/2CVII
mp

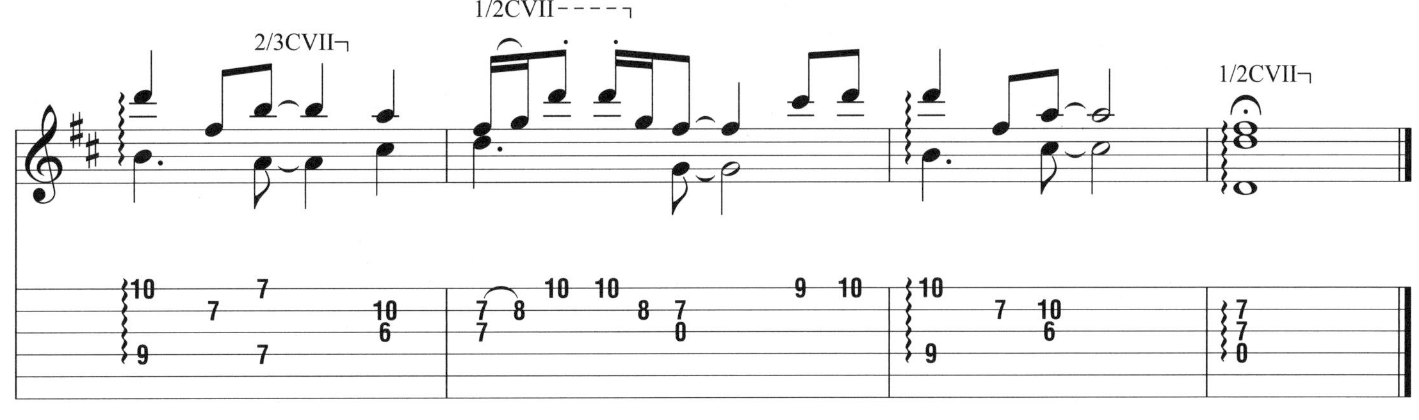
2/3CVII
1/2CVII
1/2CVII

Havana

Words and Music by Camila Cabello, Louis Bell, Pharrell Williams, Adam Feeney, Ali Tamposi, Jeffery Lamar Williams, Brian Lee, Andrew Wotman, Brittany Hazzard and Kaan Gunesberk

Moderately slow, freely ♩ = 82

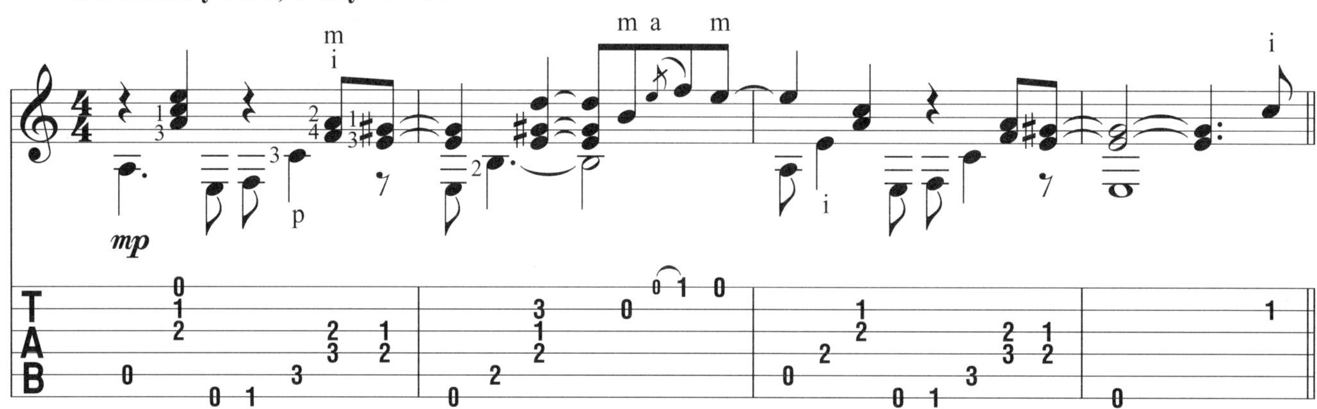

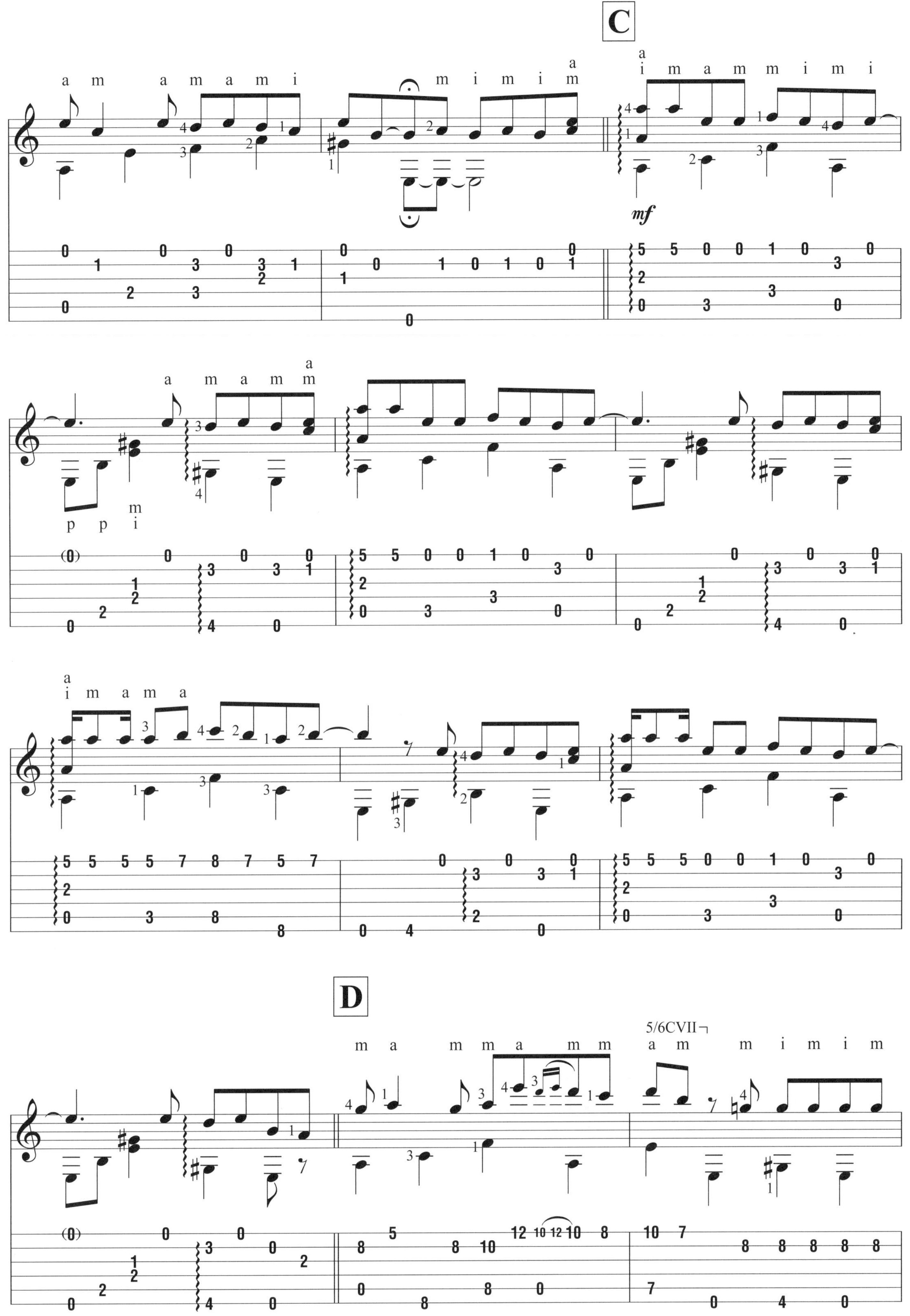
C
mf
D
5/6CVII

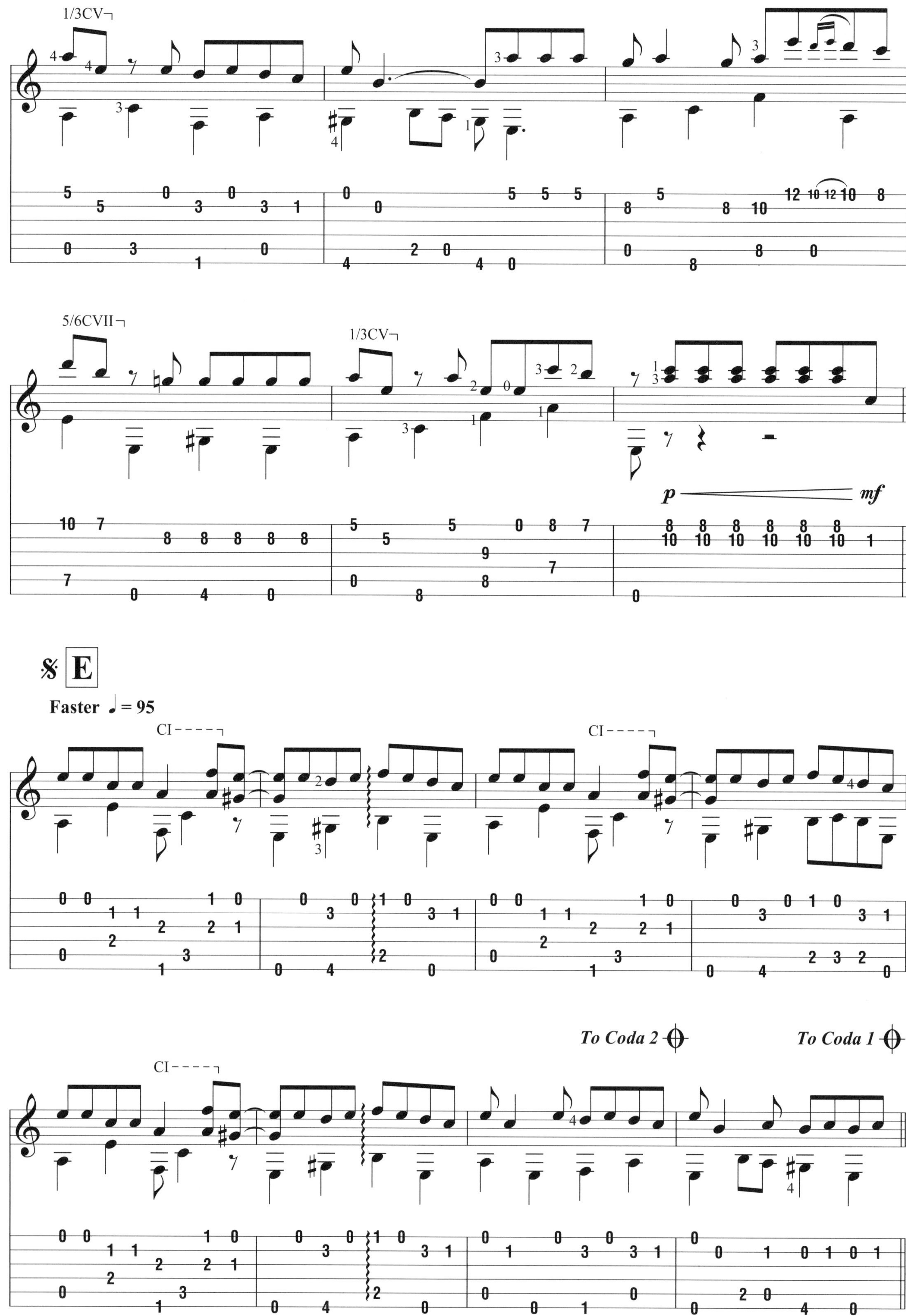

1/3CV
5/6CVII
1/3CV
p
mf
E
Faster ♩ = 95
CI
CI
CI
To Coda 2
To Coda 1

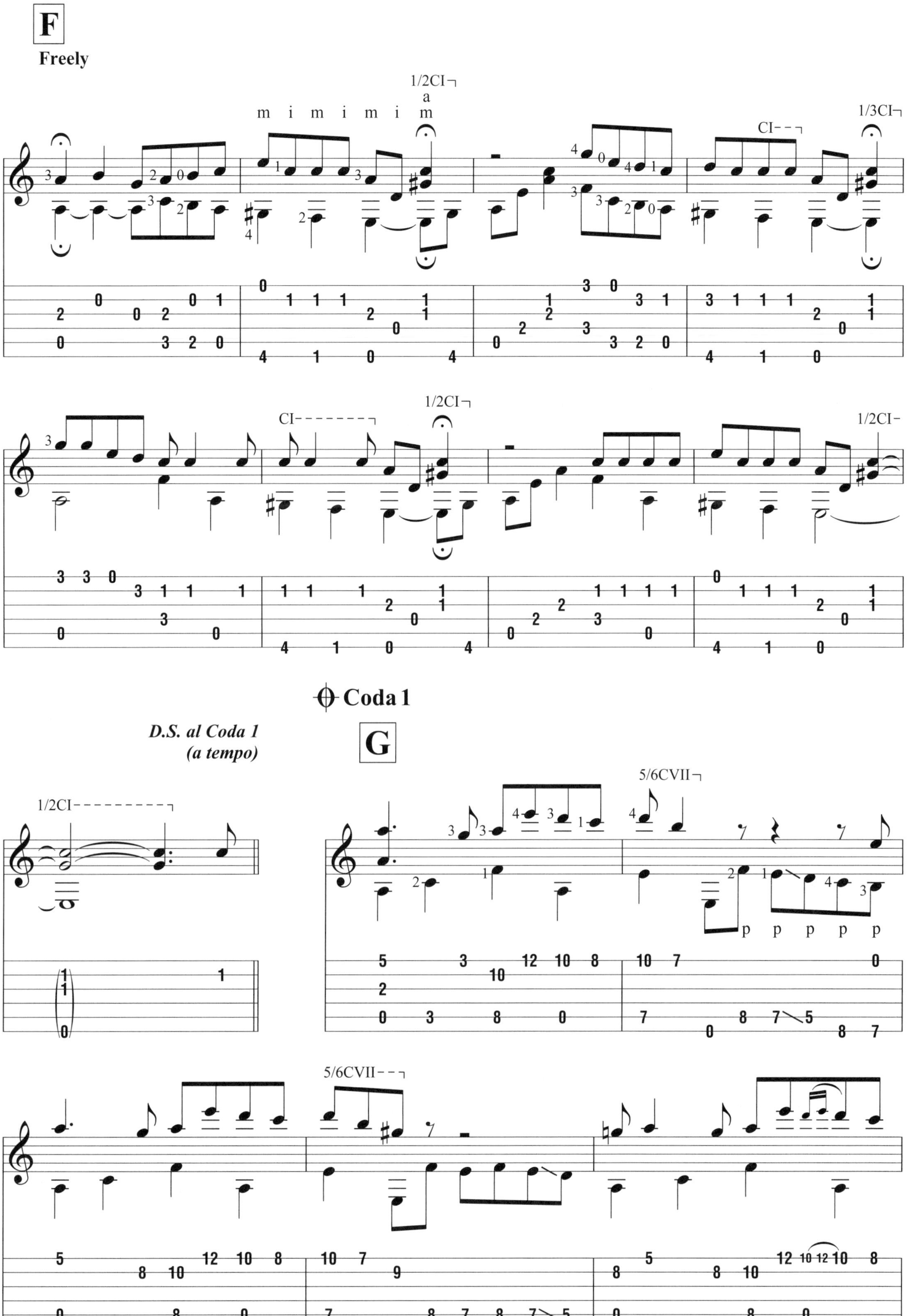

F
Freely
1/2CI
a
m i m i m i m
CI
1/3CI
1/2CI
CI
1/2CI
Coda 1
D.S. al Coda 1
(a tempo)
G
1/2CI
5/6CVII
p p p p p
5/6CVII

D.S. al Coda 2

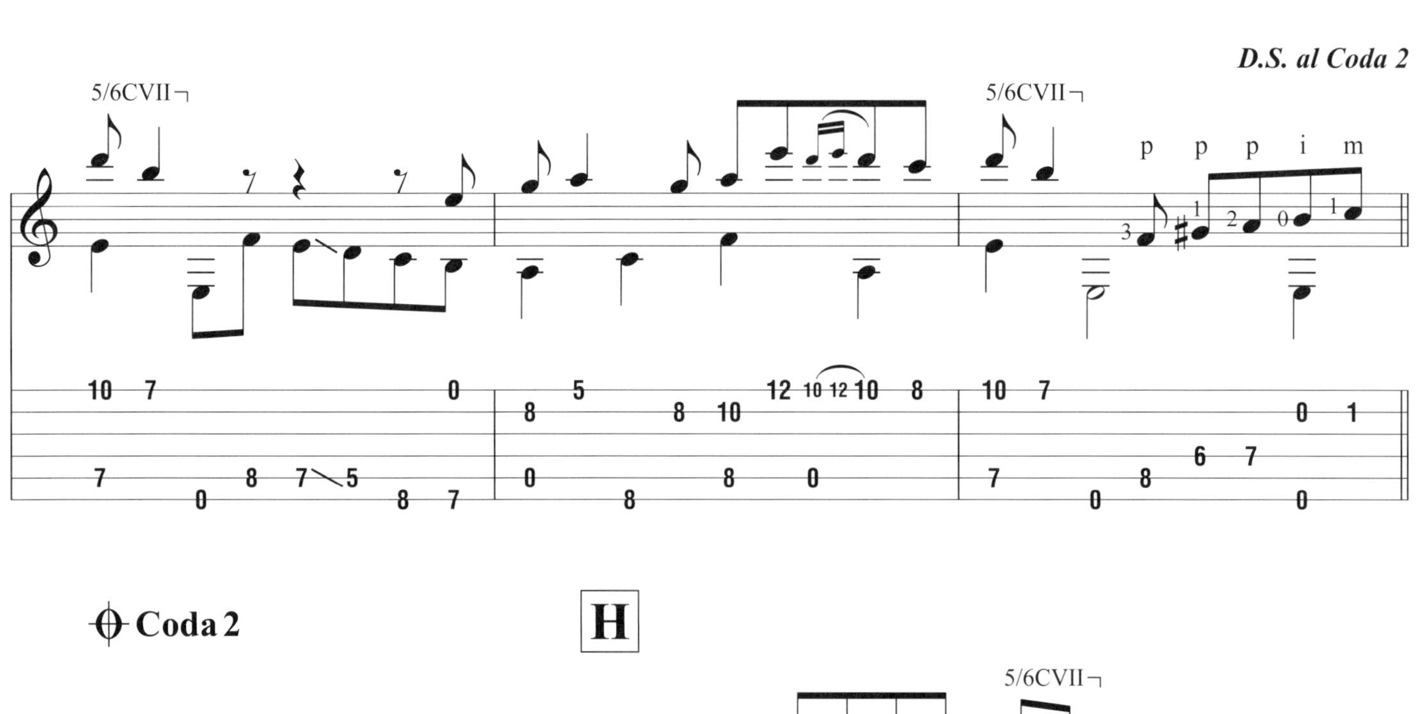

Coda 2

H

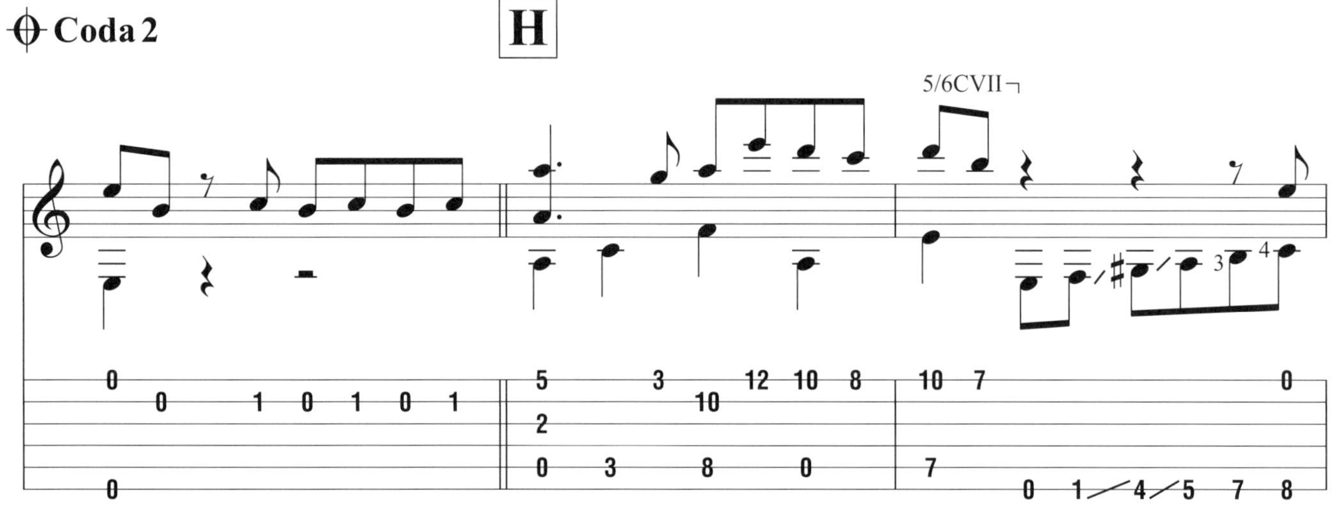

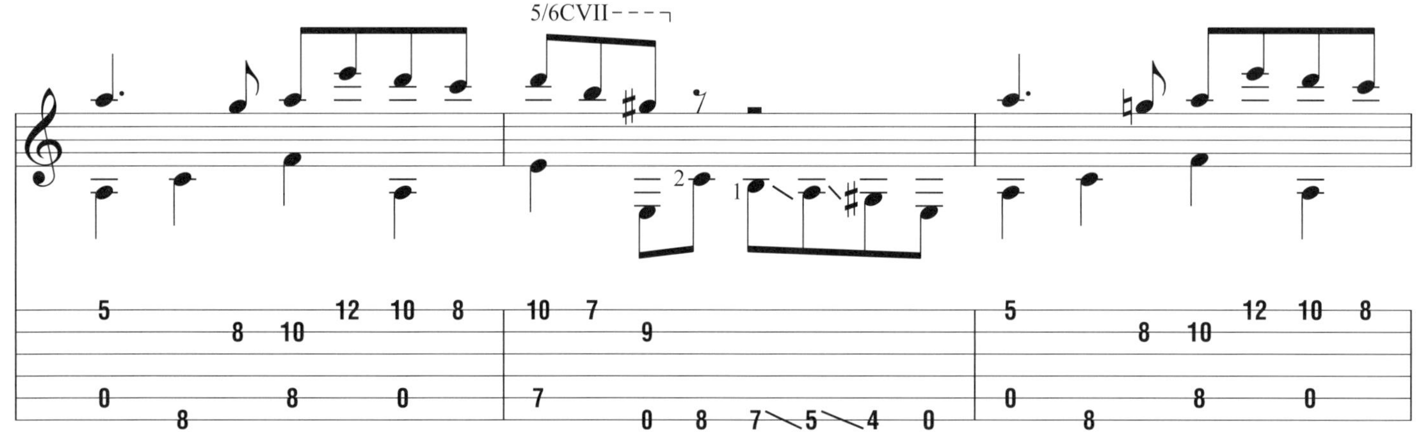

Paradise

Words and Music by Guy Berryman, Jon Buckland,
Will Champion, Chris Martin and Brian Eno

Drop D tuning:
(low to high) D-A-D-G-B-E

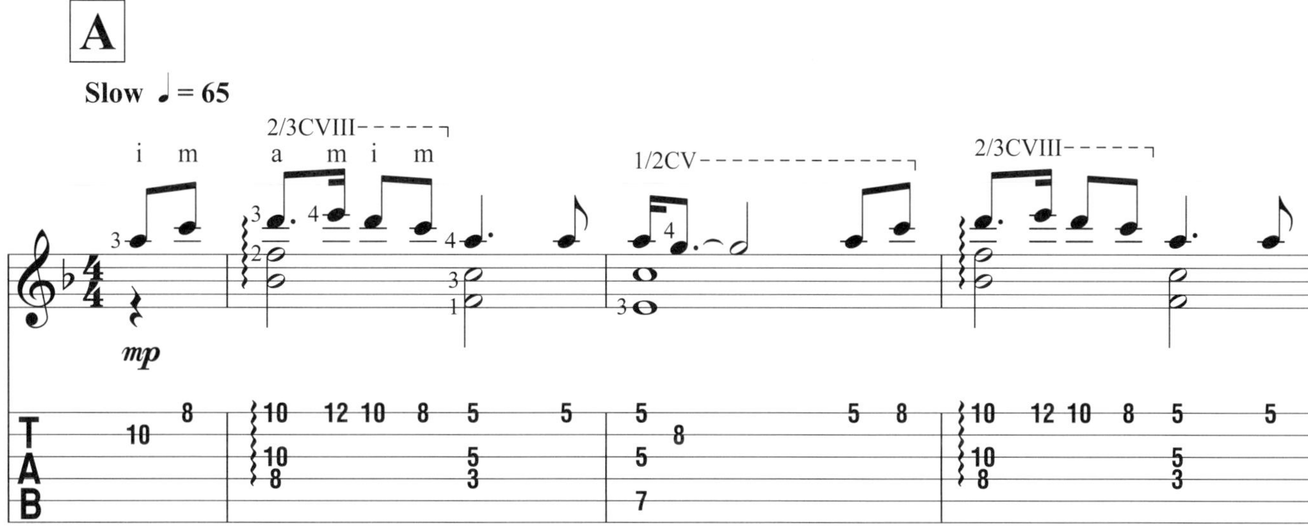

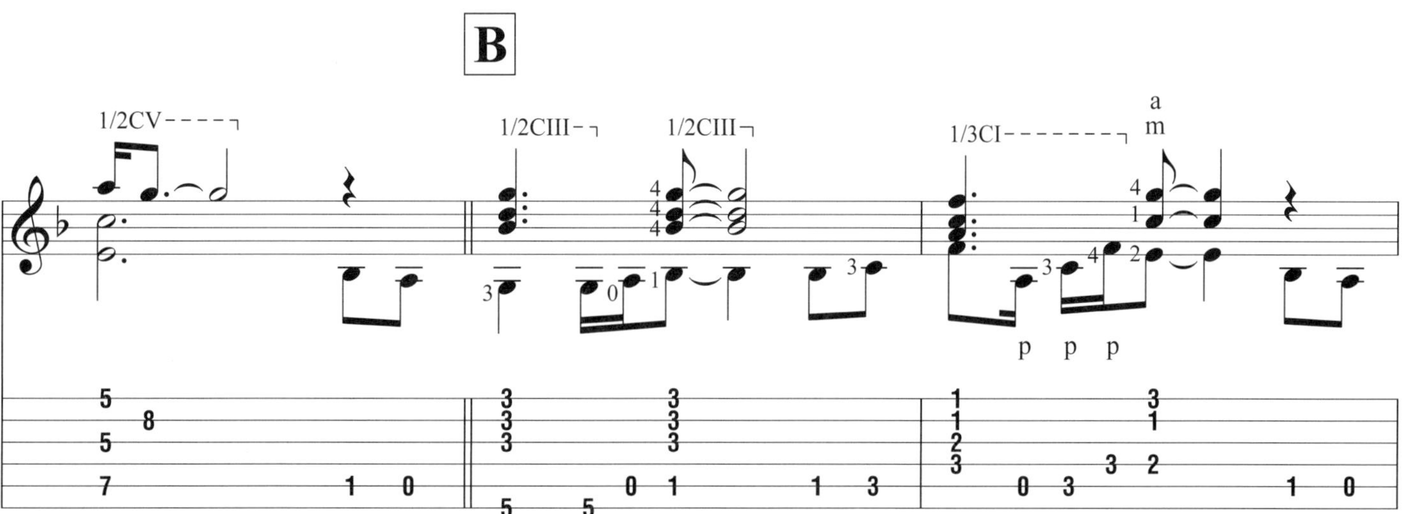

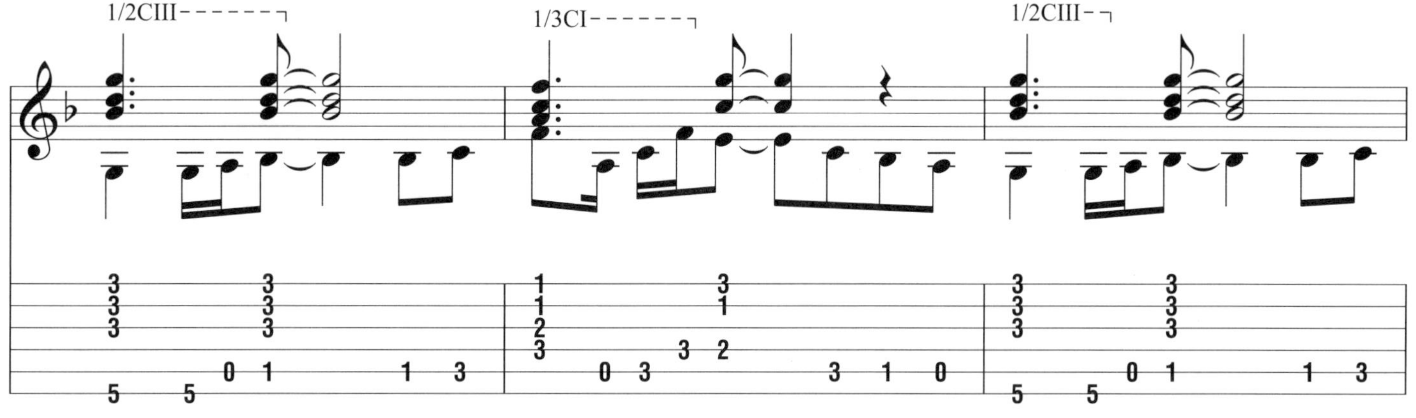

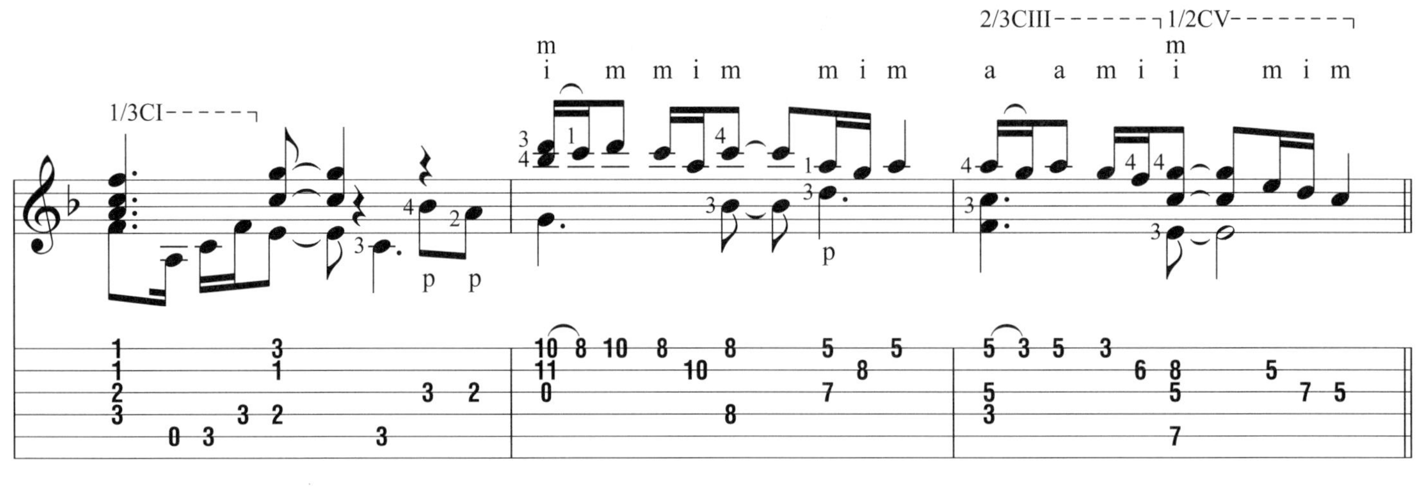
2/3CIII
1/2CV
1/3CI
m
i m m i m m i m
a a m i i m i m
p p
p

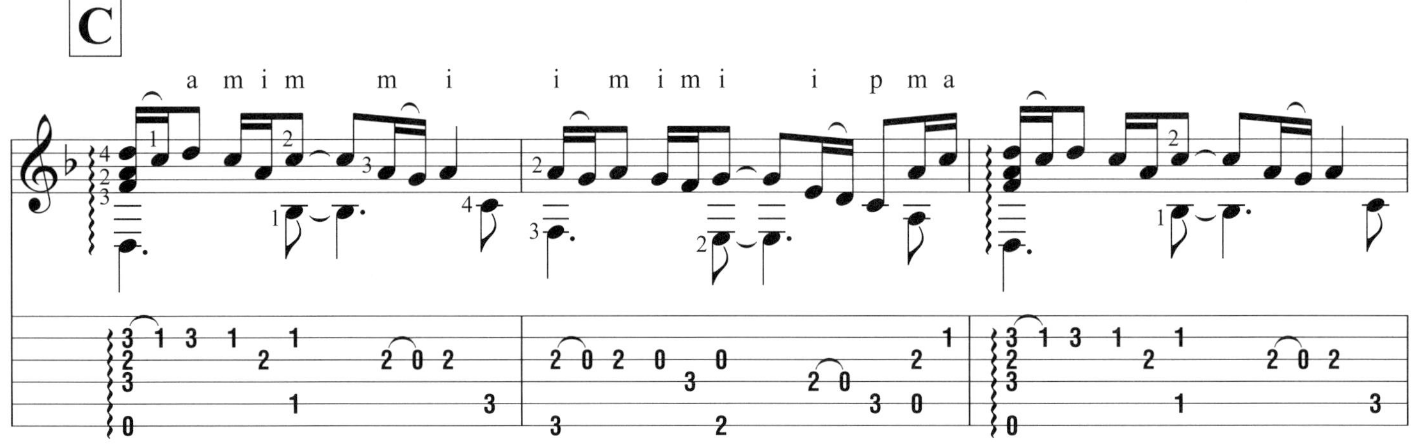
C
a m i m m i
i m i m i i p m a

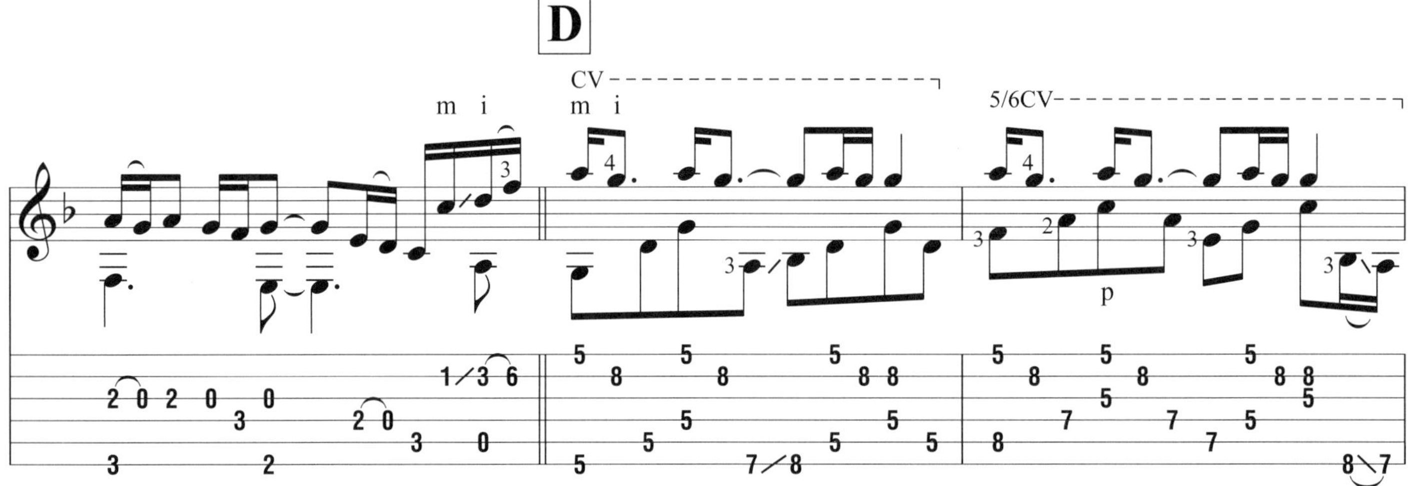
D
CV
5/6CV
m i
m i
p

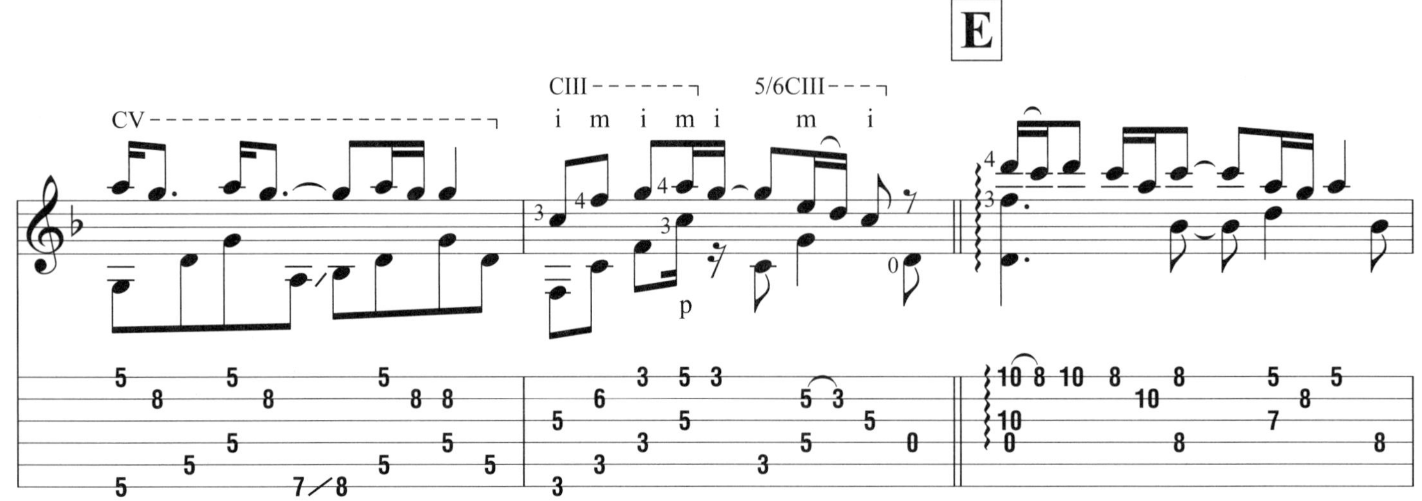
E
CV
CIII
5/6CIII
i m i m i m i
p

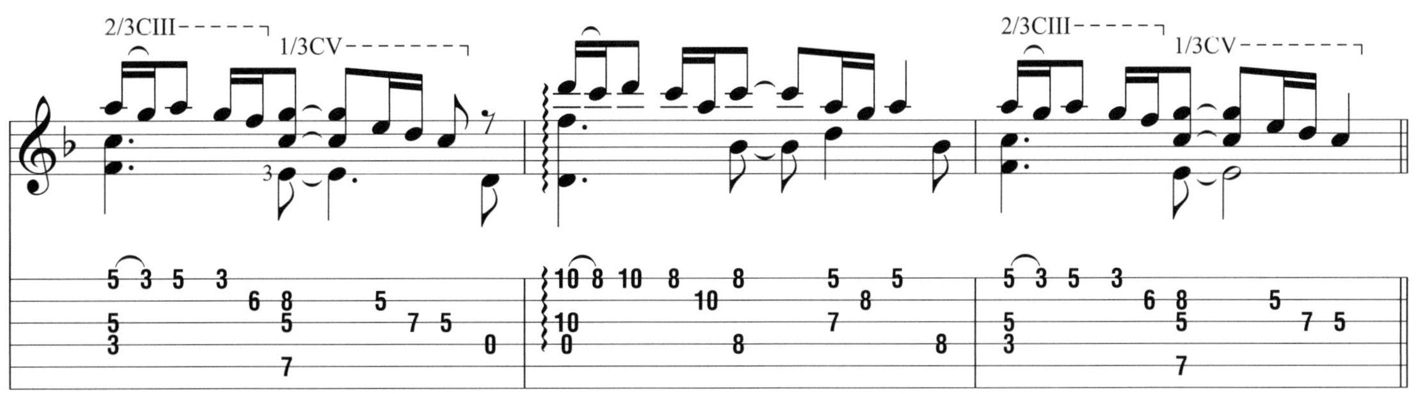
2/3CIII
1/3CV
2/3CIII
1/3CV

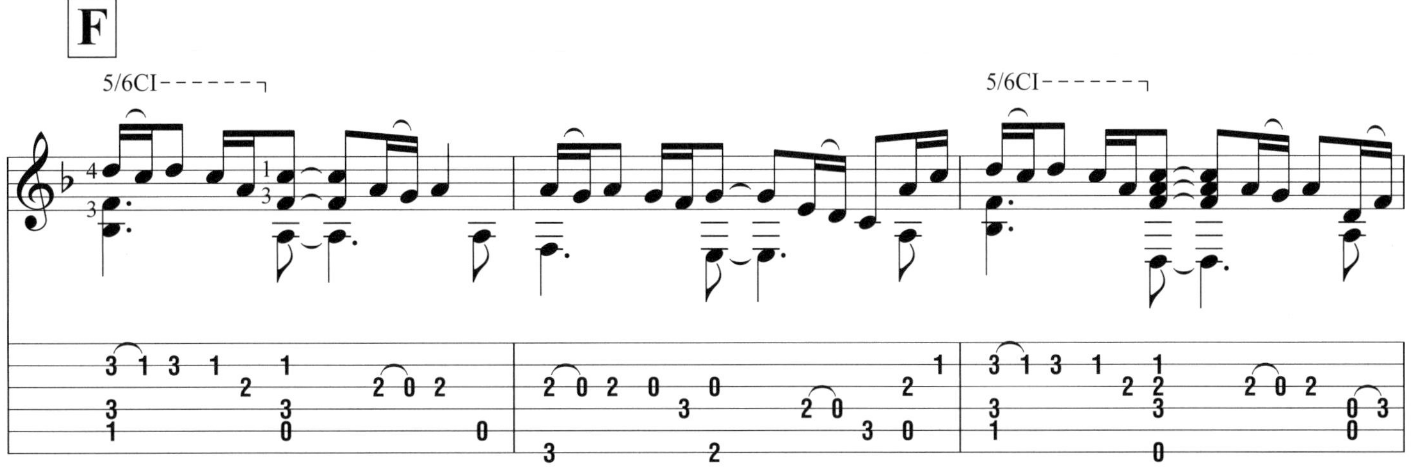
F
5/6CI
5/6CI

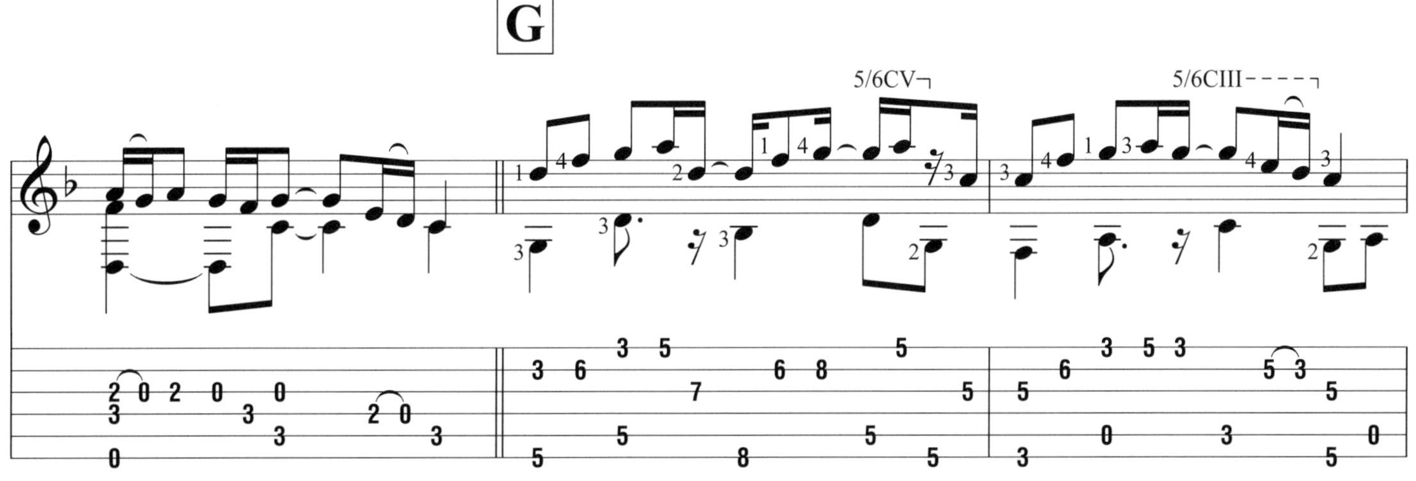
G
5/6CV
5/6CIII

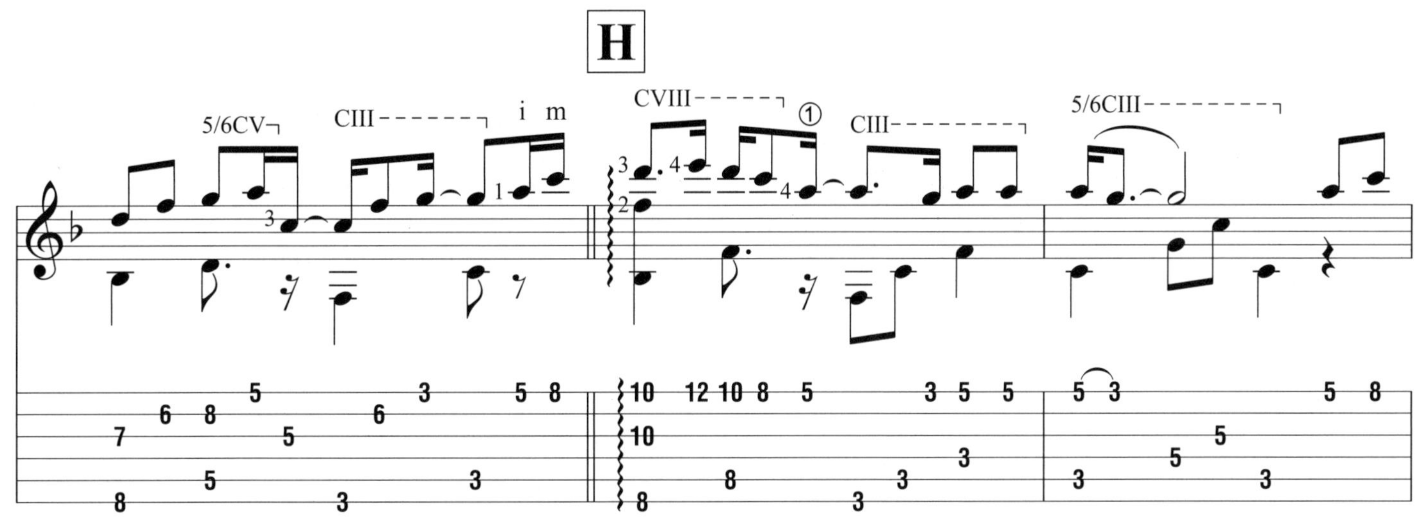
H
5/6CV
CIII
i m
CVIII
①
CIII
5/6CIII

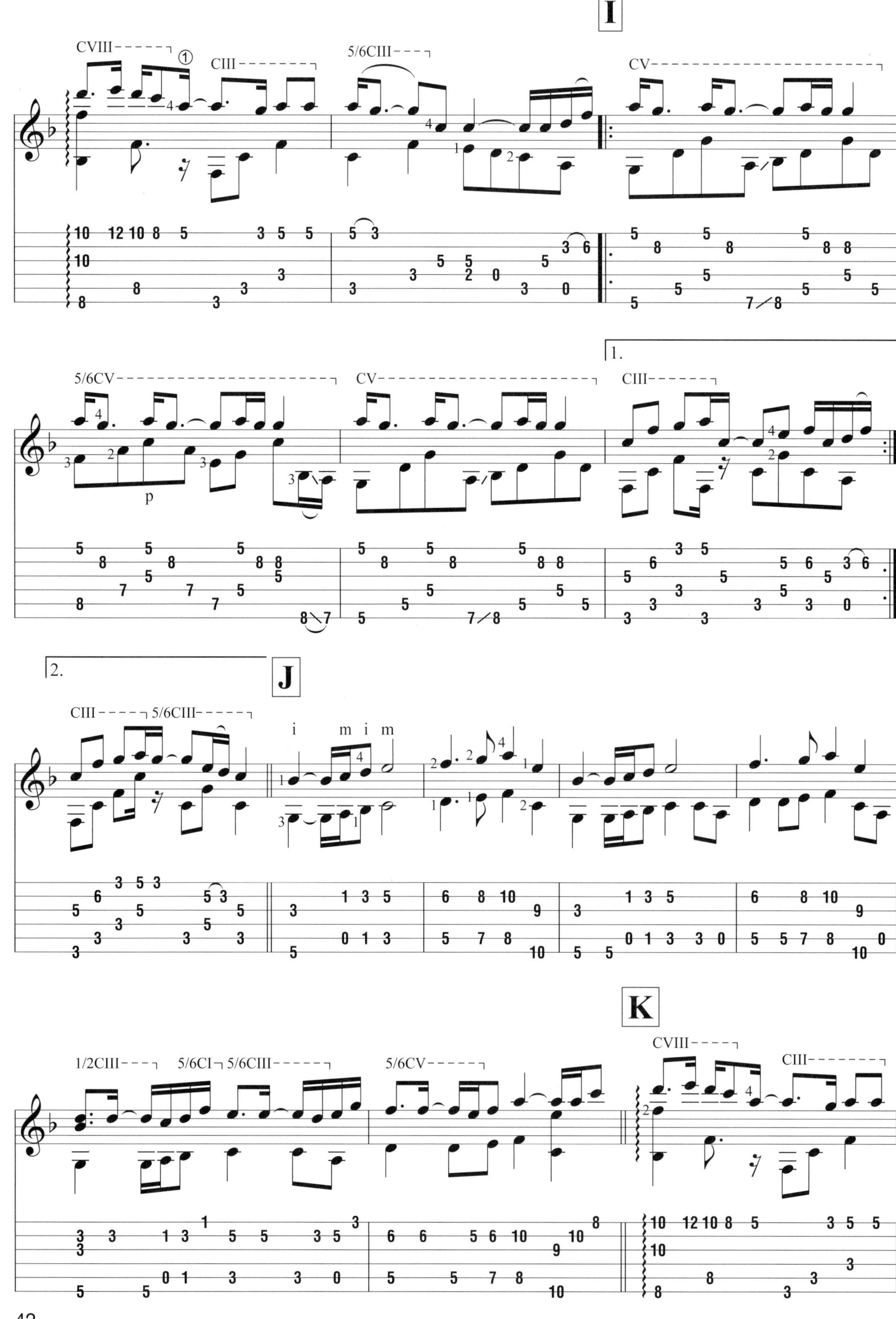
I
CVIII
CIII
5/6CIII
CV
5/6CV
CV
1.
CIII
2.
J
CIII
5/6CIII
i m i m
K
1/2CIII
5/6CI
5/6CIII
5/6CV
CVIII
CIII

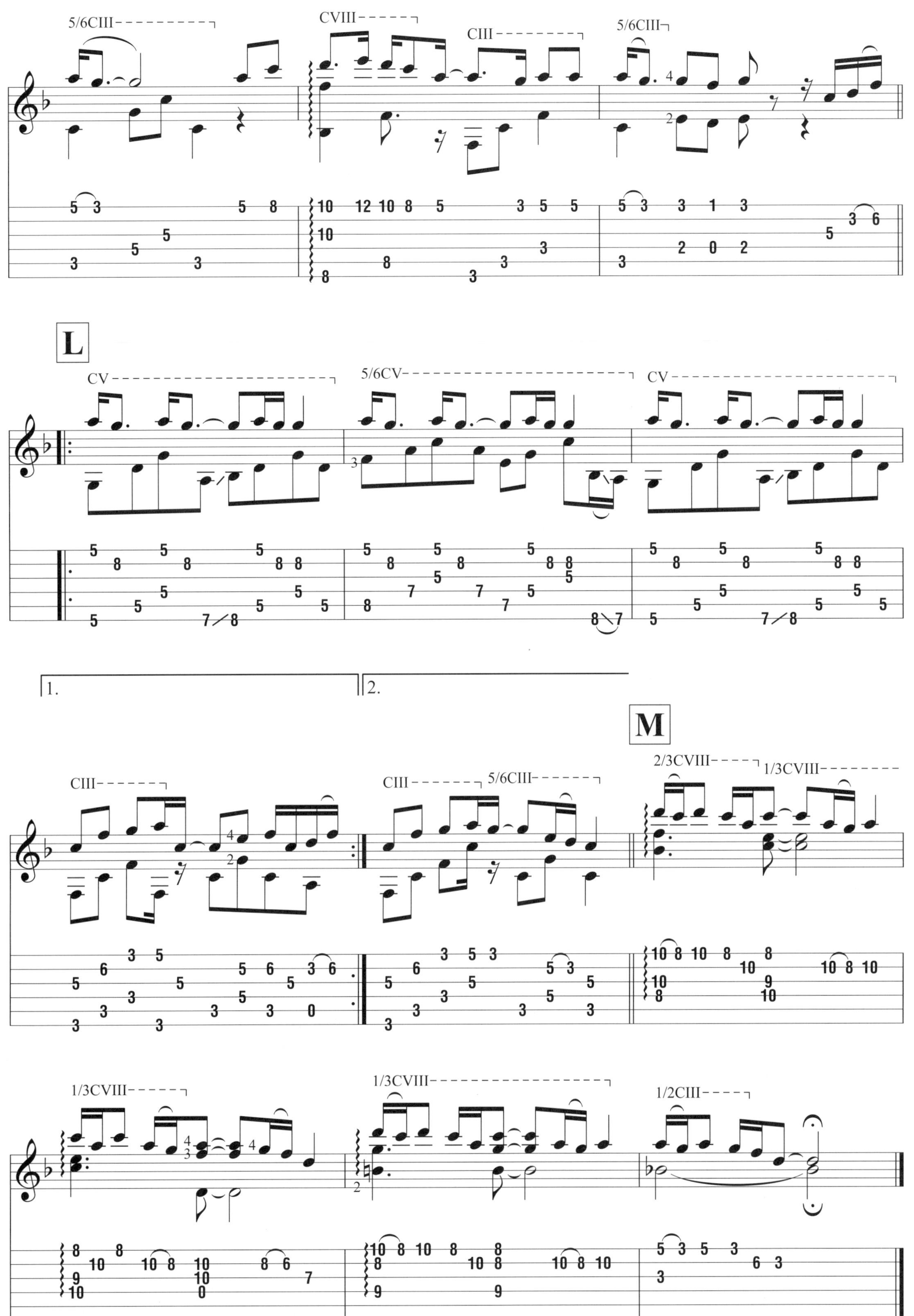
5/6CIII
CVIII
CIII
5/6CIII
L
CV
5/6CV
CV
1.
2.
M
CIII
CIII
5/6CIII
2/3CVIII
1/3CVIII
1/3CVIII
1/3CVIII
1/2CIII

Hello

Words and Music by Adele Adkins and Greg Kurstin

Drop D tuning:
(low to high) D-A-D-G-B-E

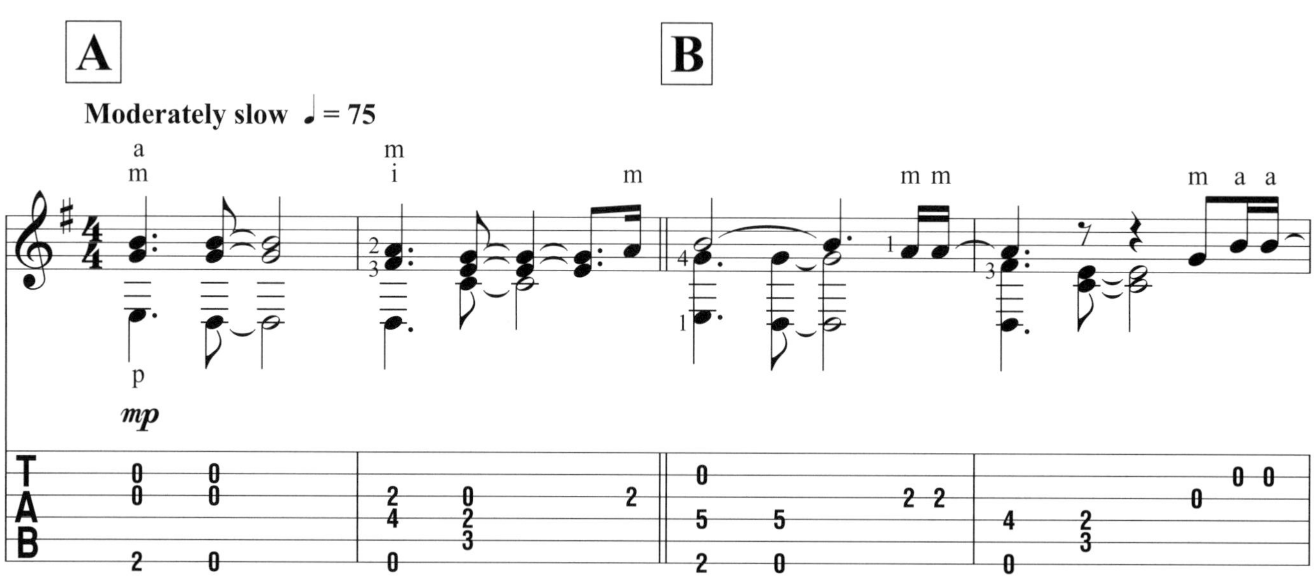

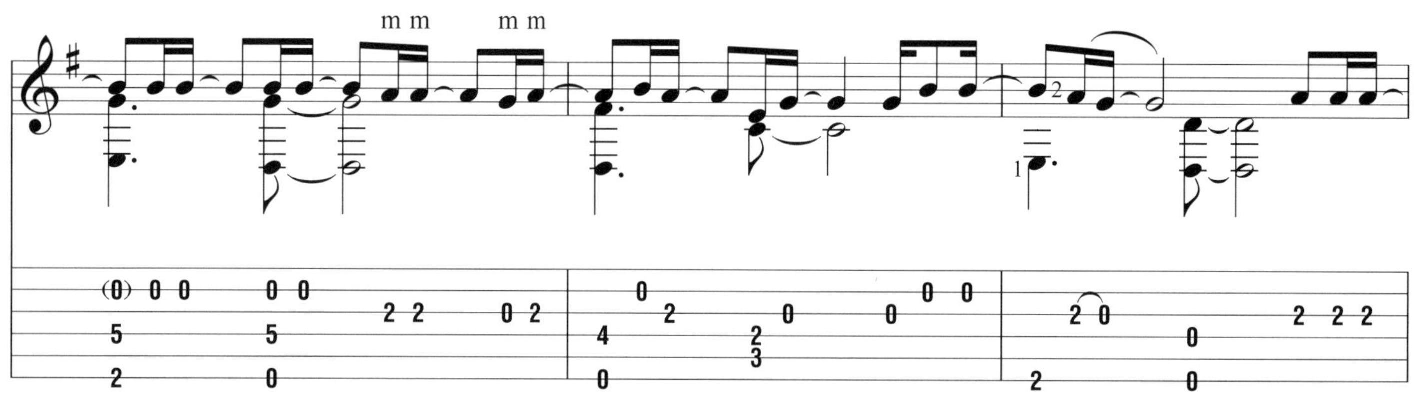

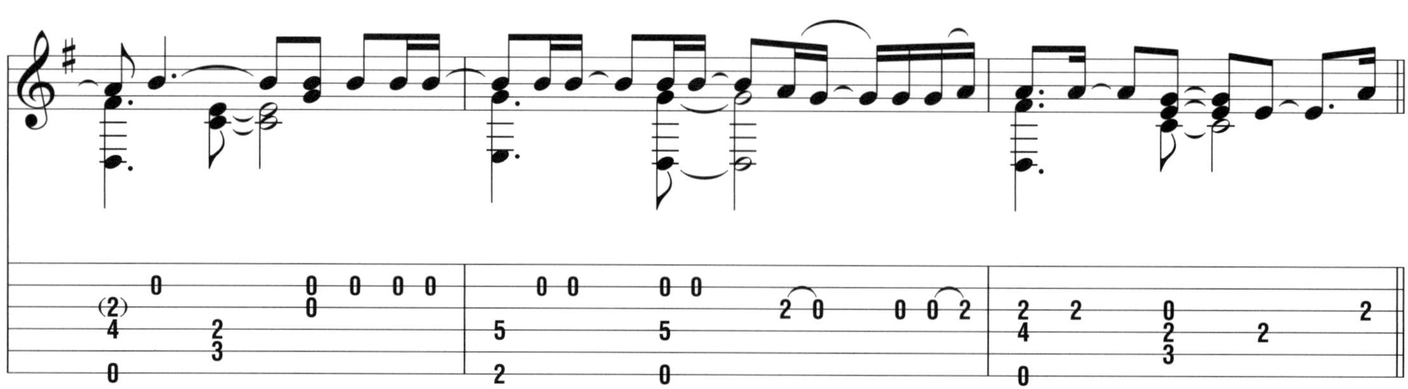

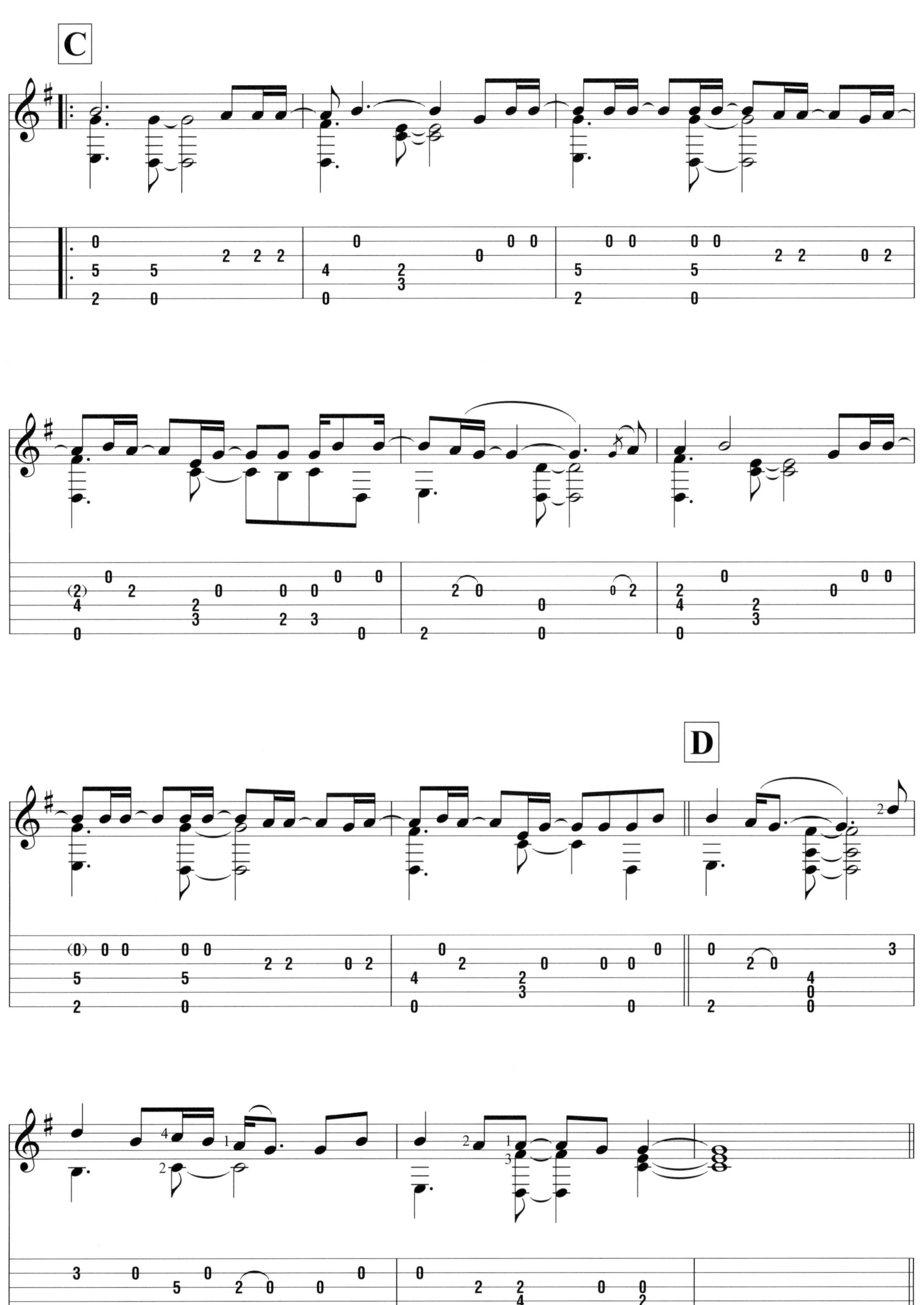
C
D

E

m a
5/6CVII
mf

2/3CVII

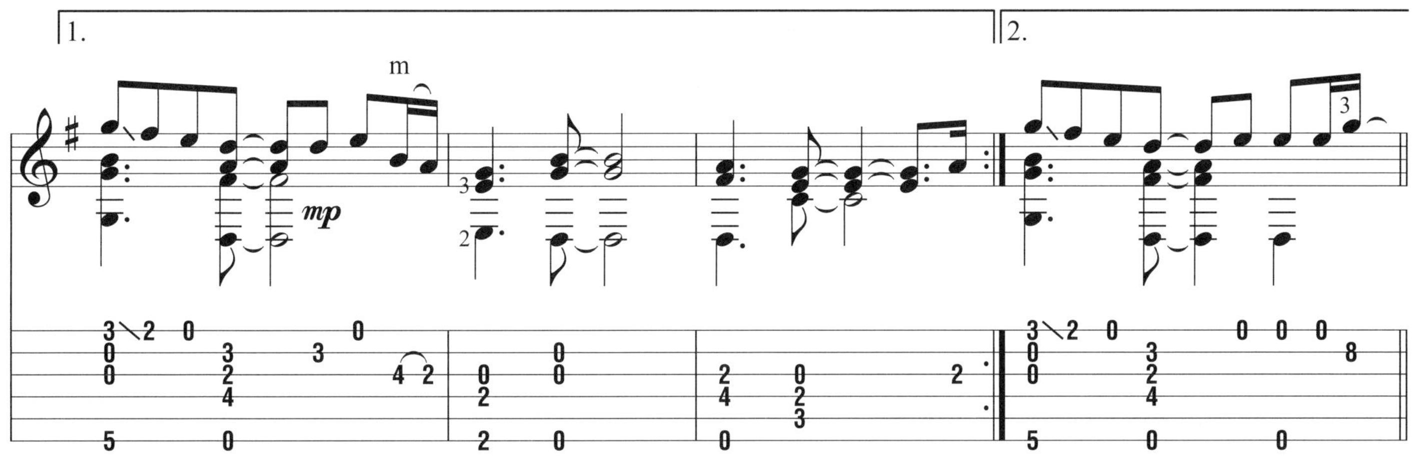
1.
2.
mp

F

D.S. al Coda

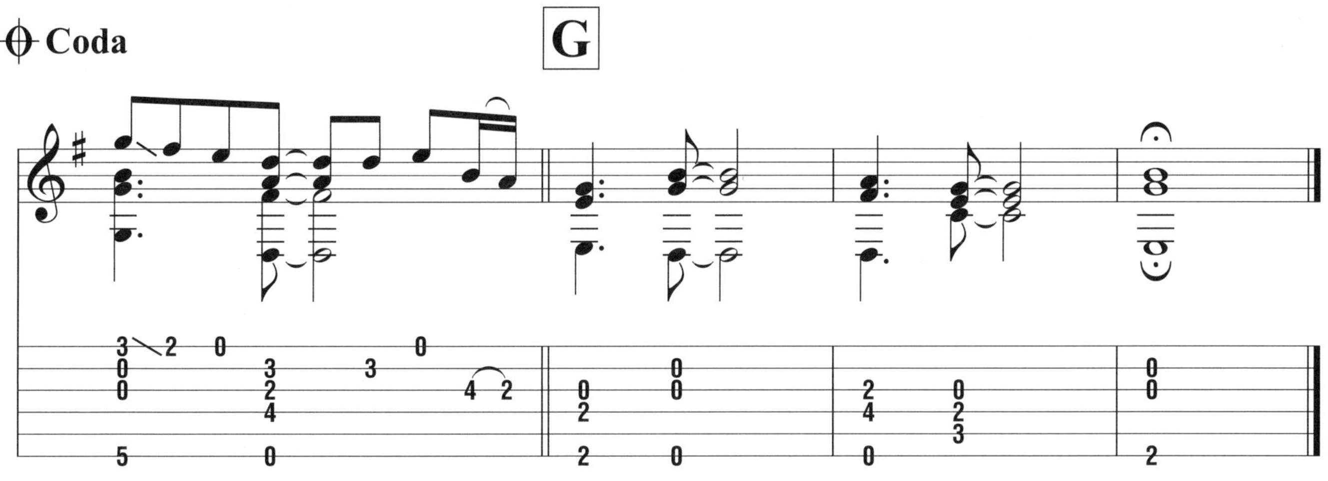
Coda
G

Radioactive

Words and Music by Daniel Reynolds, Benjamin McKee,
Daniel Sermon, Alexander Grant and Josh Mosser

Drop D tuning;
(low to high) D-A-D-G-B-E

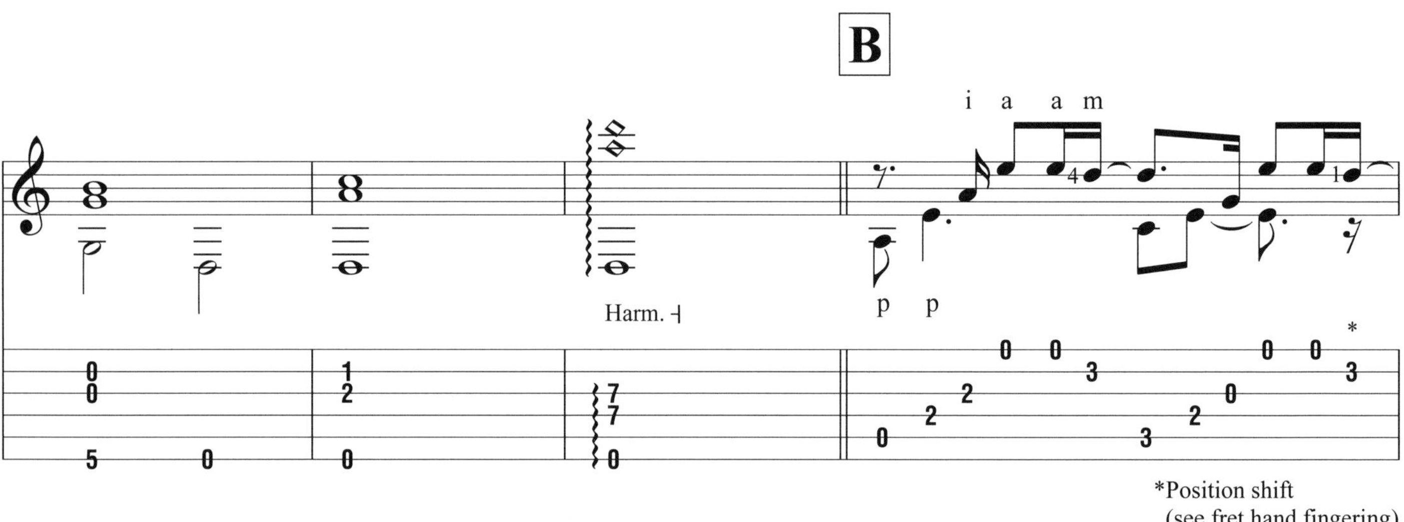

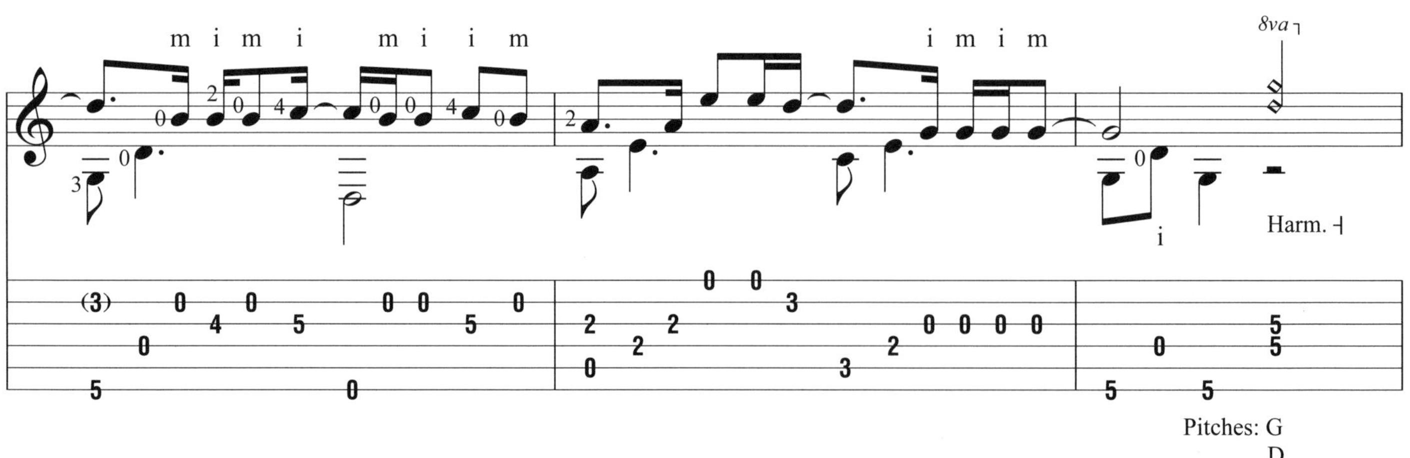

loco

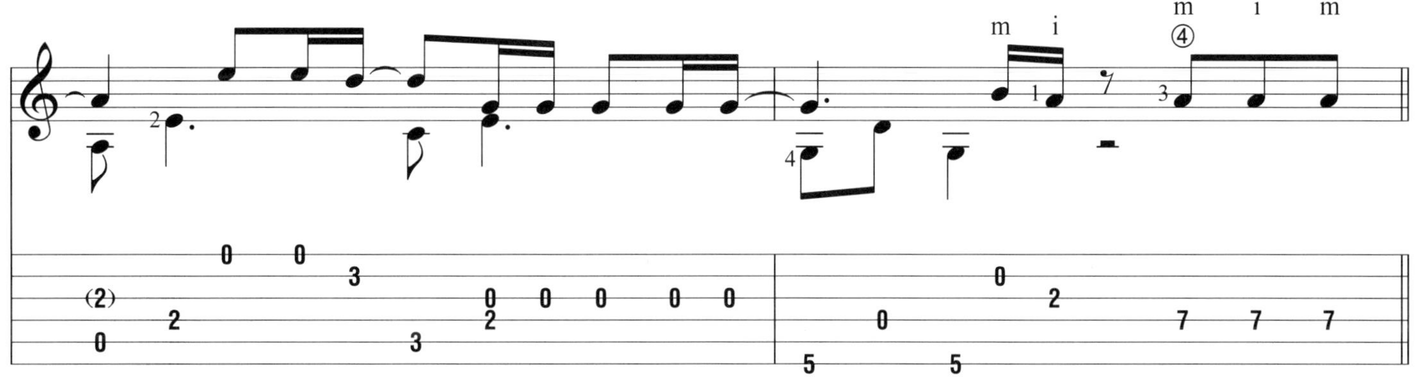
m i
m i m

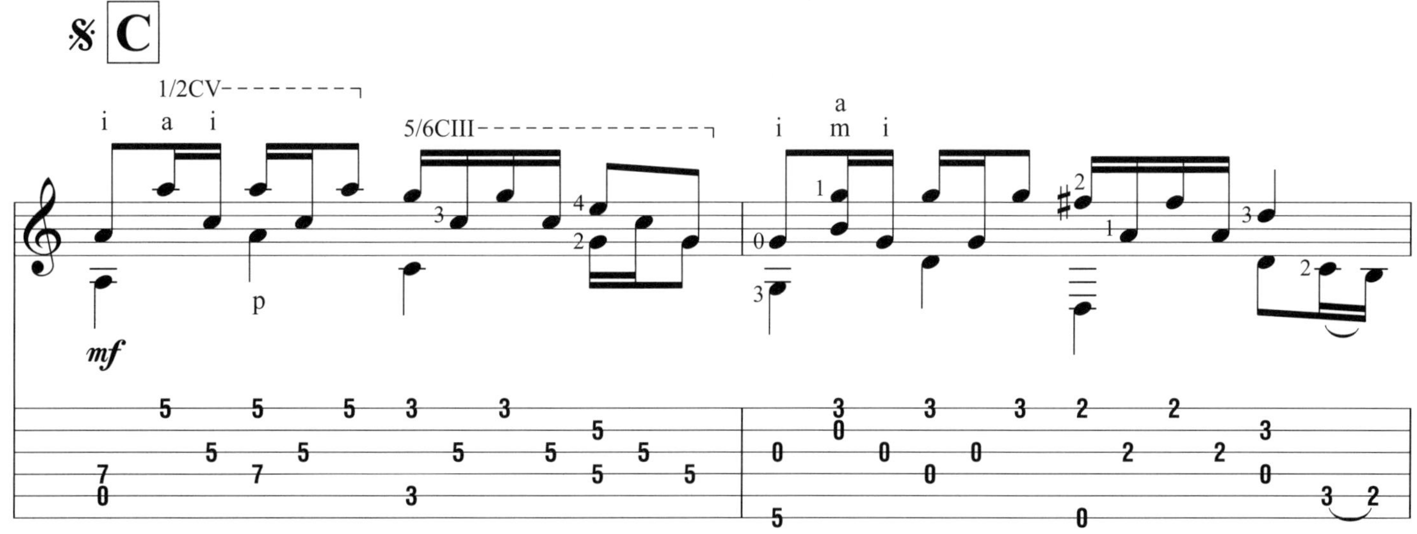
C
1/2CV
5/6CIII
i a i
p
mf
a
i m i

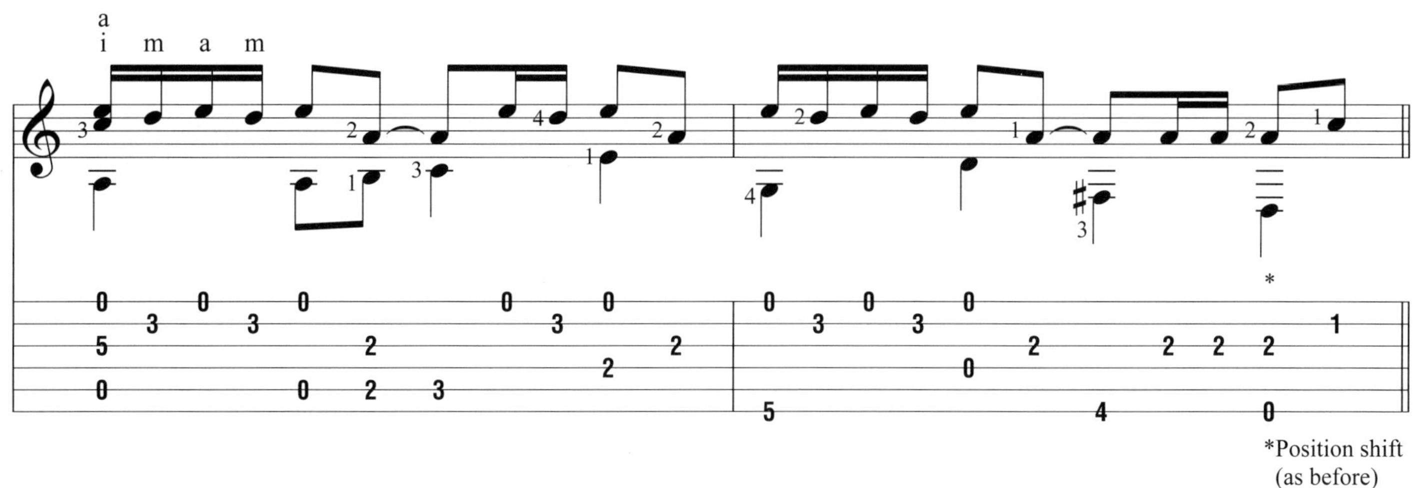
a
i m a m
*Position shift
(as before)

D
a m i
a
m
5/6CV
To Coda 2
To Coda 1
E
p i m a

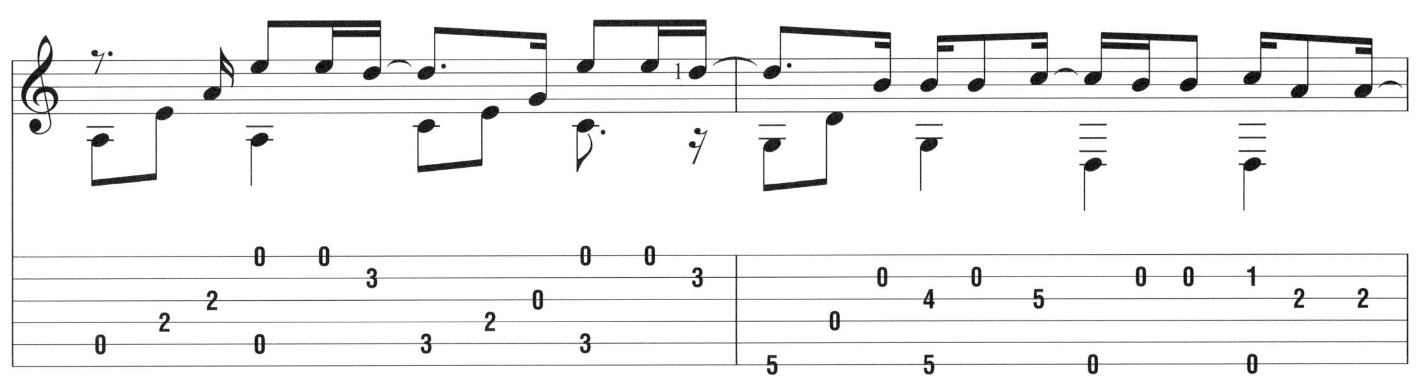

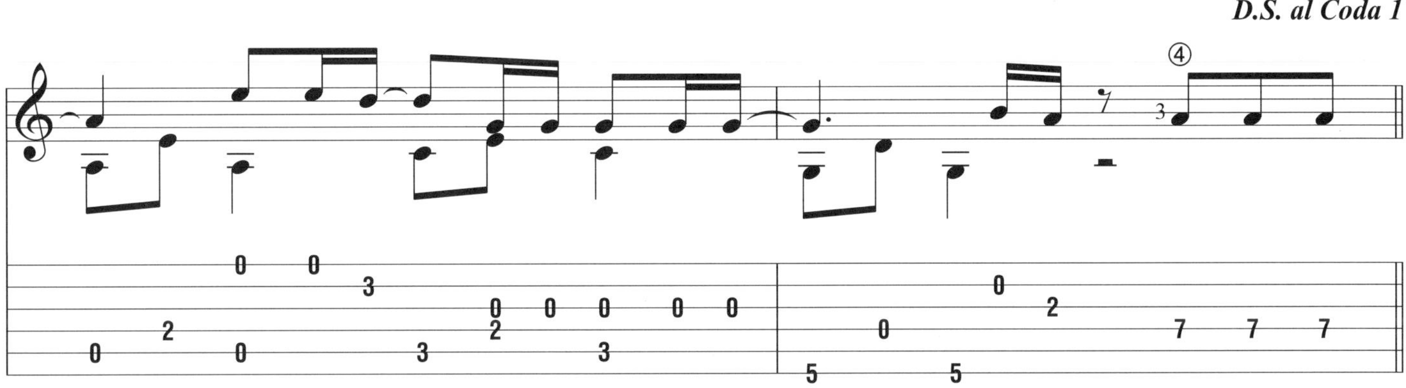
D.S. al Coda 1
④

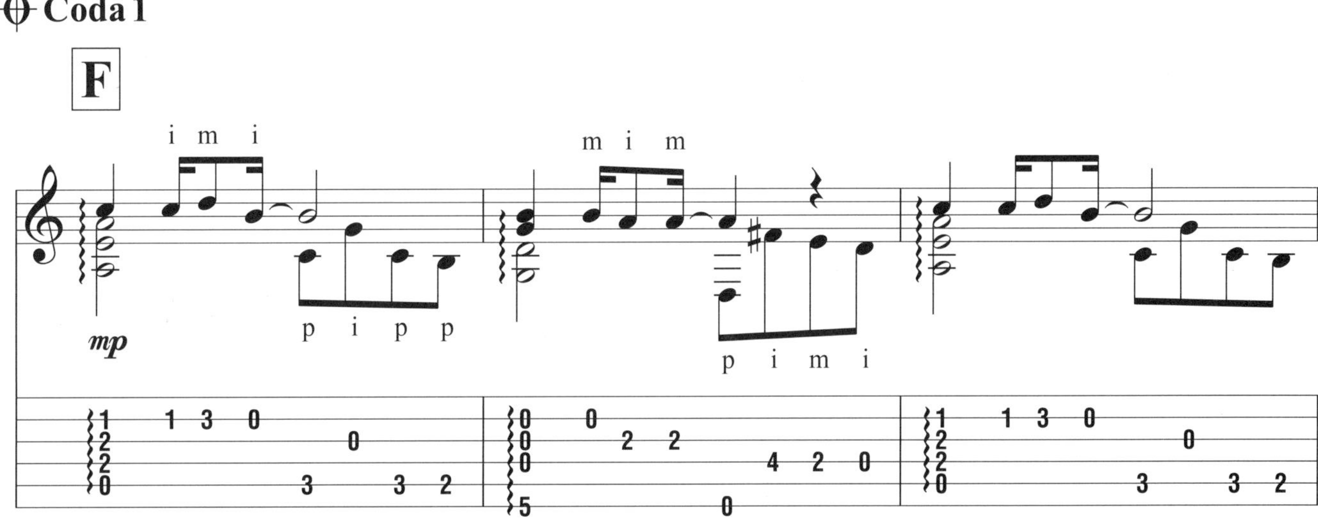
Coda 1
F
i m i
m i m
mp
p i p p
p i m i

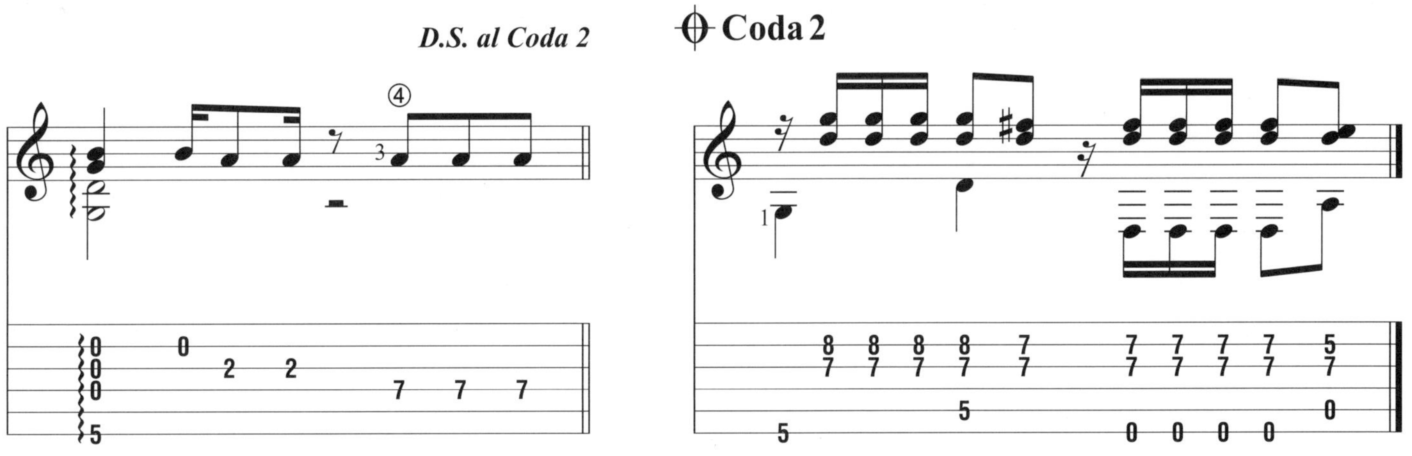
D.S. al Coda 2
Coda 2
④

Royals

Words and Music by Ella Yelich-O'Connor and Joel Little

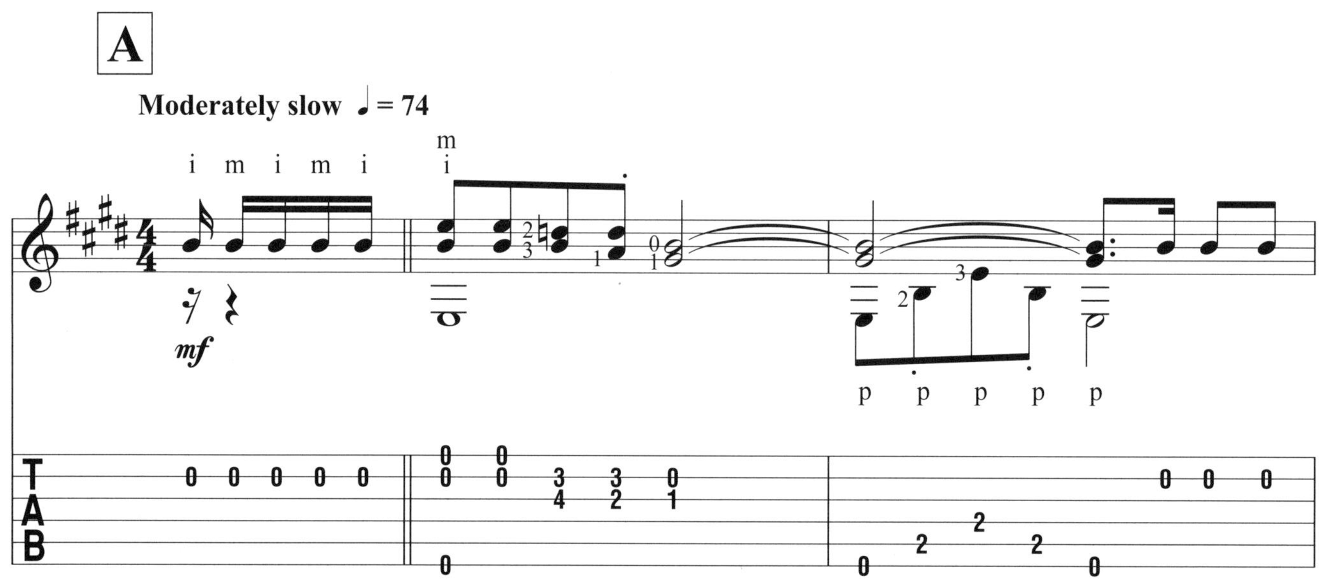

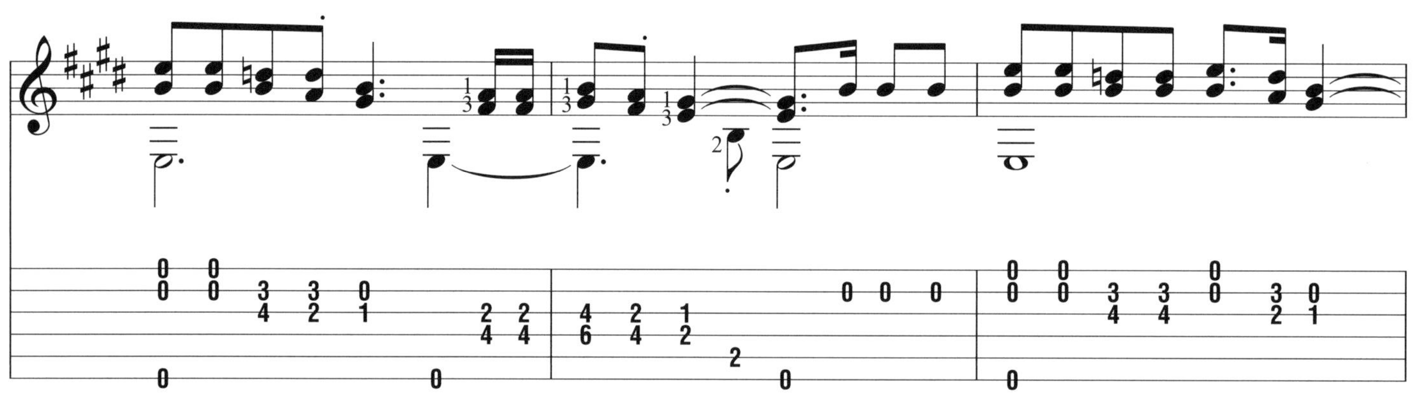

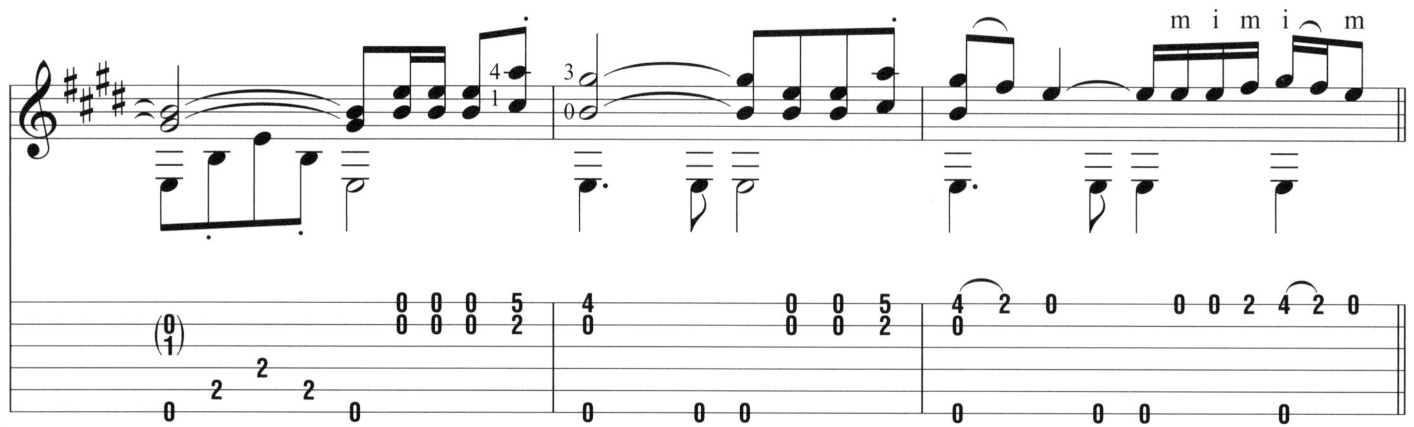

B
2/3CII
C
1/2CII

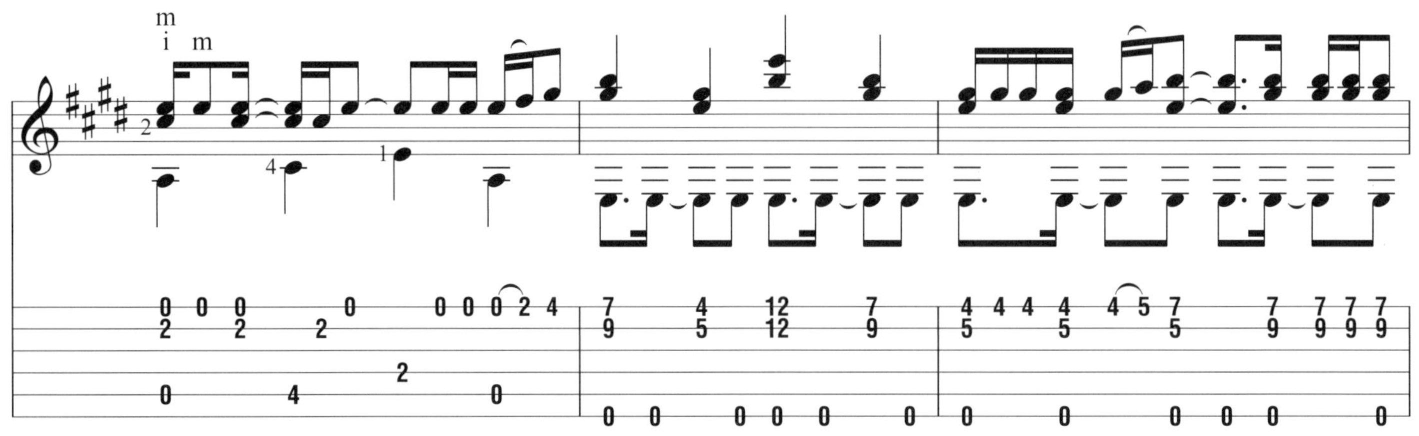

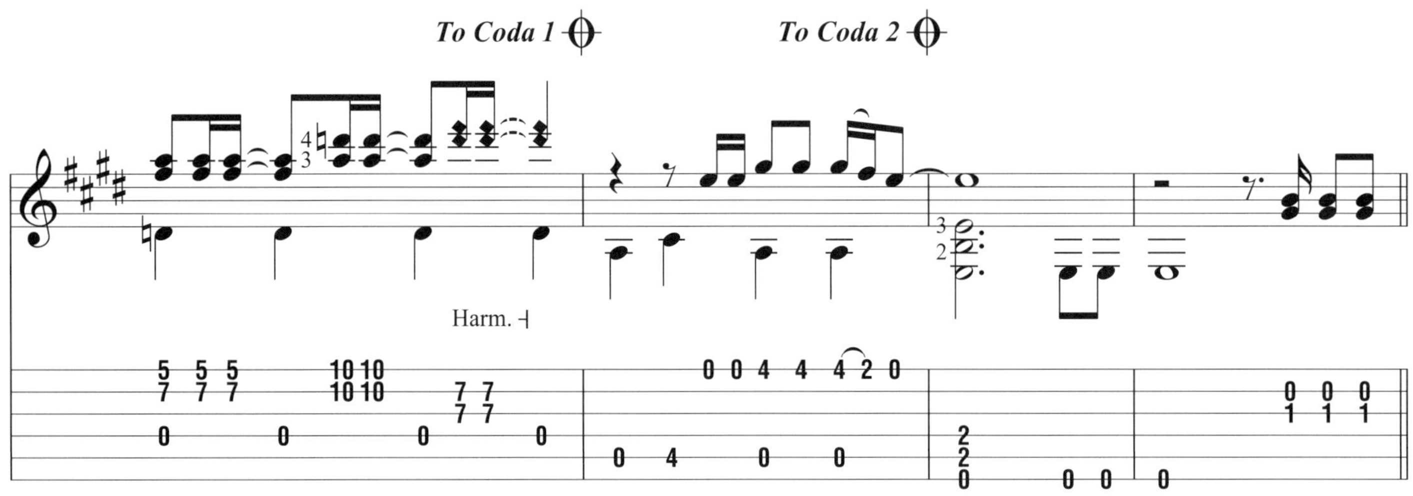

D

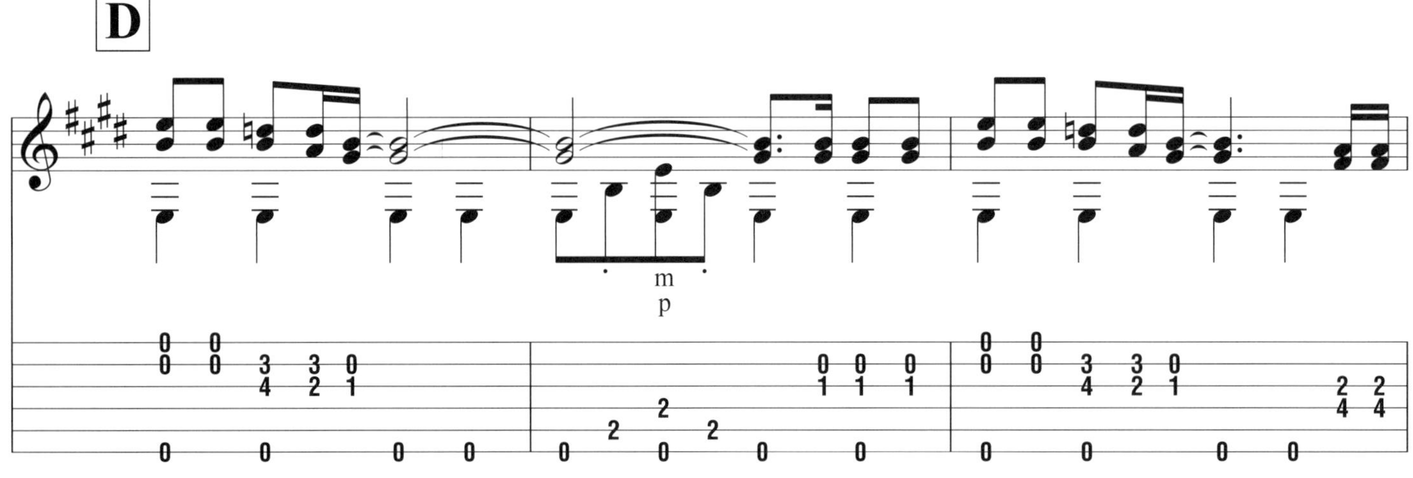

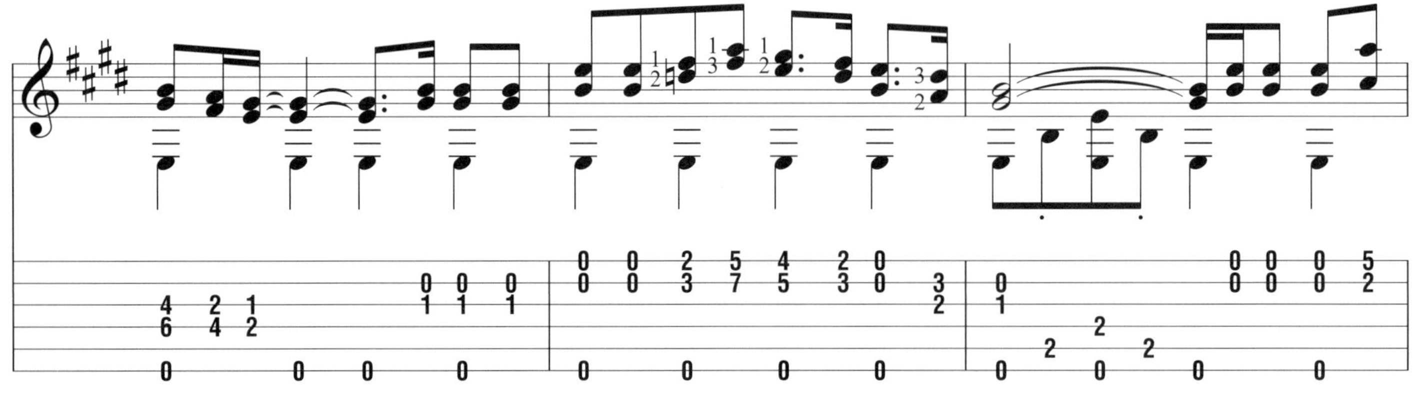

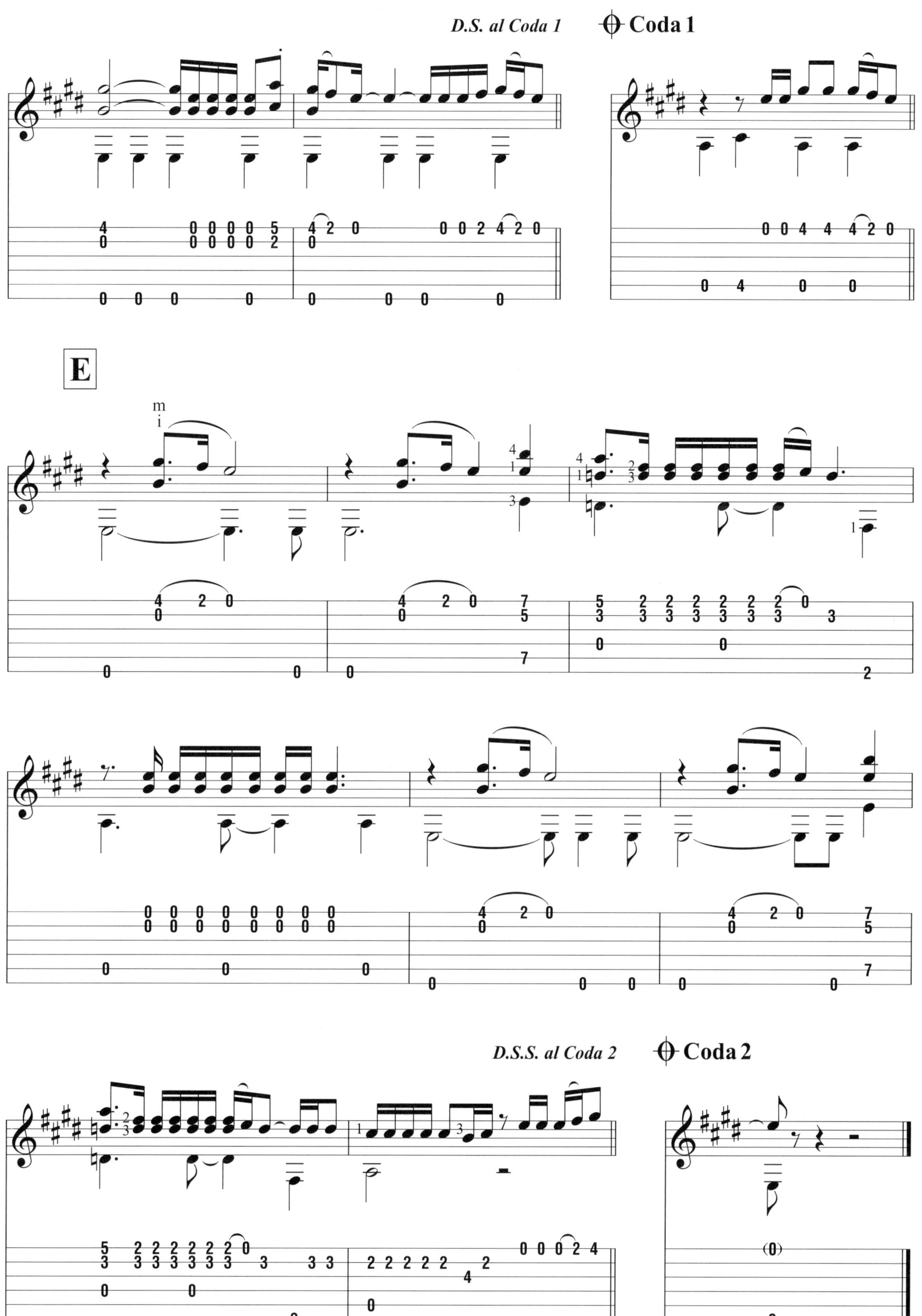
D.S. al Coda 1
Coda 1
E
m
i
D.S.S. al Coda 2
Coda 2

This Is Me

from THE GREATEST SHOWMAN

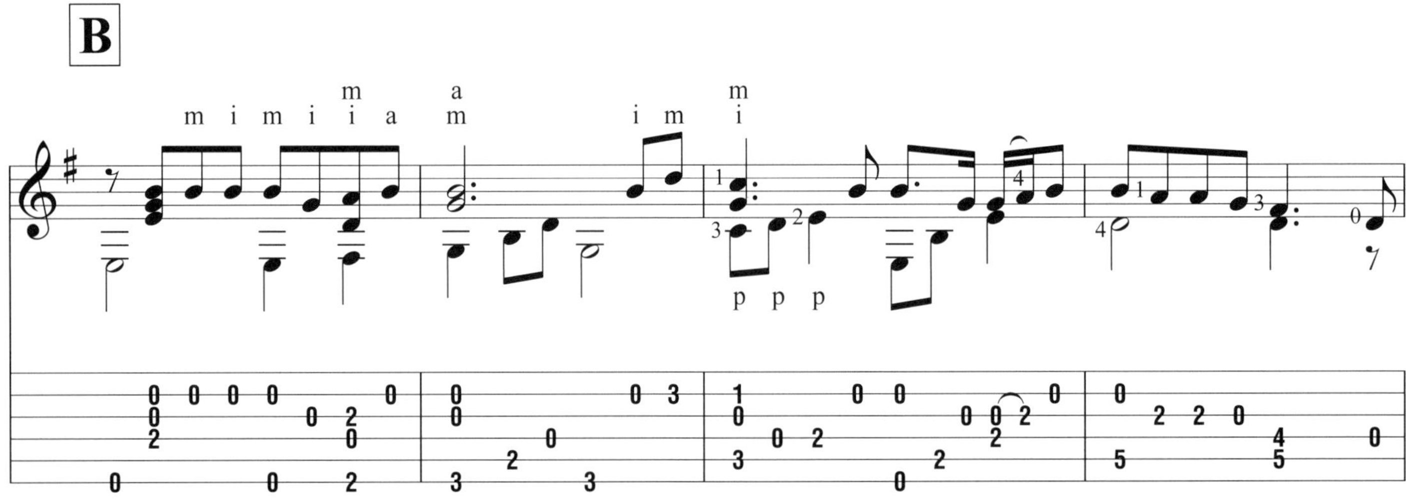

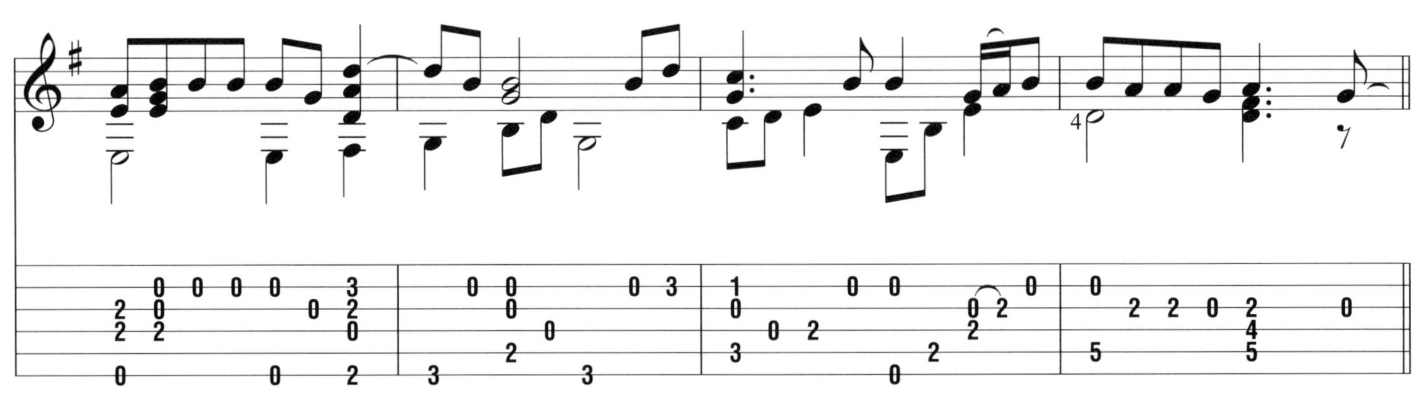

C

i a a m i m i m i i m i m i i m

mf

𝄋 D

a m i m i m i m i i m i i m i

𝄋𝄋 E

m m
i i i m i

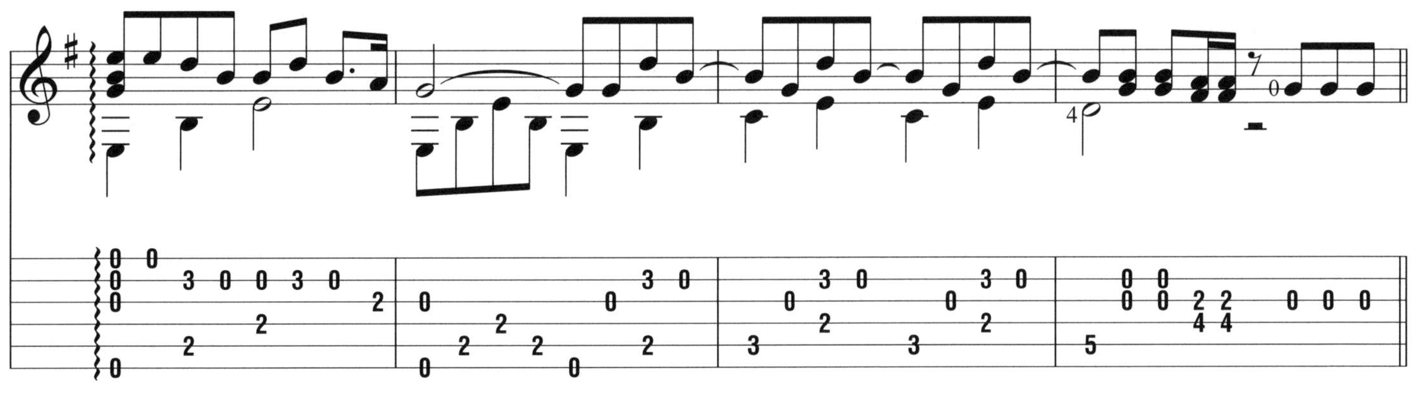

F

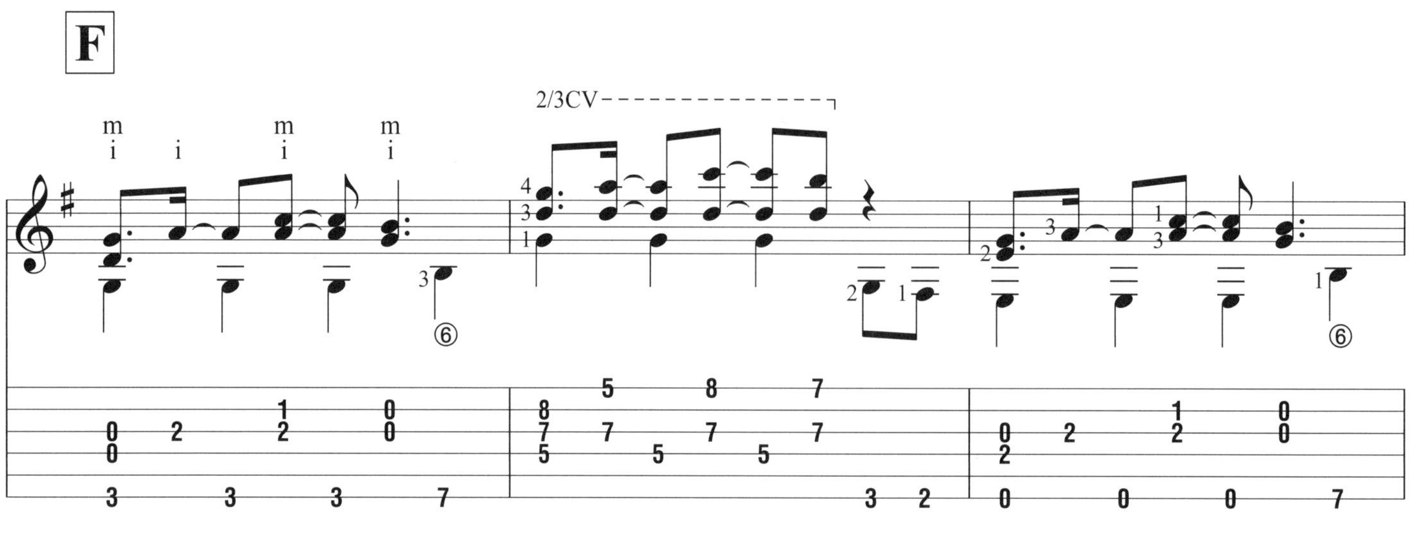

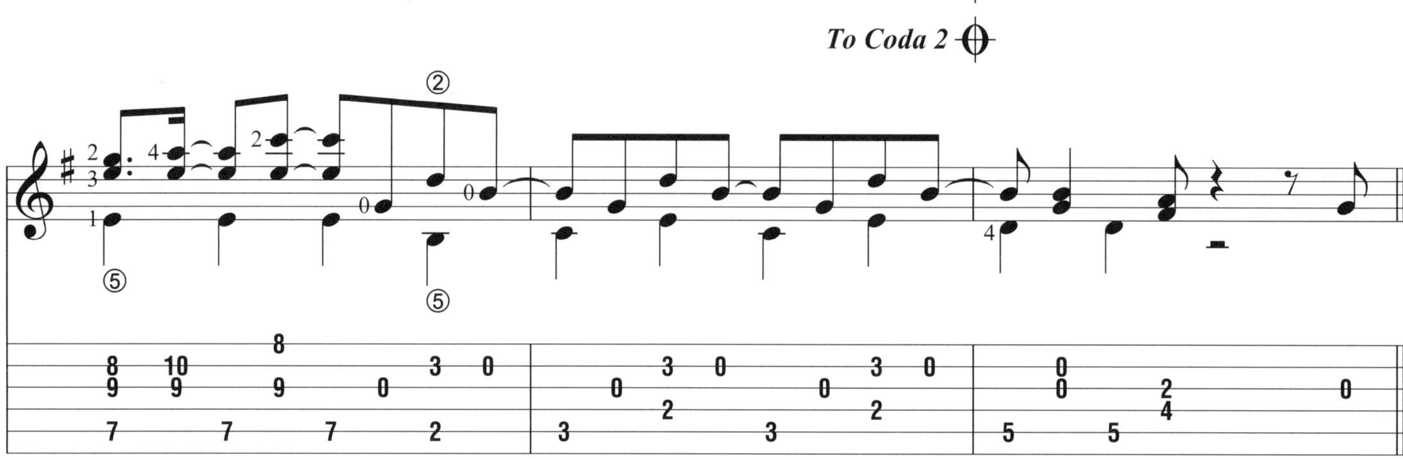

G

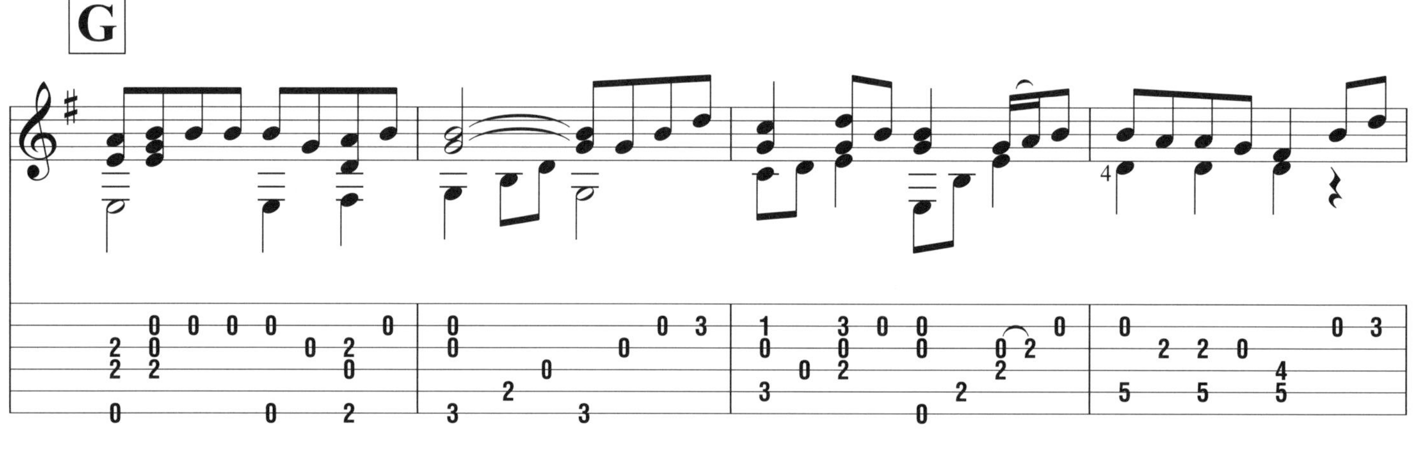

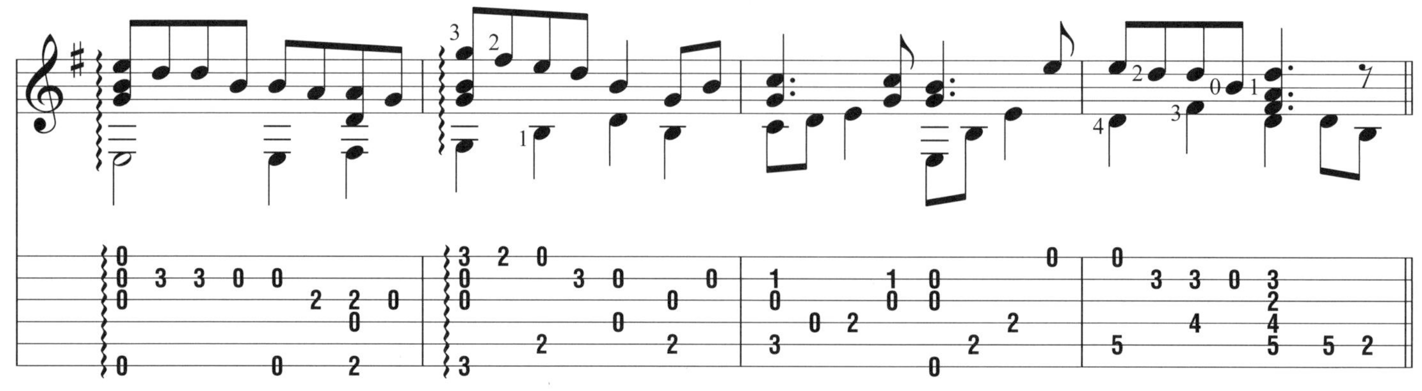

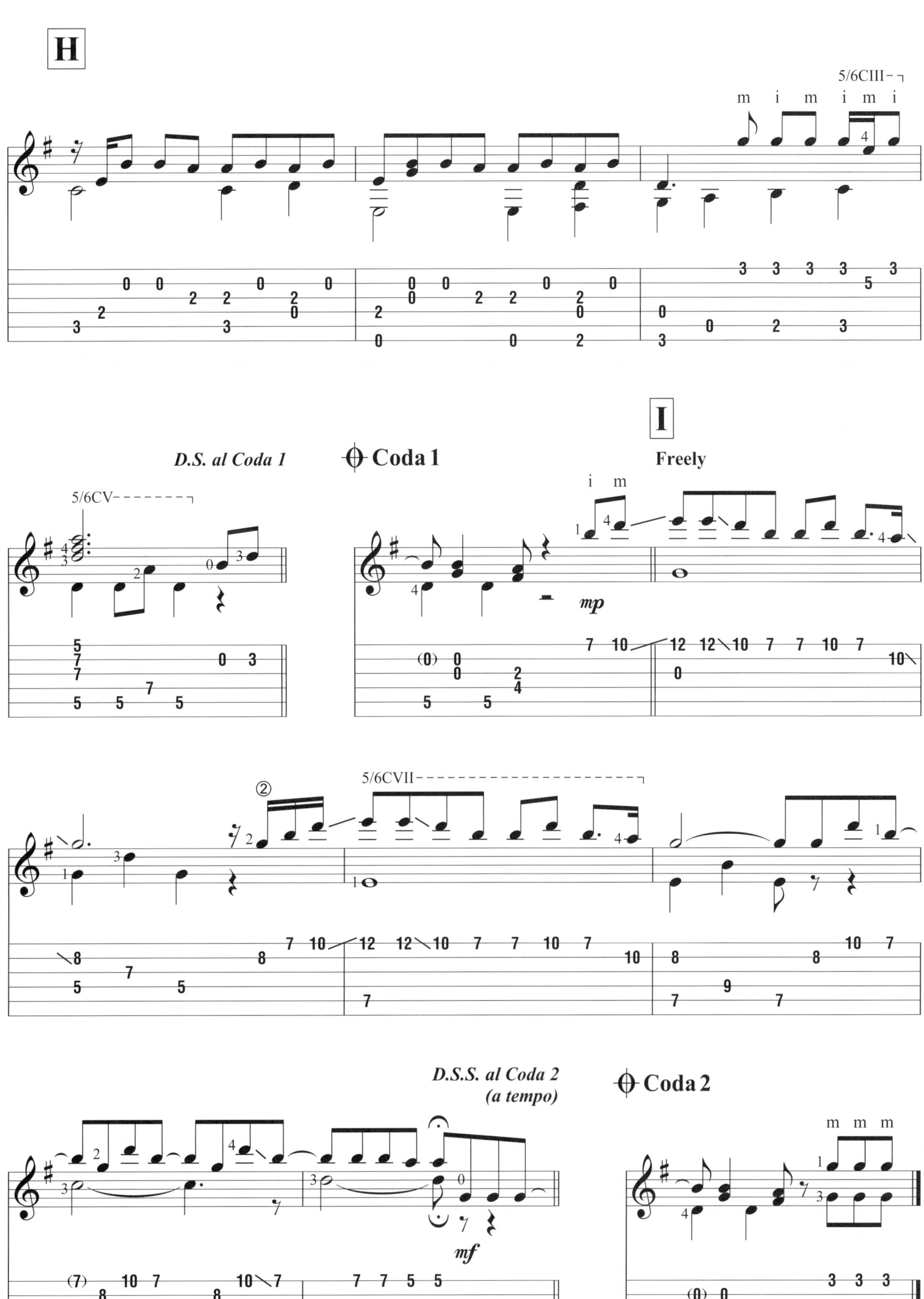
H
5/6CIII
D.S. al Coda 1
Coda 1
I
Freely
5/6CV
mp
5/6CVII
D.S.S. al Coda 2
(a tempo)
Coda 2
mf

A Thousand Years

from the Summit Entertainment film THE TWILIGHT SAGA: BREAKING DAWN - PART 1

Words and Music by David Hodges and Christina Perri

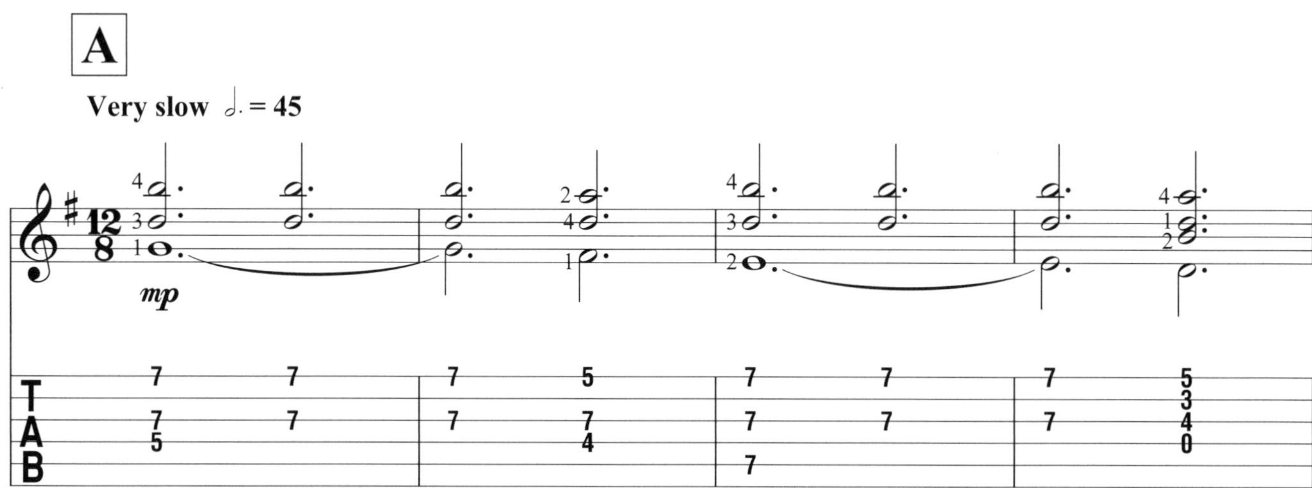

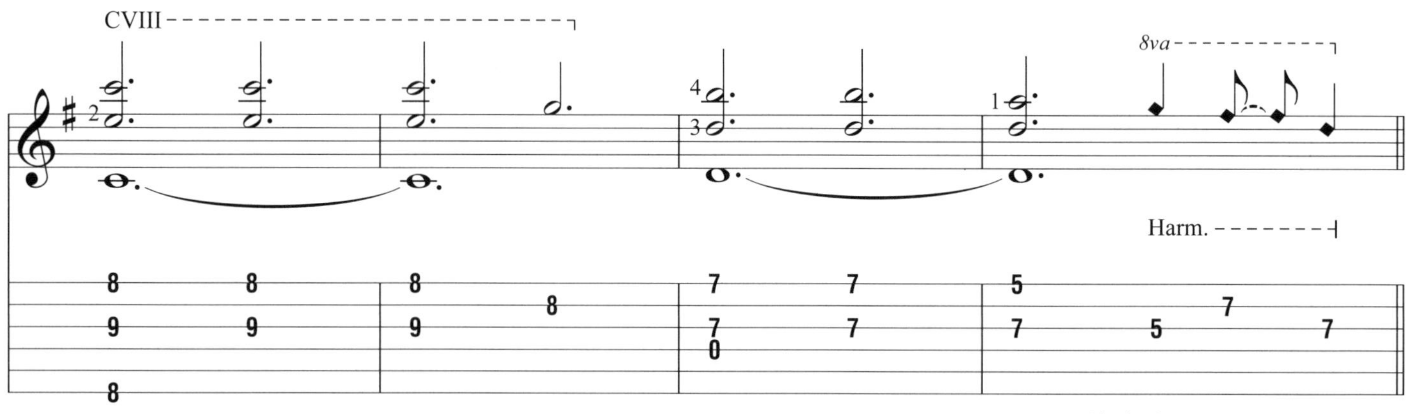

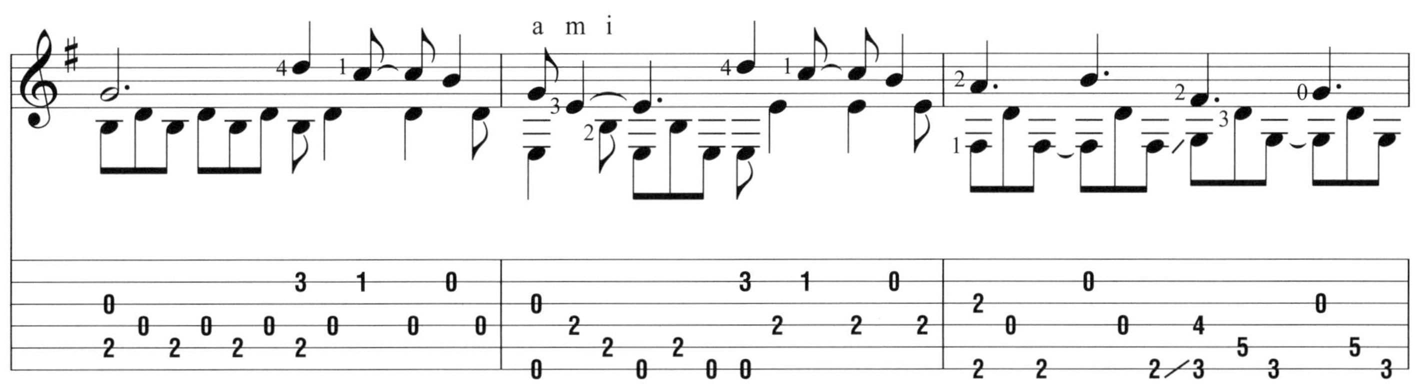
a m i
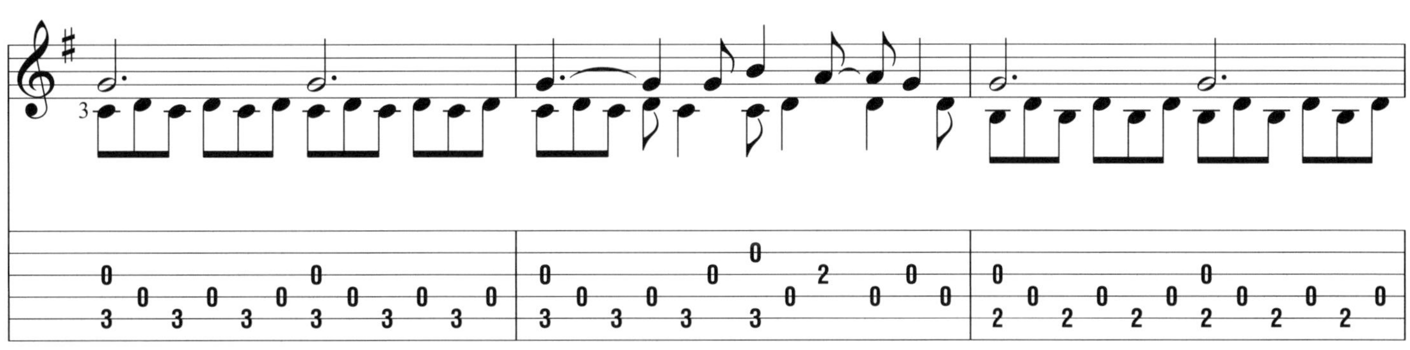

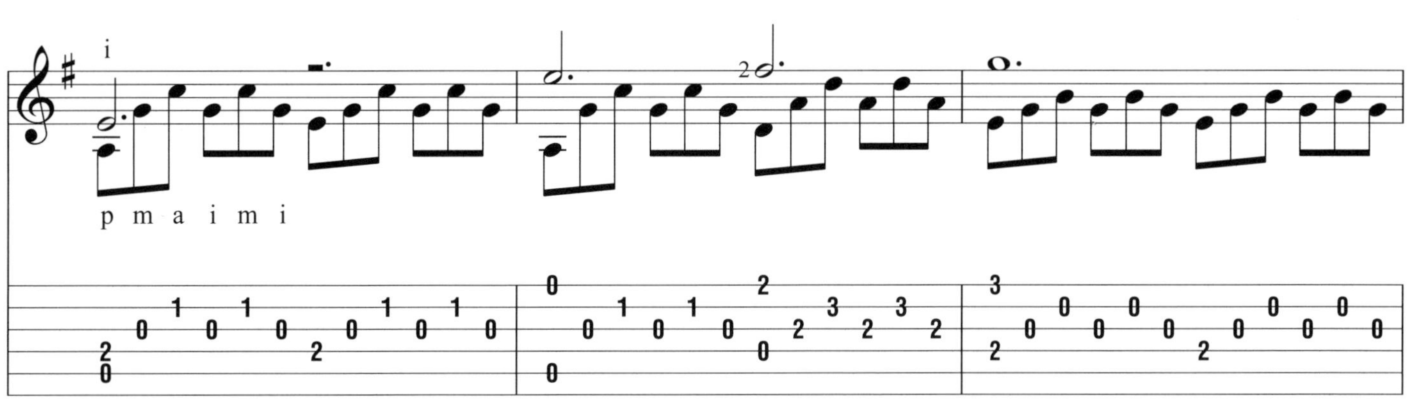
i
p m a i m i

C
CIII
m i a
mf
m i i m i m m i m
1.
1/2CII
mp
2.

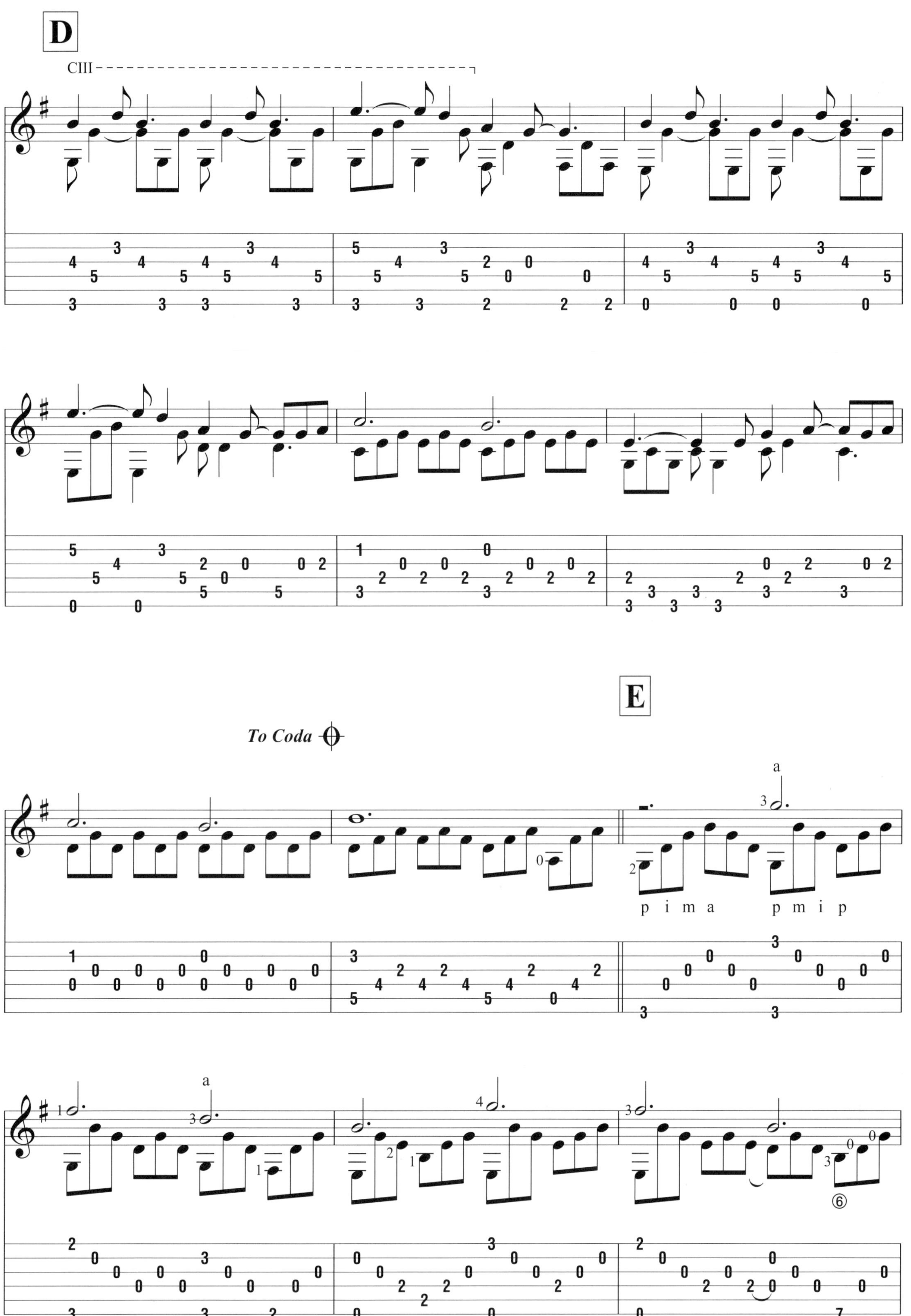
D
CIII
To Coda
E
p i m a p m i p

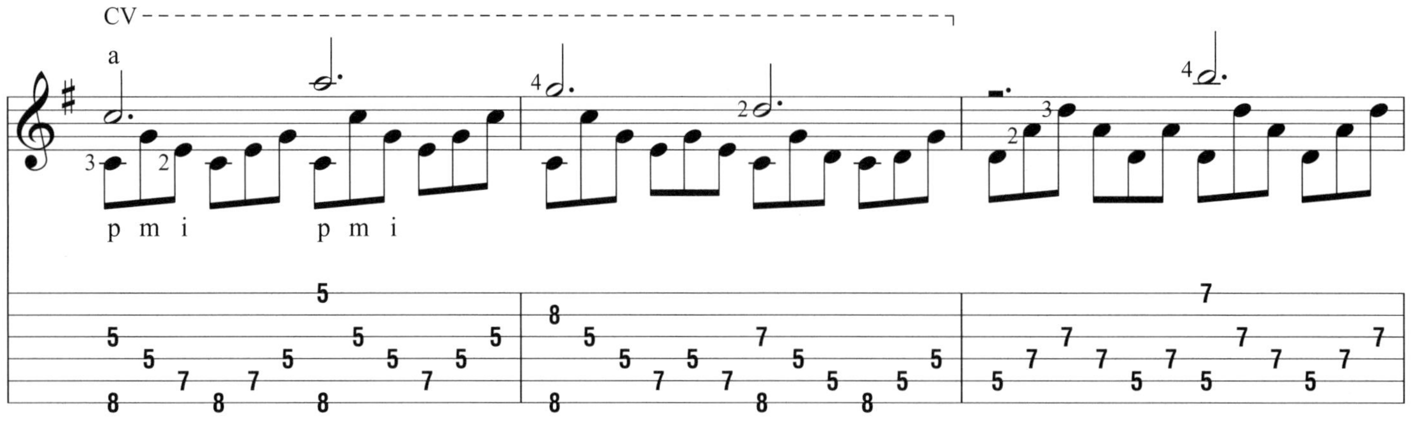
CV
a
p m i
p m i

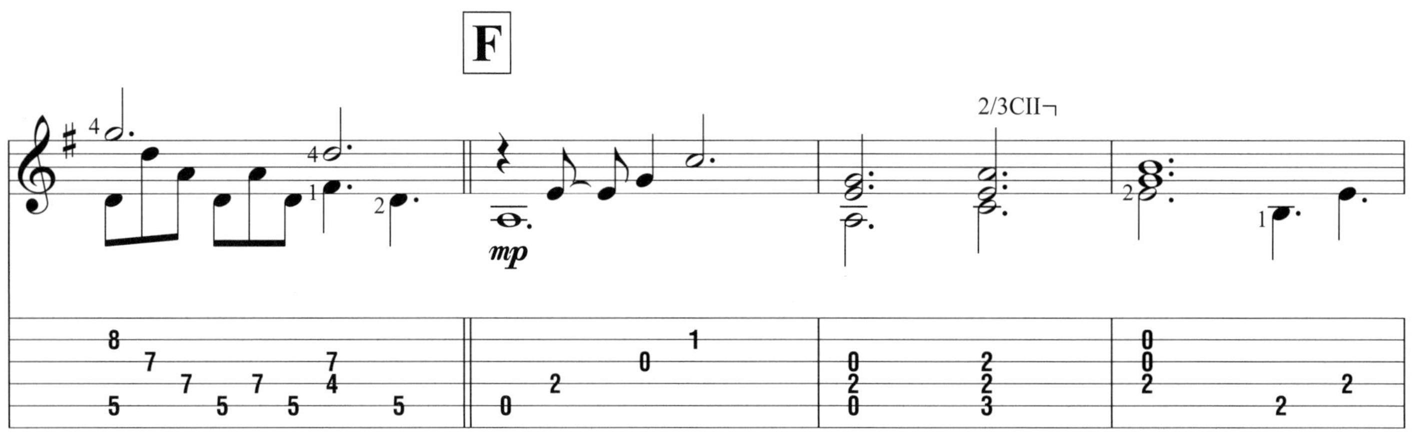
F
2/3CII
mp

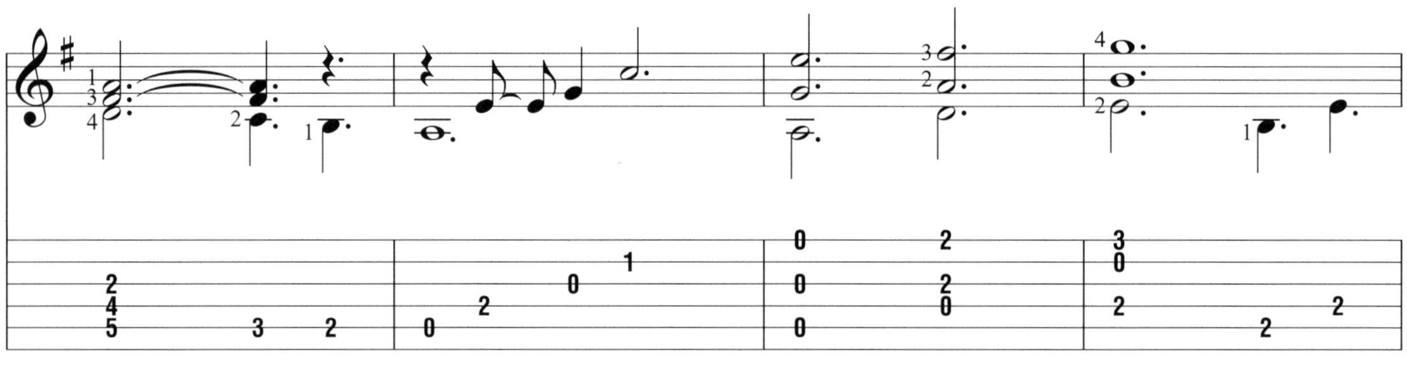

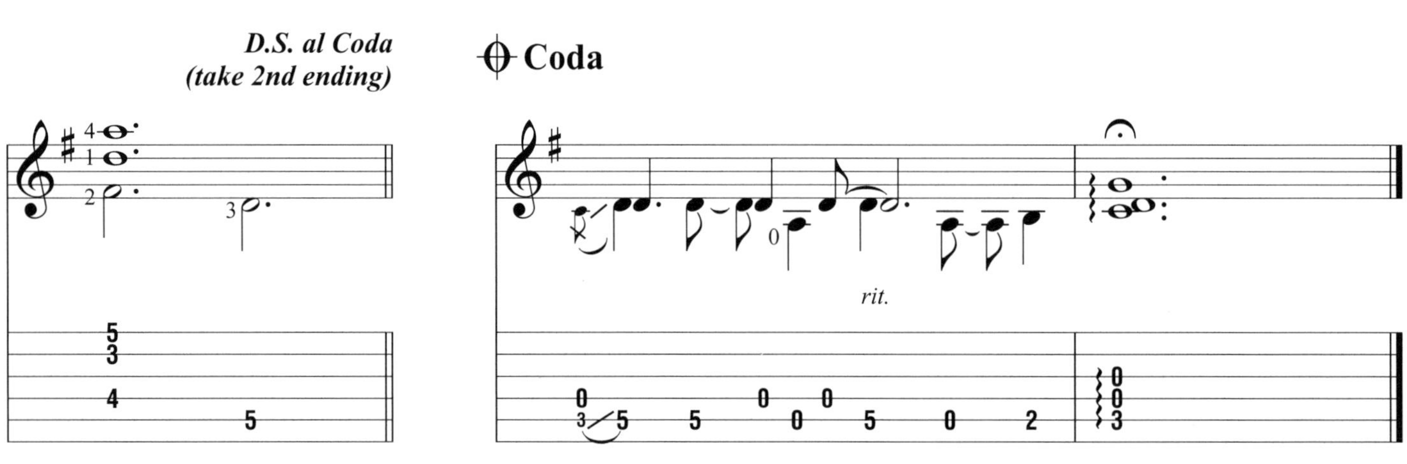
D.S. al Coda
(take 2nd ending)
Coda
rit.

Perfect

Words and Music by Ed Sheeran

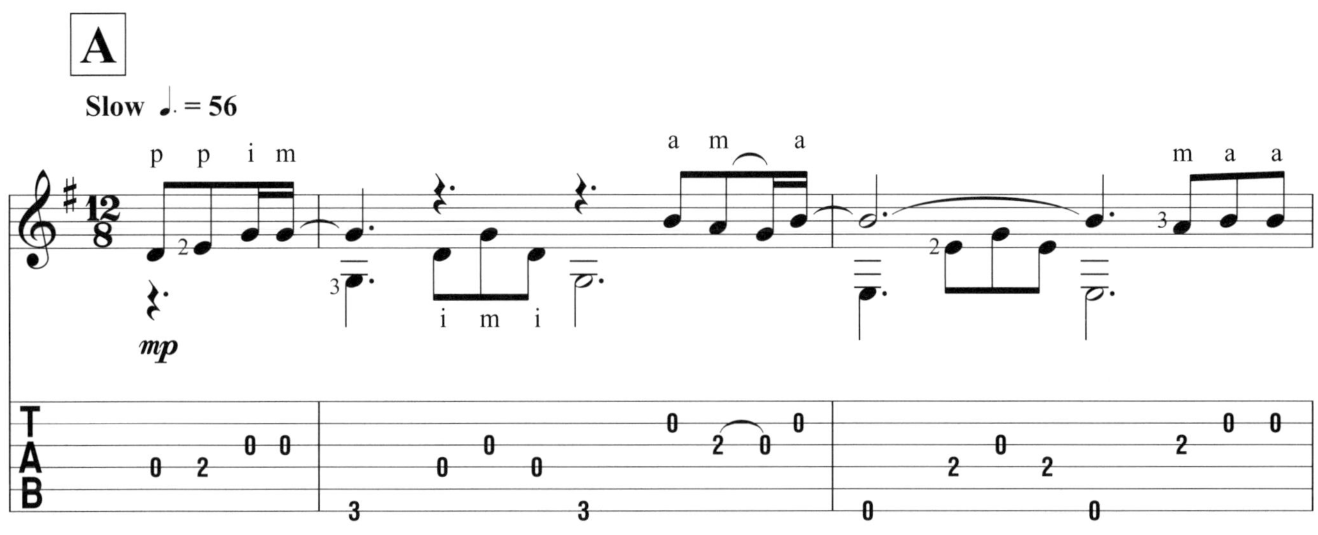

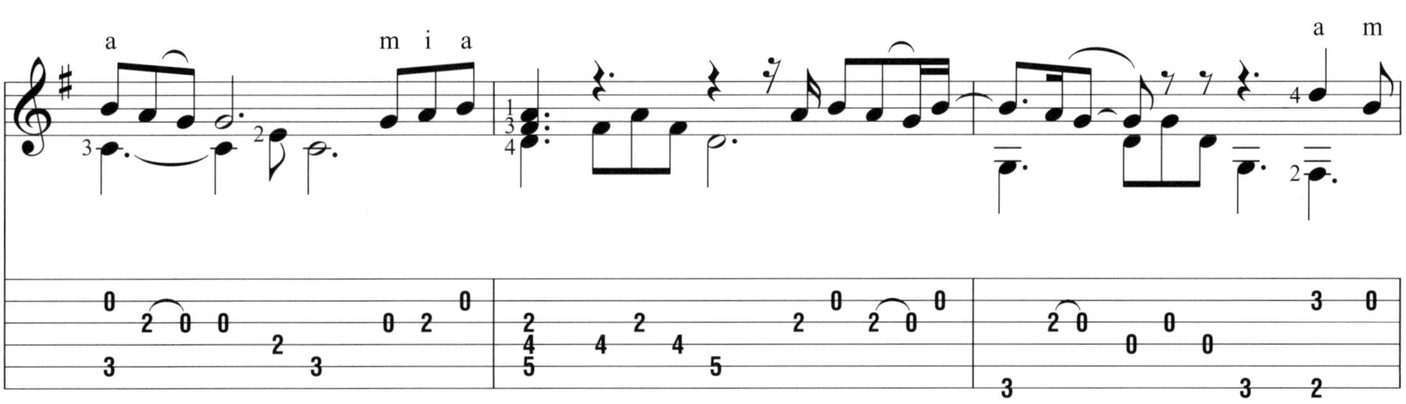

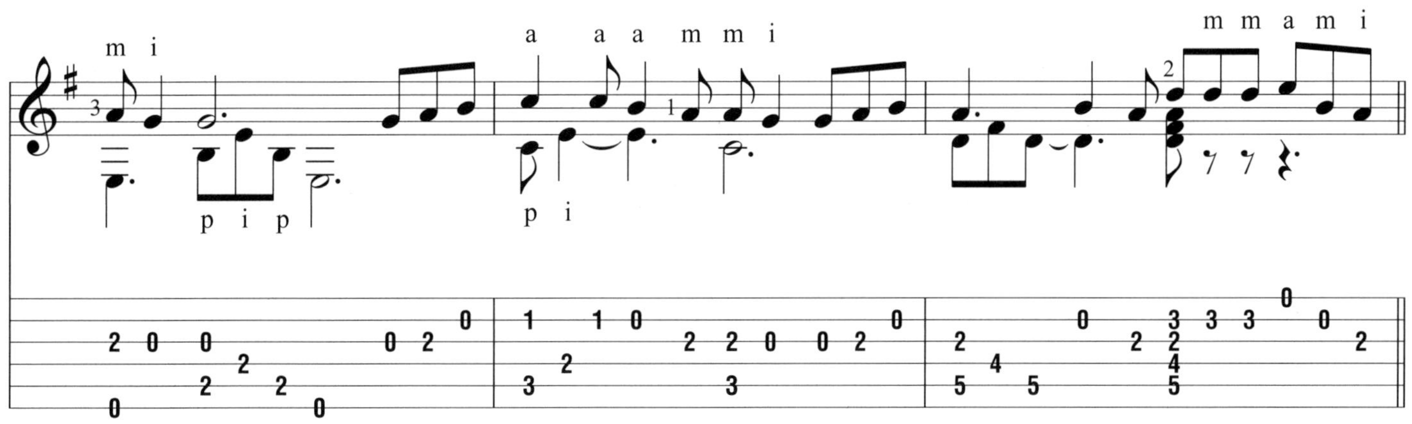

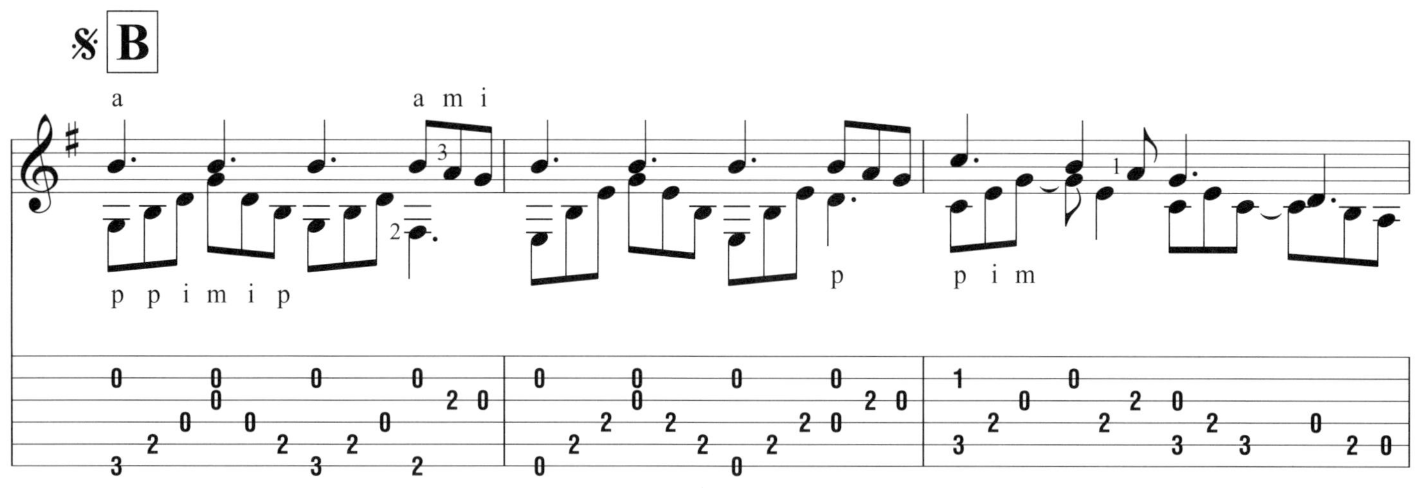
B
a
a m i
p p i m i p
p
p i m

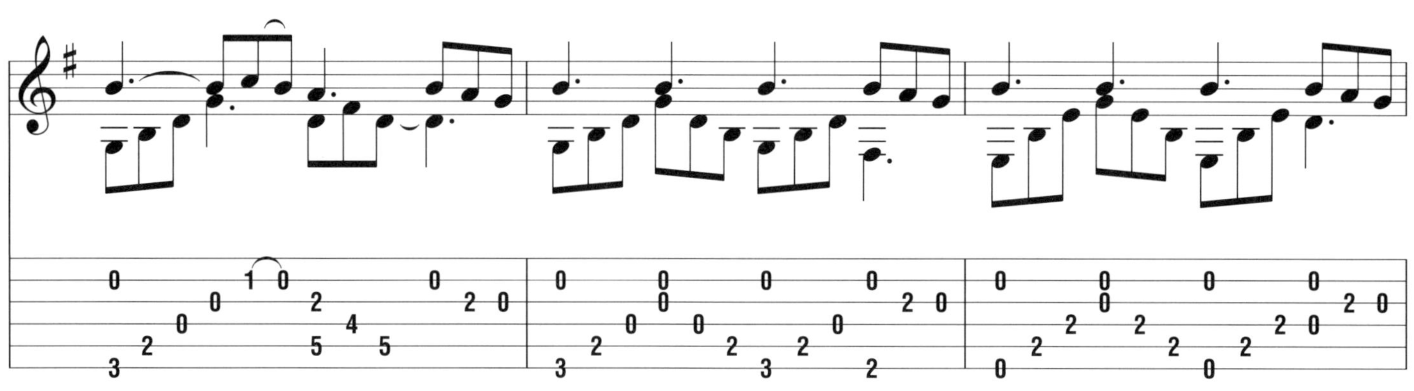

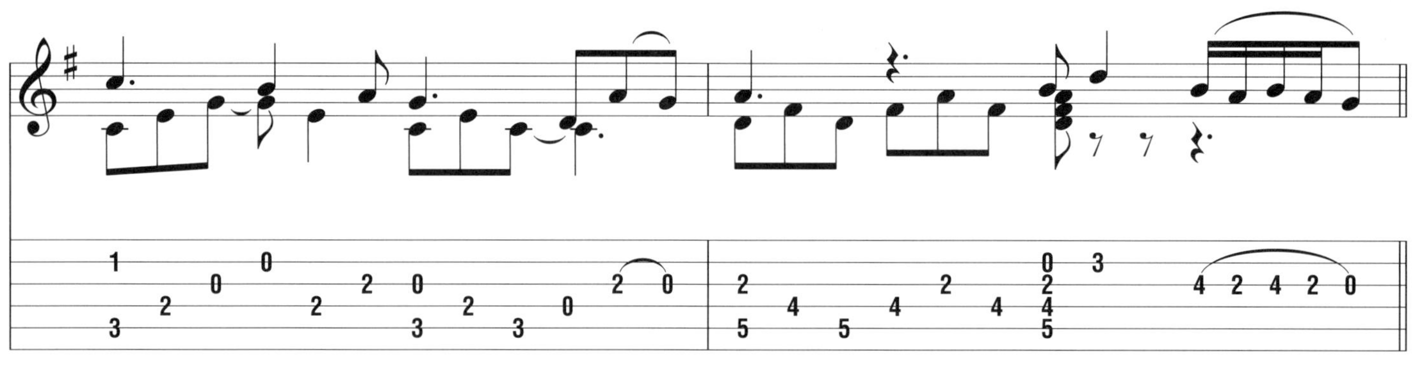

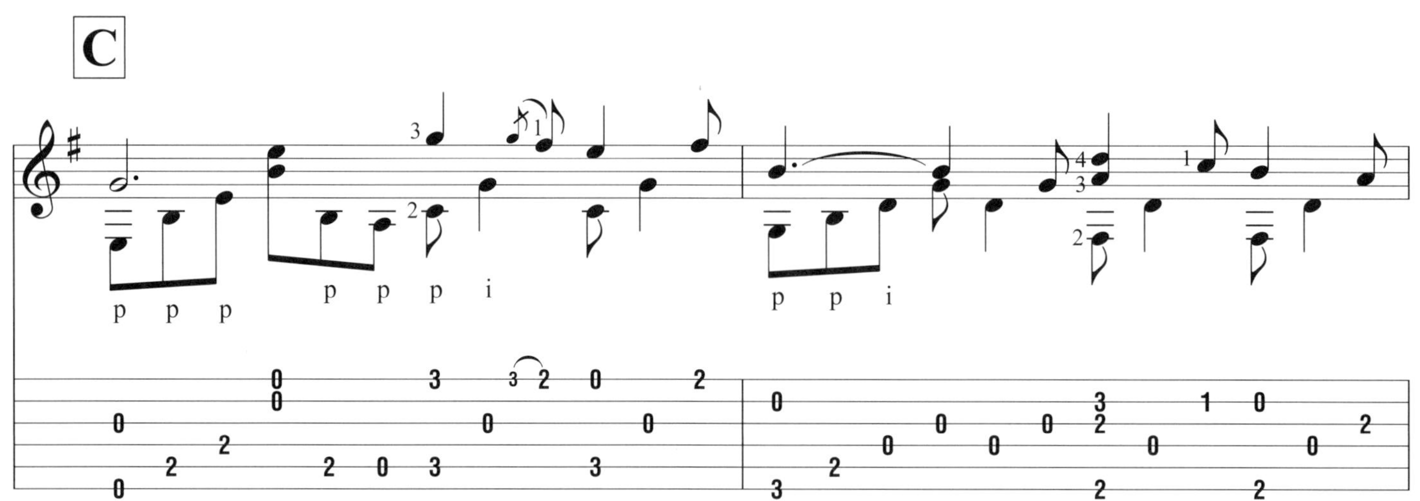
C
p p p
p p p i
p p i

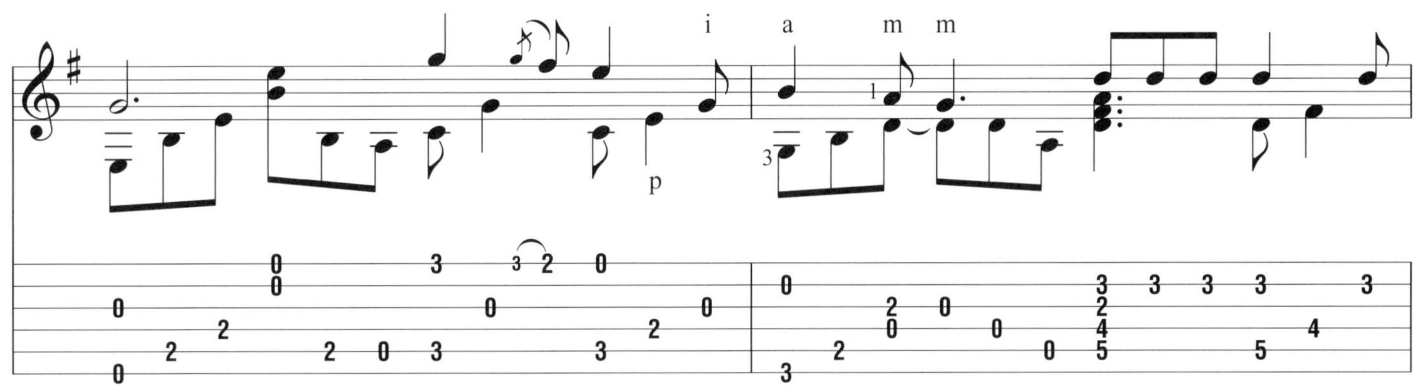

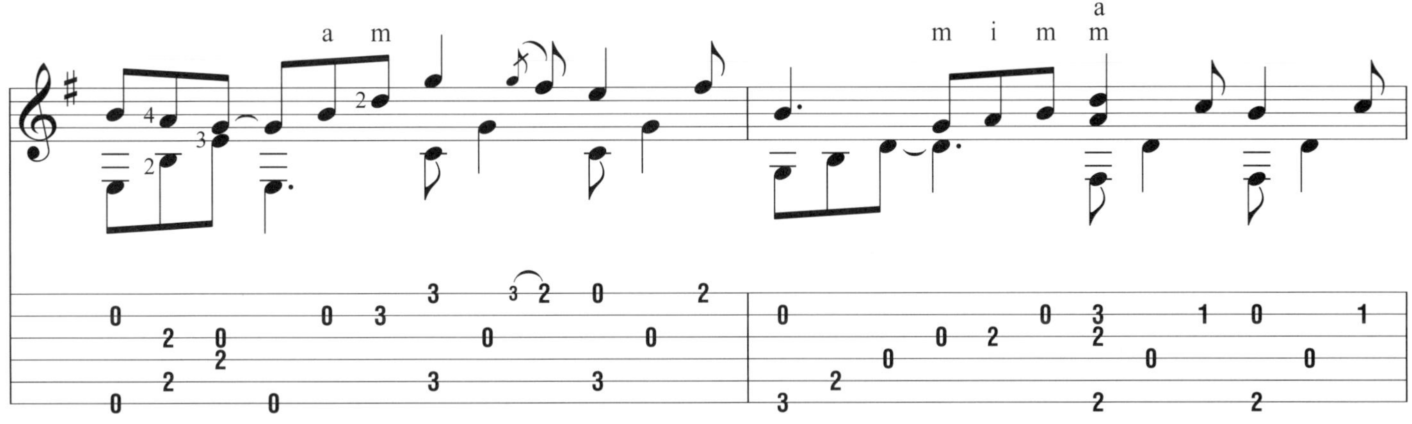

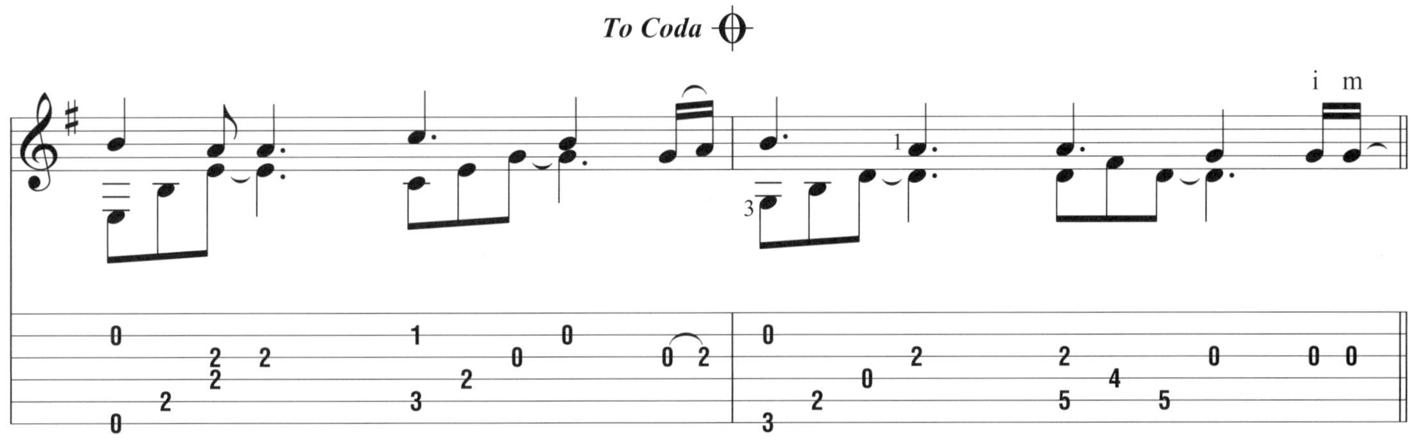
To Coda

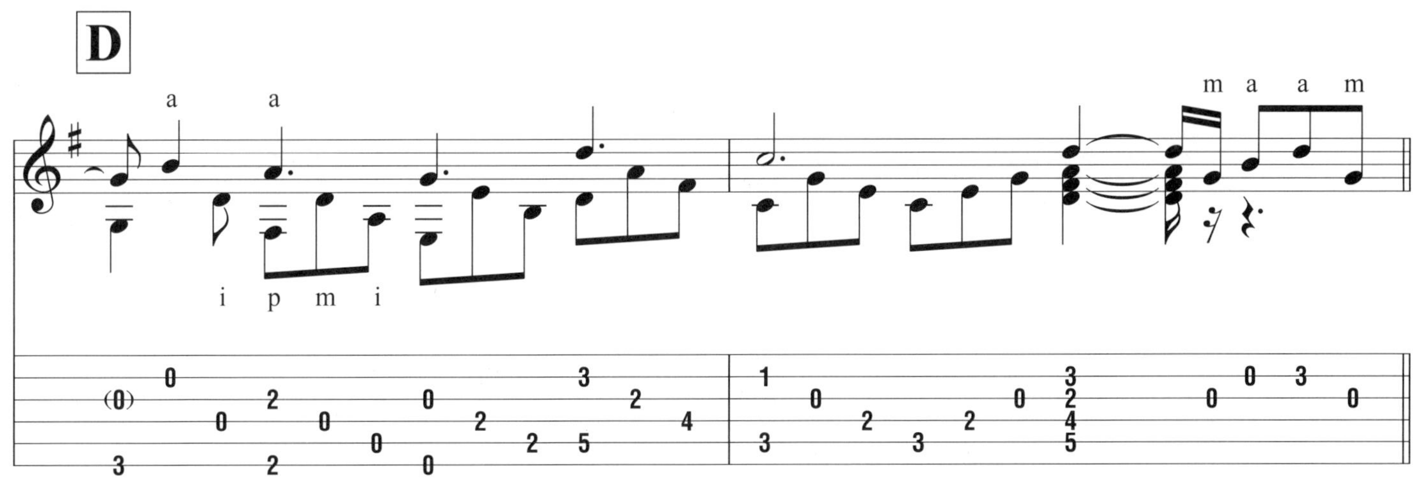
D

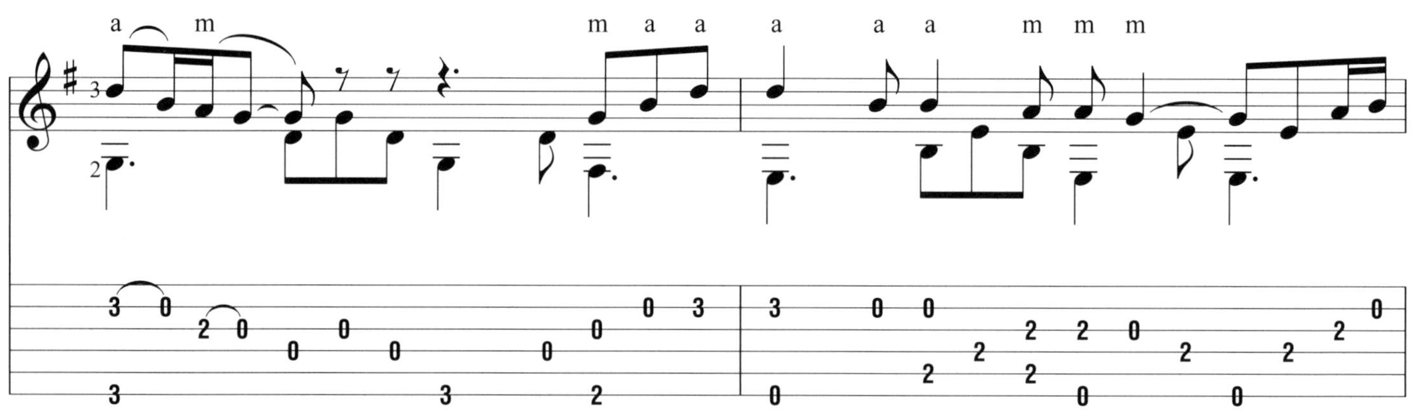

D.S. al Coda

Coda
F
a m i
m
i m i
G

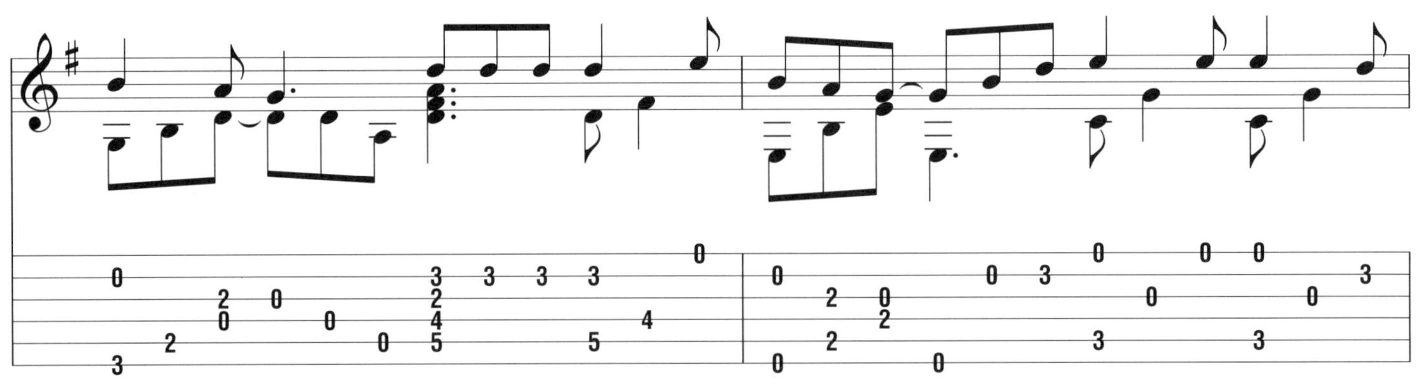

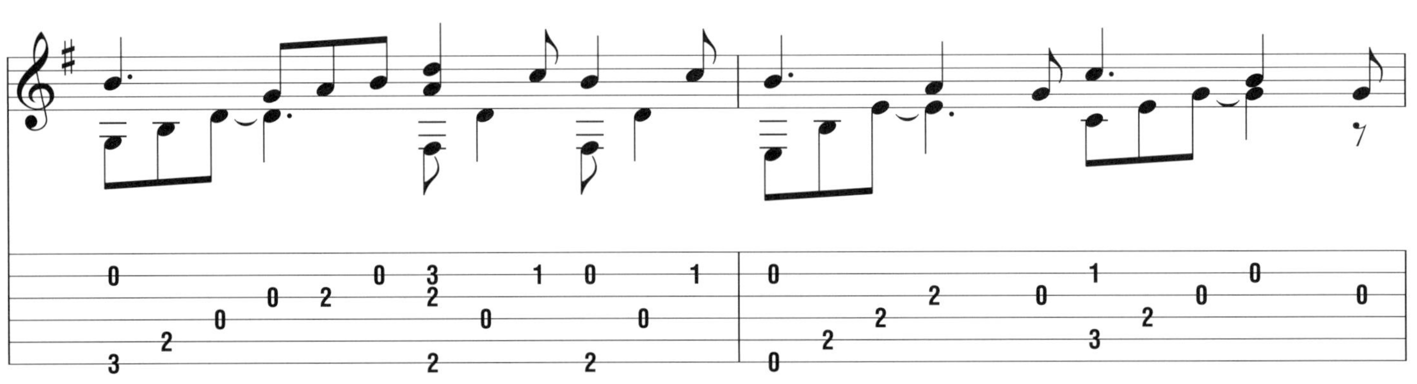

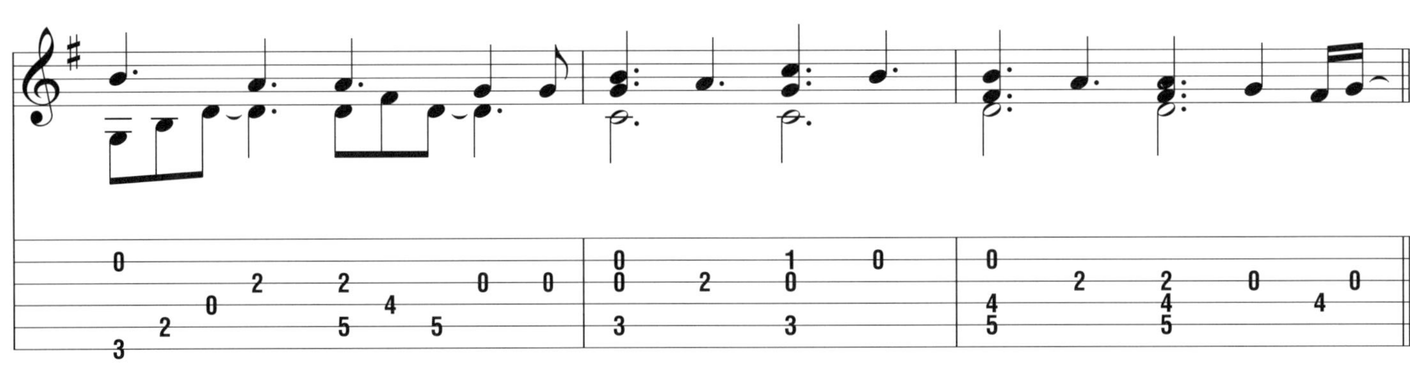

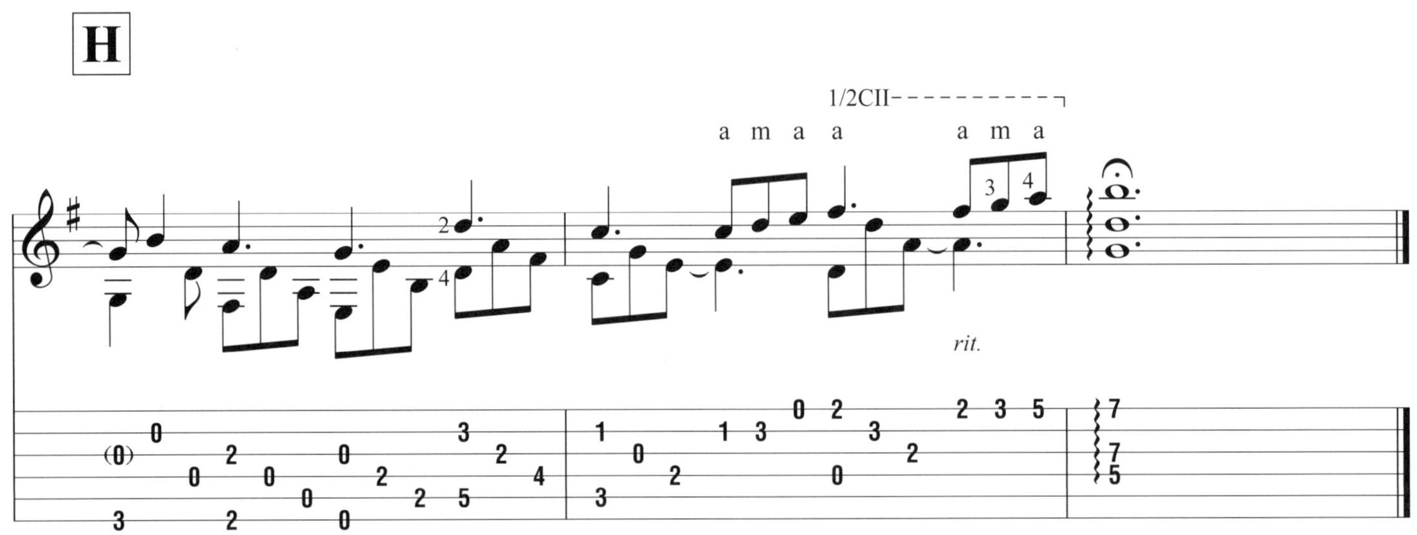
H
1/2CII
a m a a
a m a
rit.

Stay with Me

Words and Music by Sam Smith, James Napier, William Edward Phillips, Tom Petty and Jeff Lynne

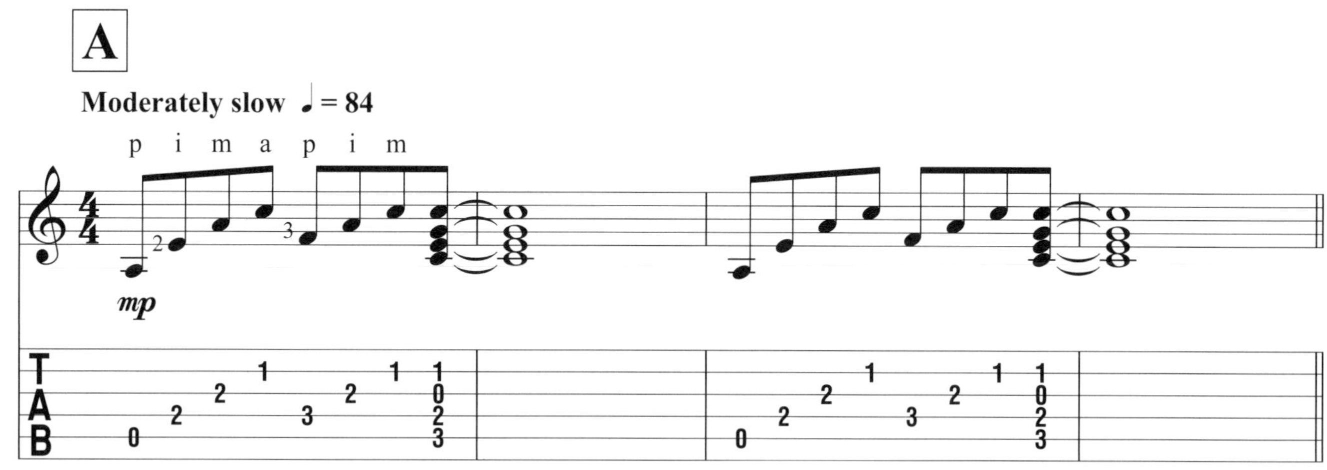

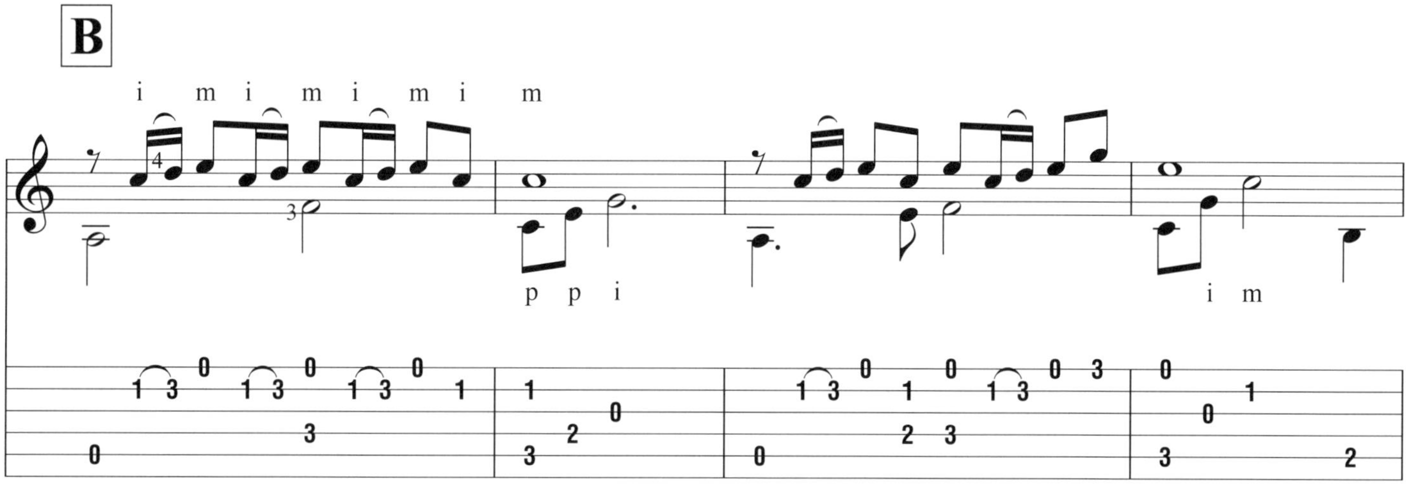

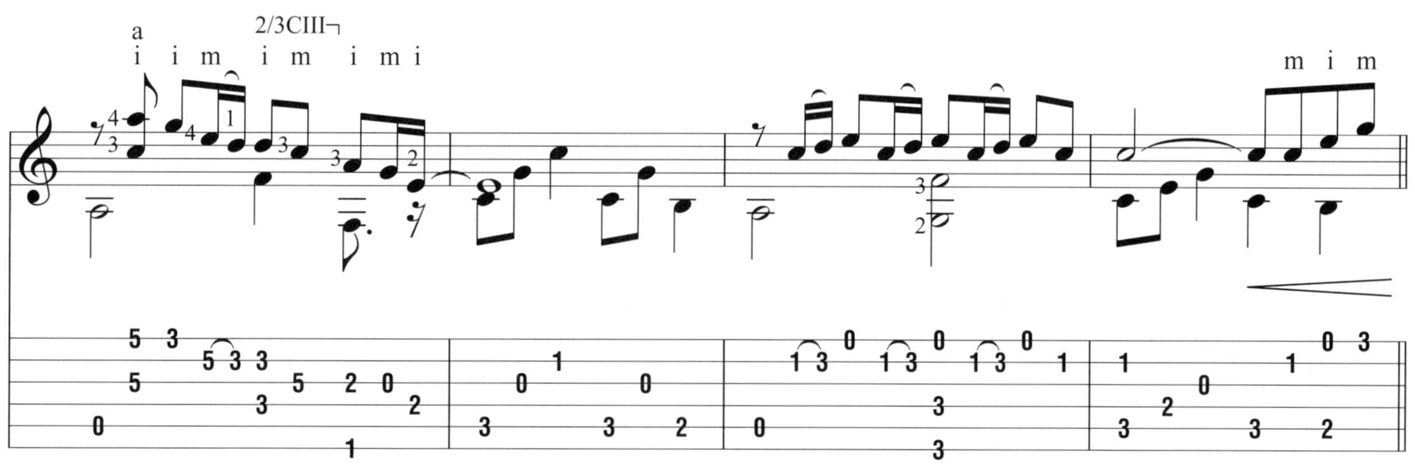

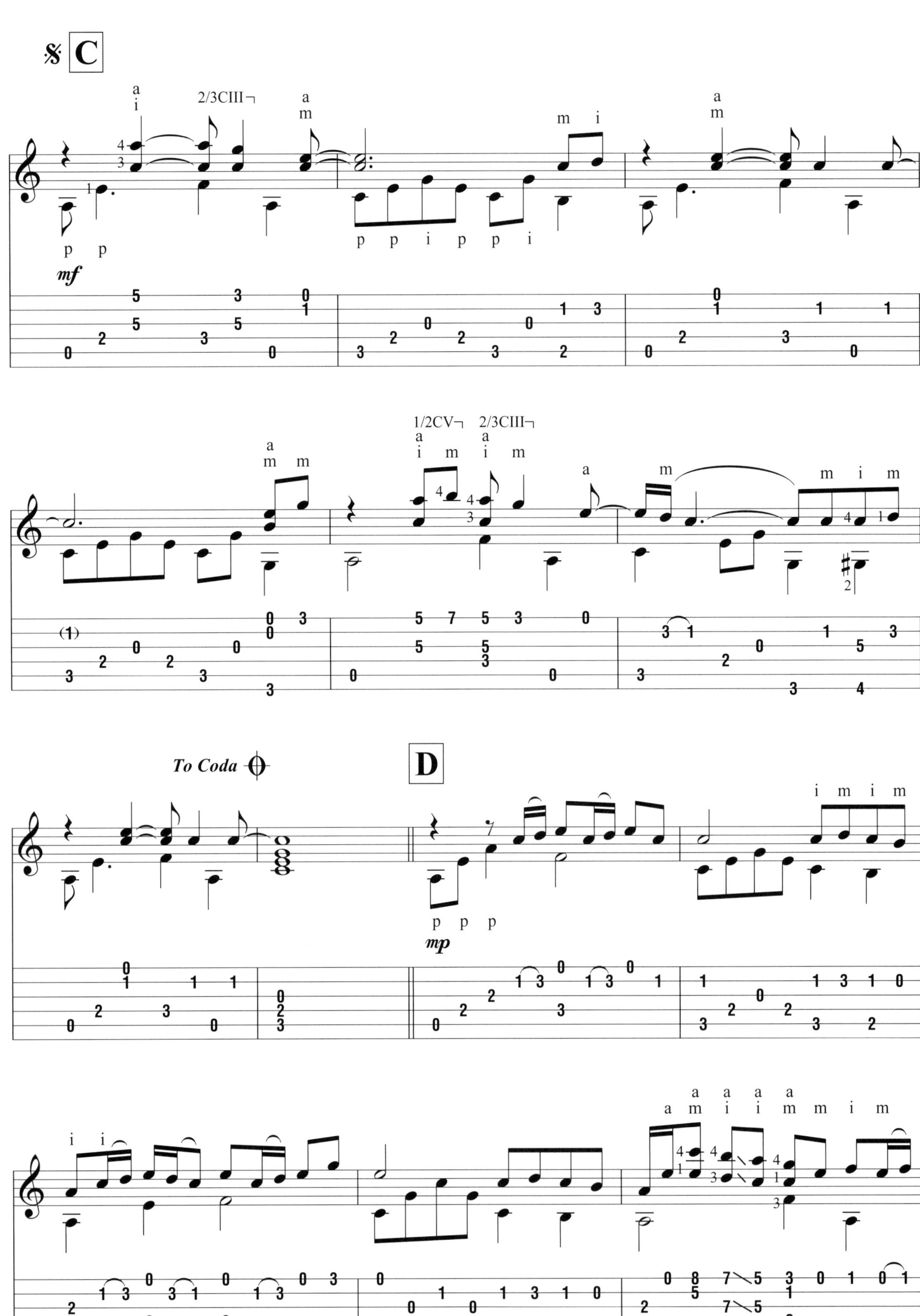
C
To Coda
D
mf
mp
2/3CIII
1/2CV

D.S. al Coda

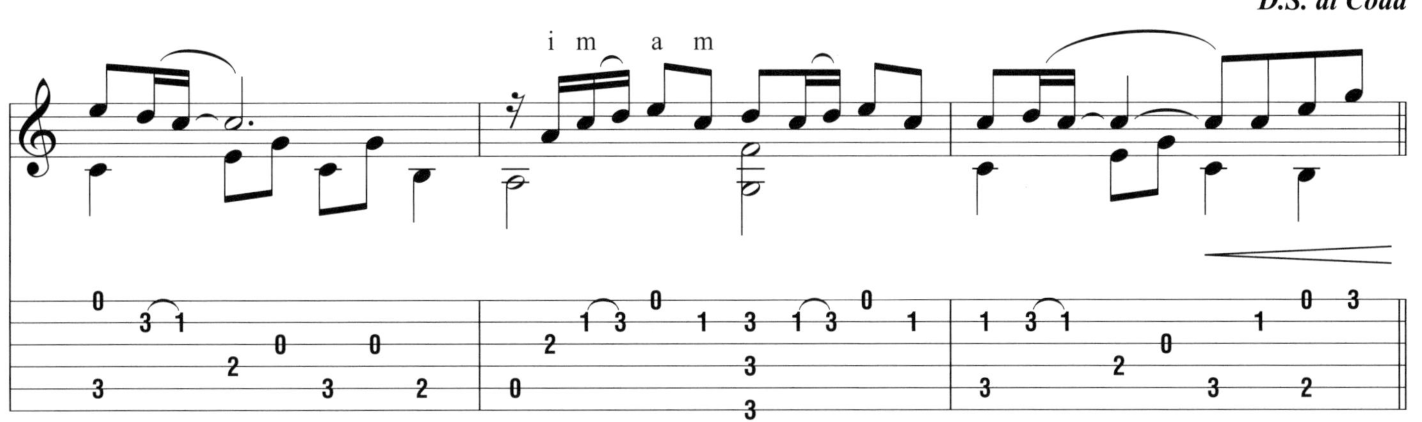
i m a m

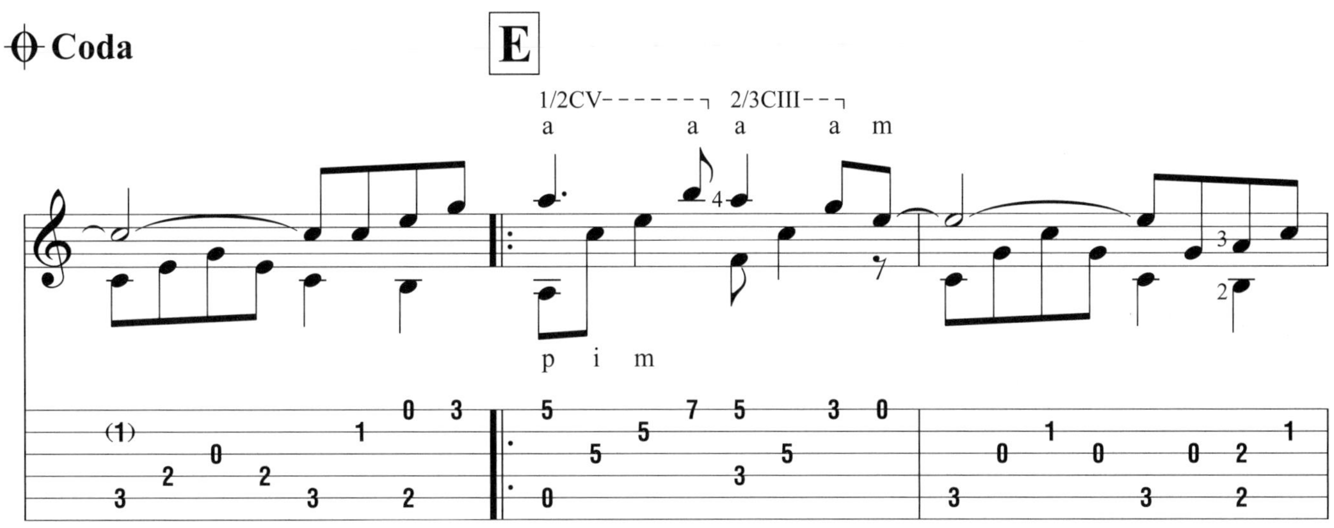
Coda
E
1/2CV
2/3CIII
a a a a m
p i m

1.
2.
mp

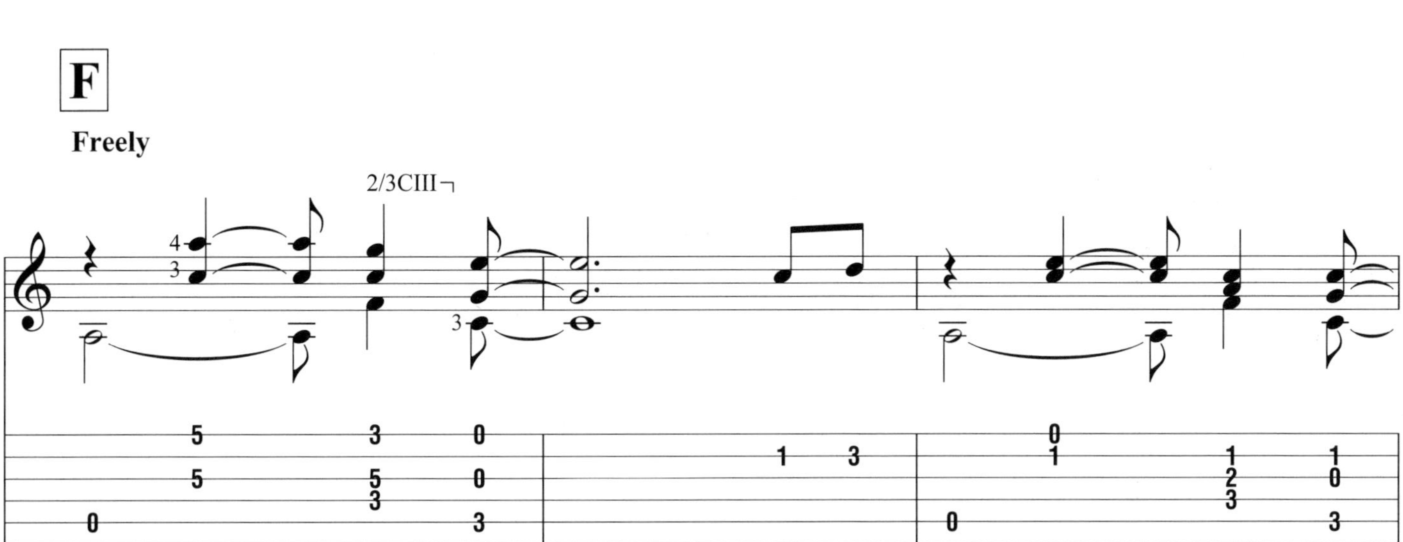
F
Freely
2/3CIII

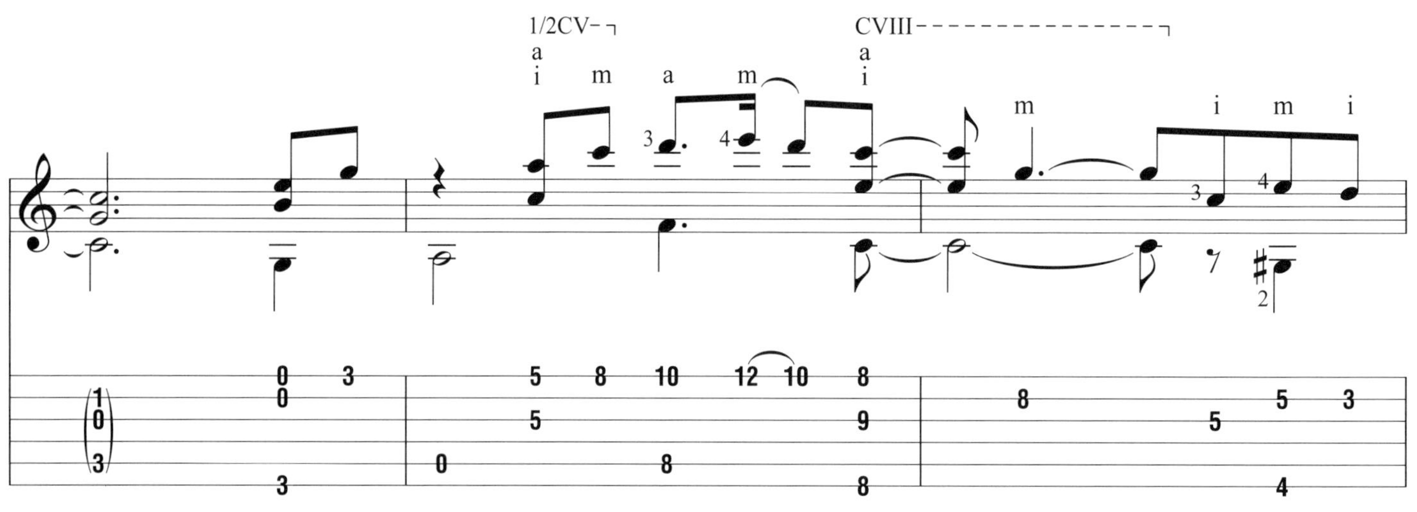

1/2CV
CVIII

G
A tempo
2/3CIII
mf

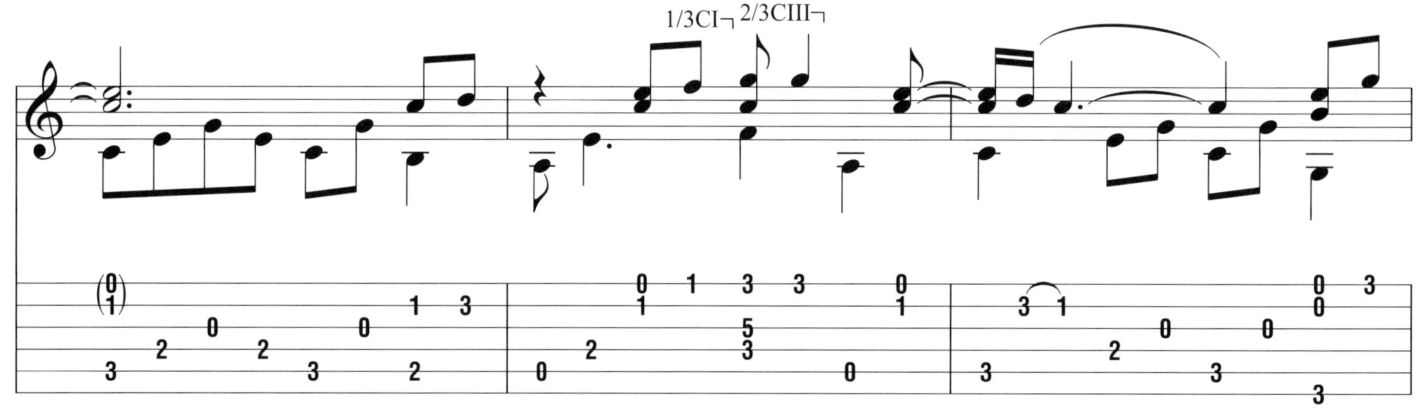

1/3CI 2/3CIII

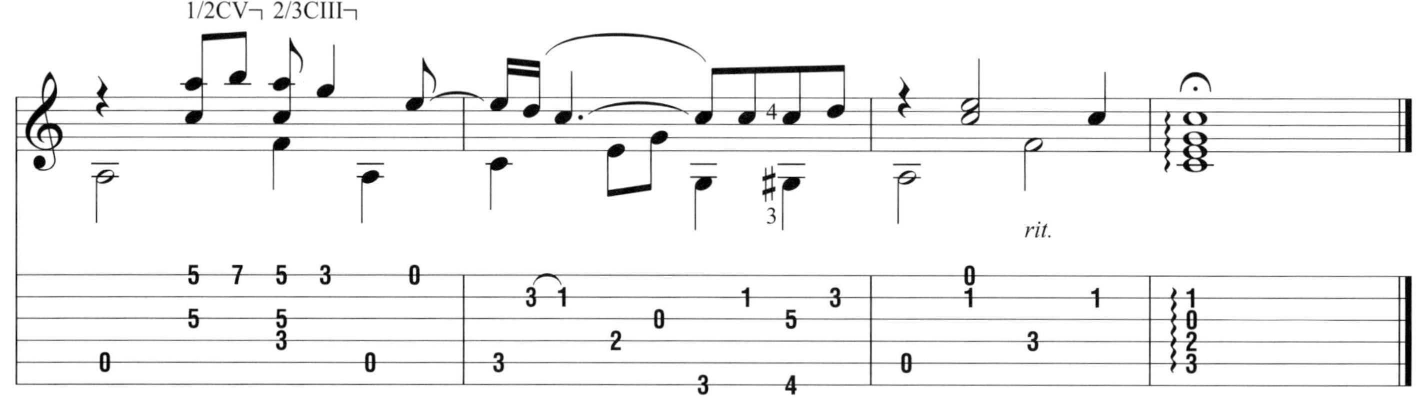

1/2CV 2/3CIII
rit.

When I Was Your Man

Words and Music by Bruno Mars, Ari Levine, Philip Lawrence and Andrew Wyatt

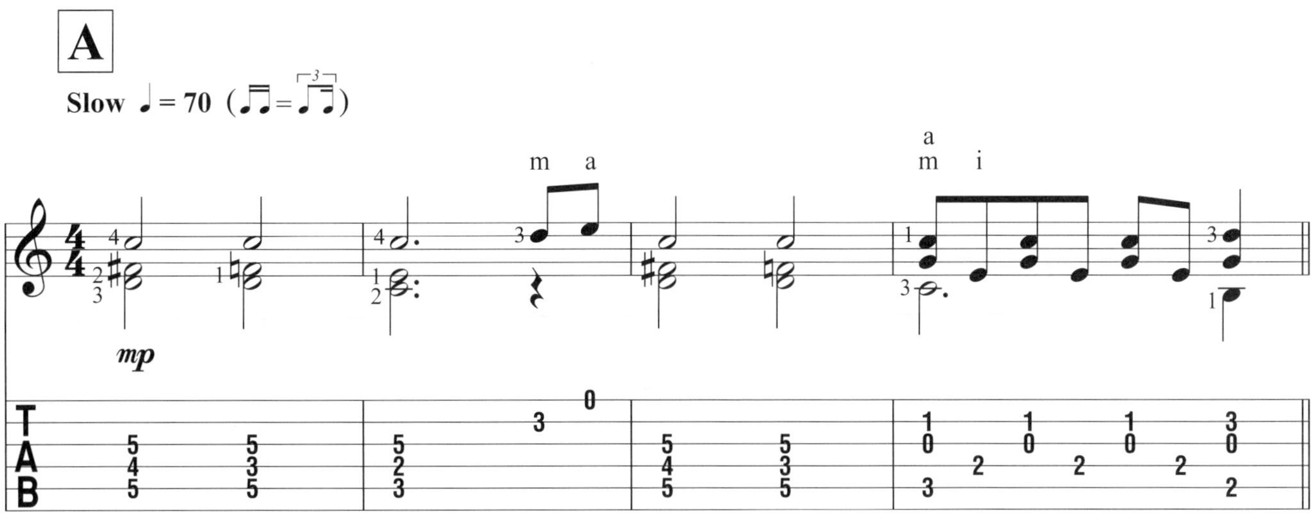

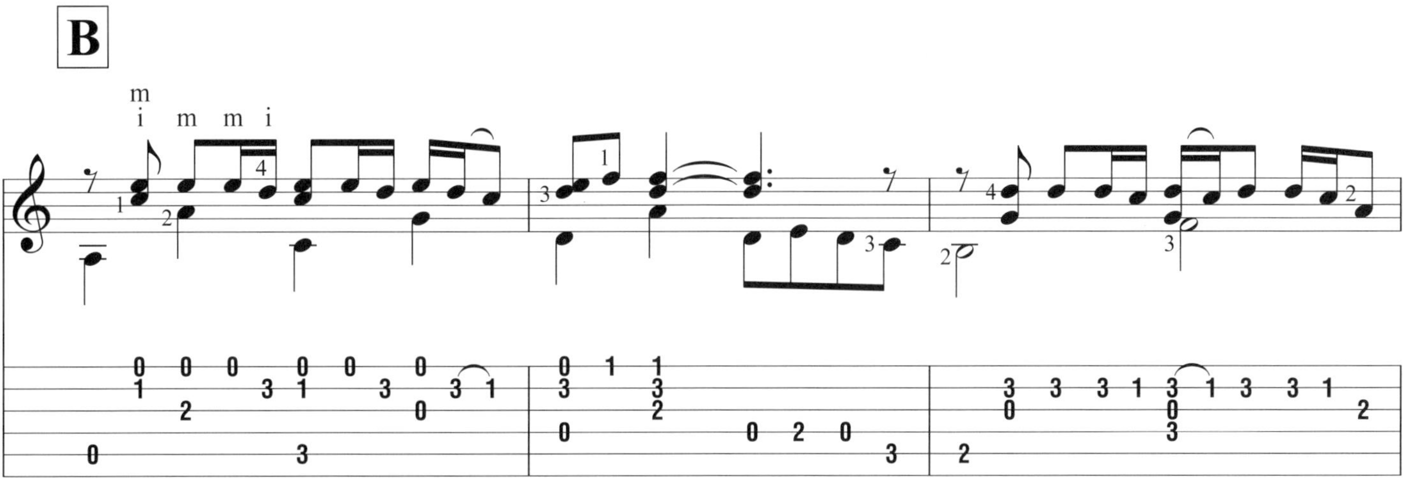

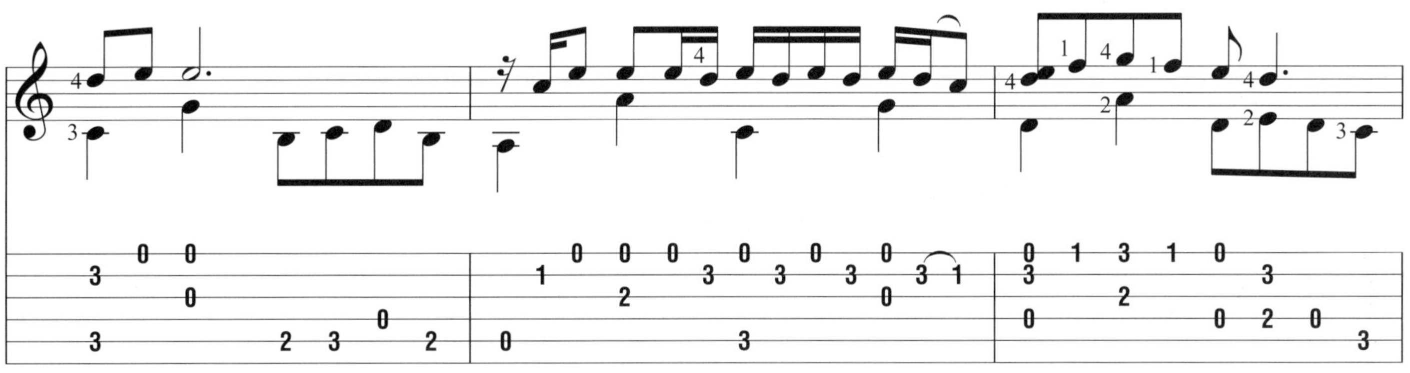

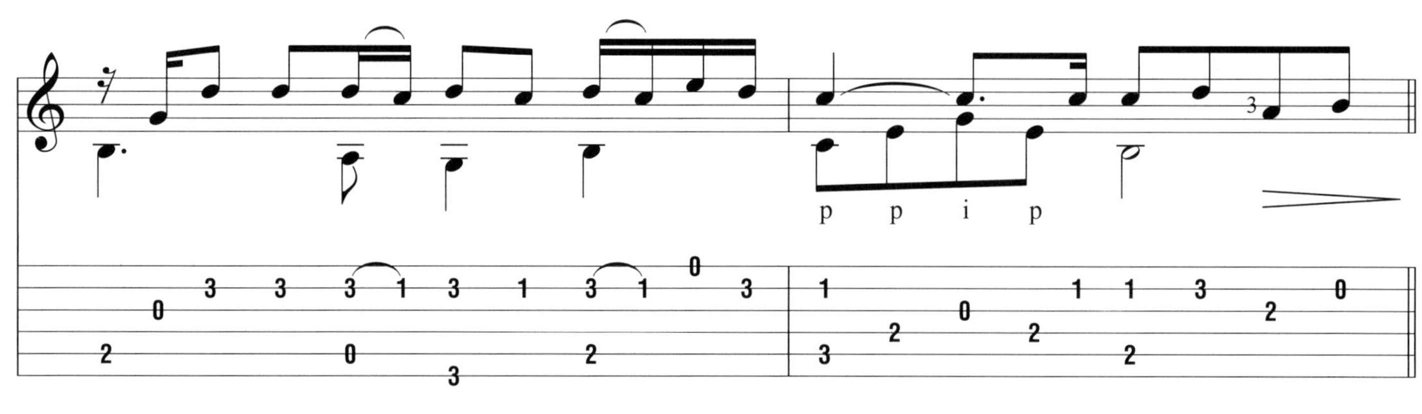
p p i p

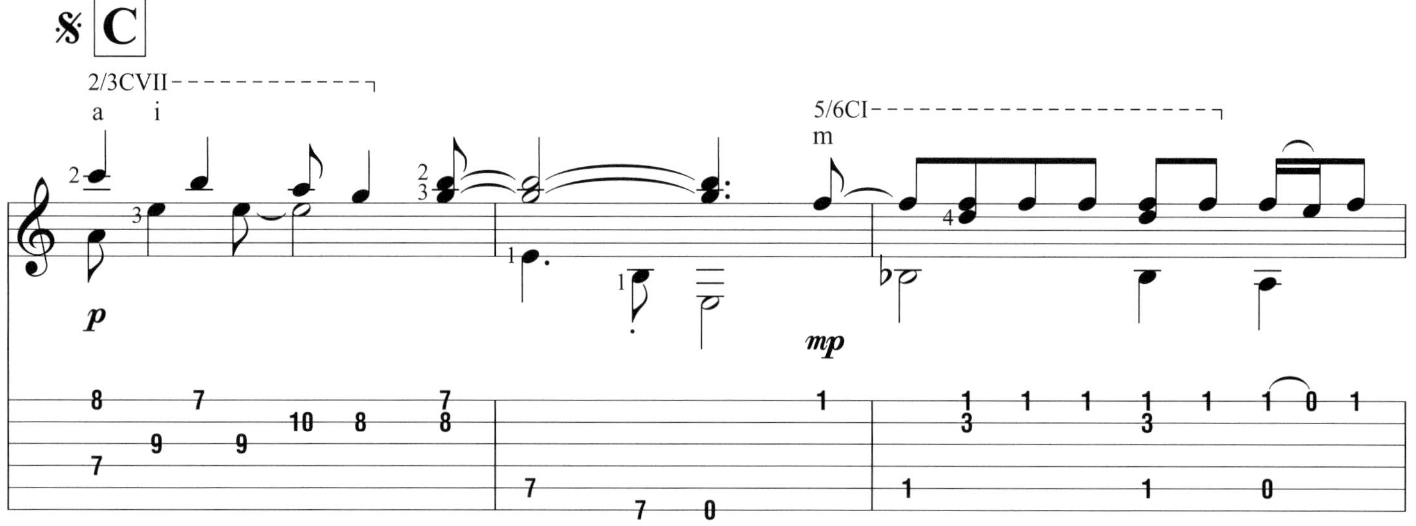
C
2/3CVII
a i
5/6CI
m
p
mp

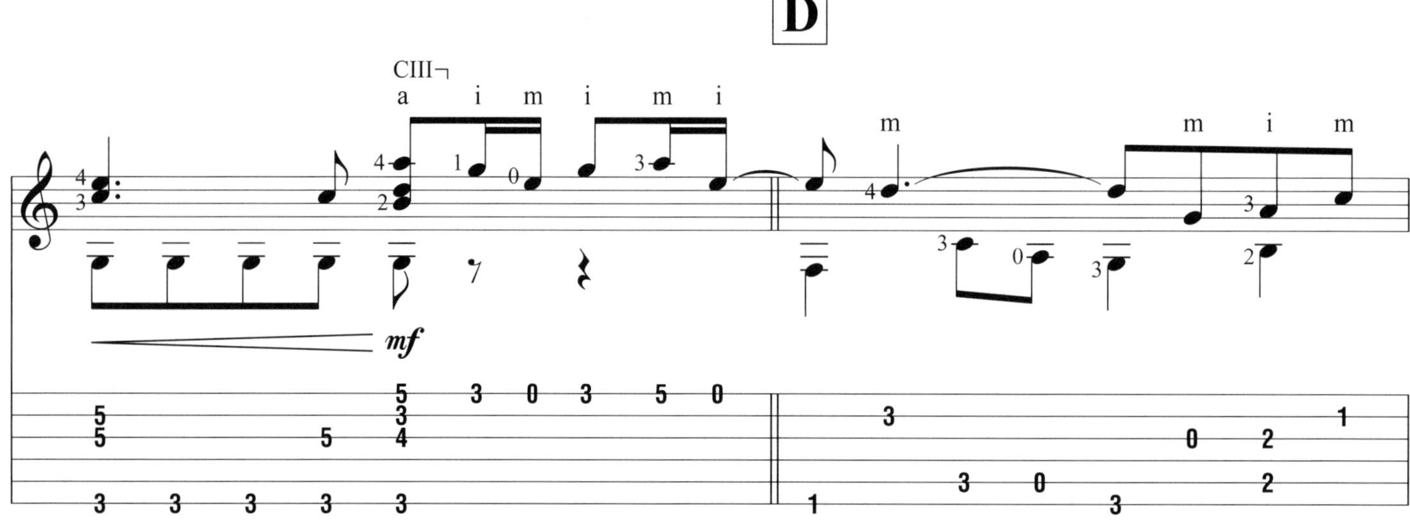
D
CIII
a i m i m i
m
m i m
mf

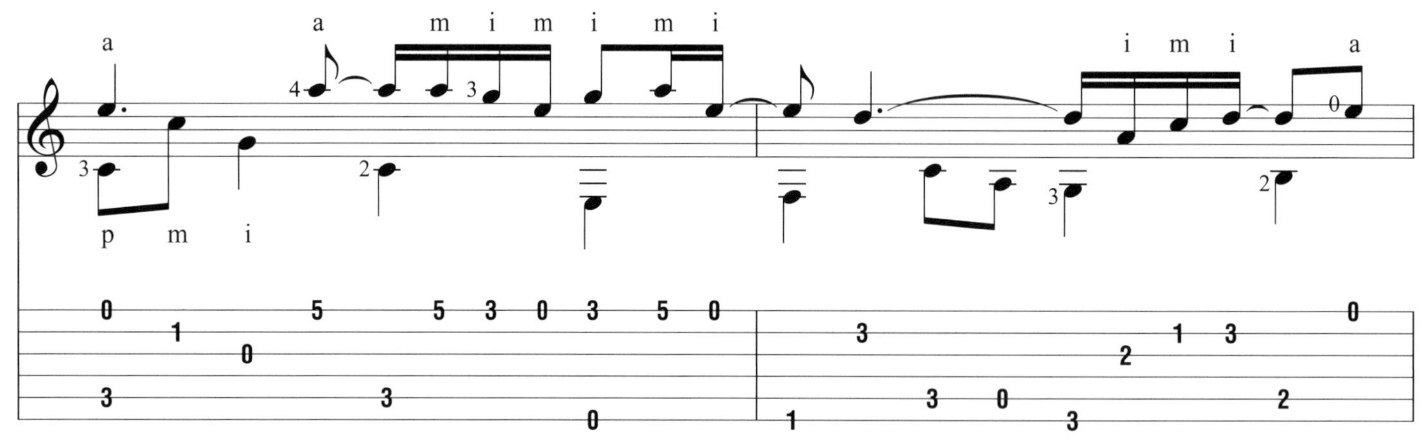
a
a m i m i m i
i m i a
p m i

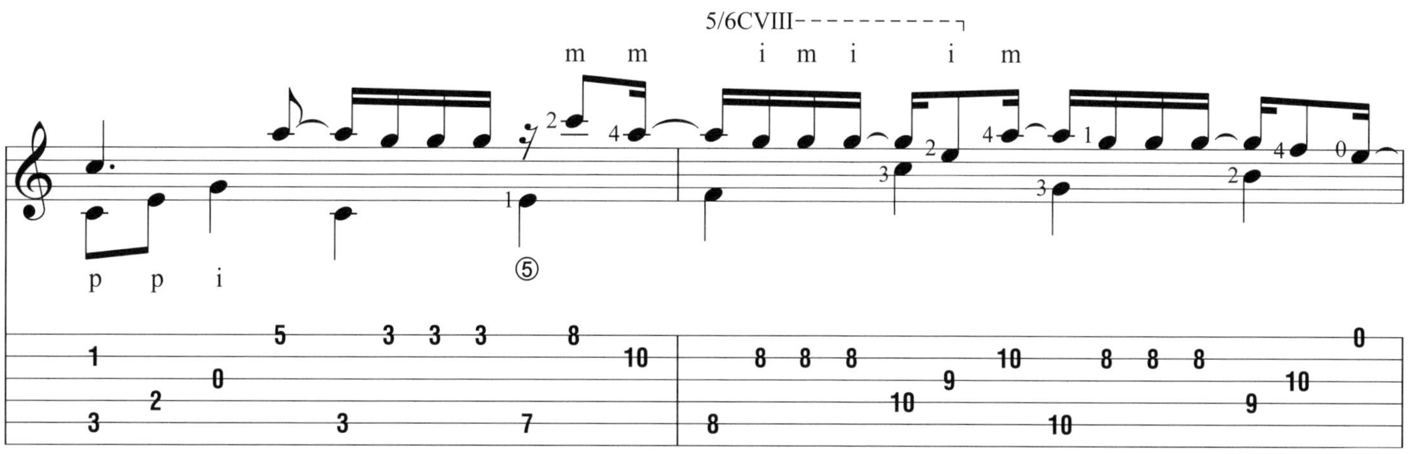
5/6CVIII

To Coda

CI

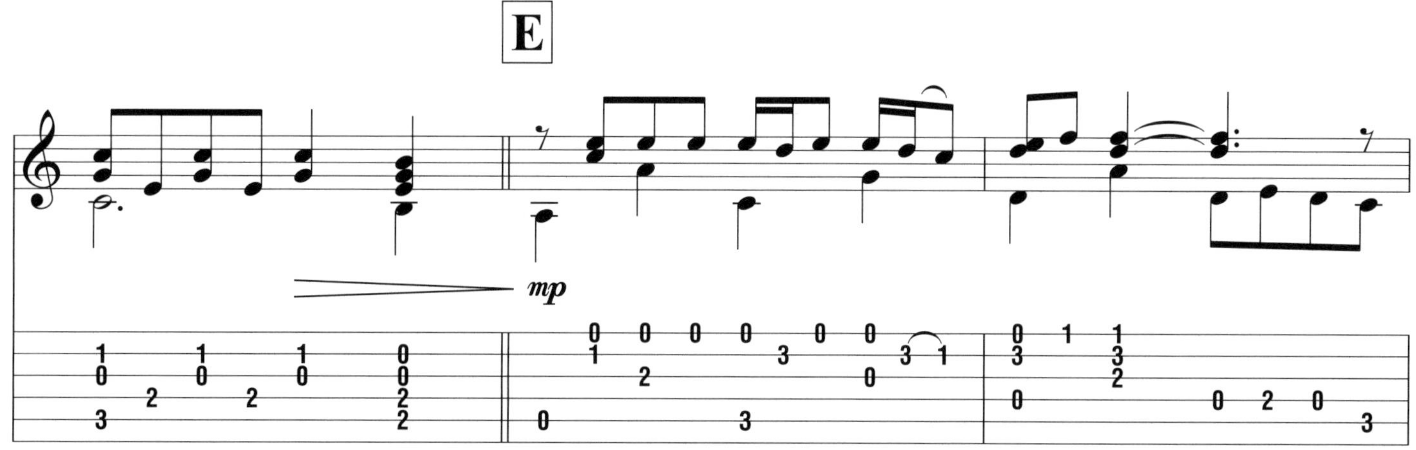
E
mp

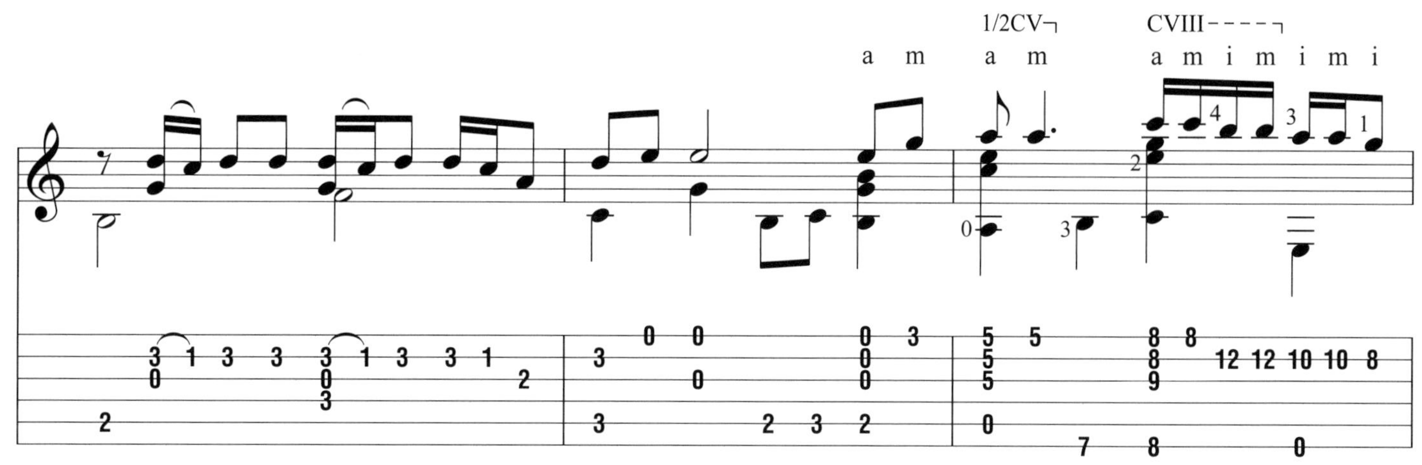
1/2CV
CVIII

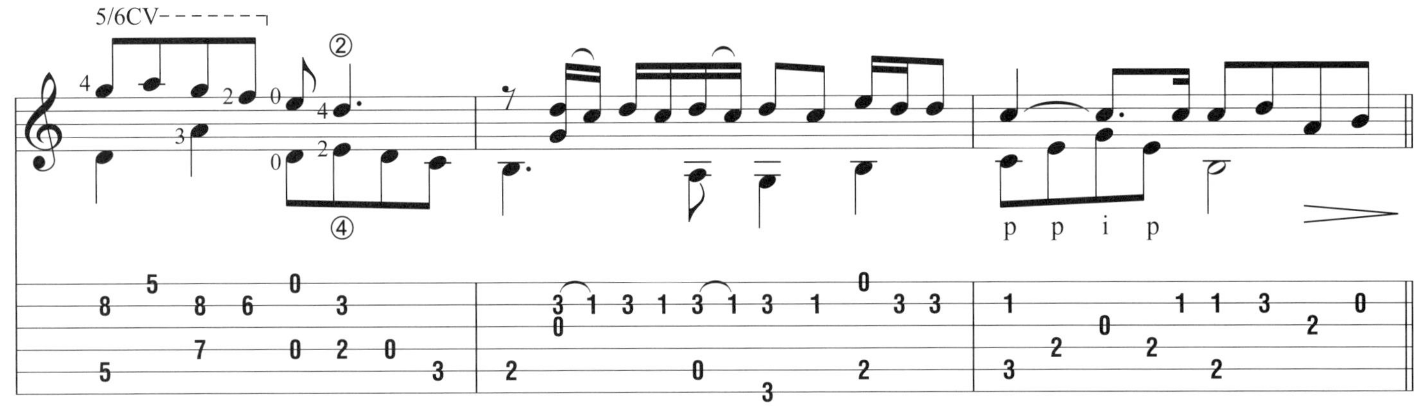
5/6CV
p p i p

Coda

F

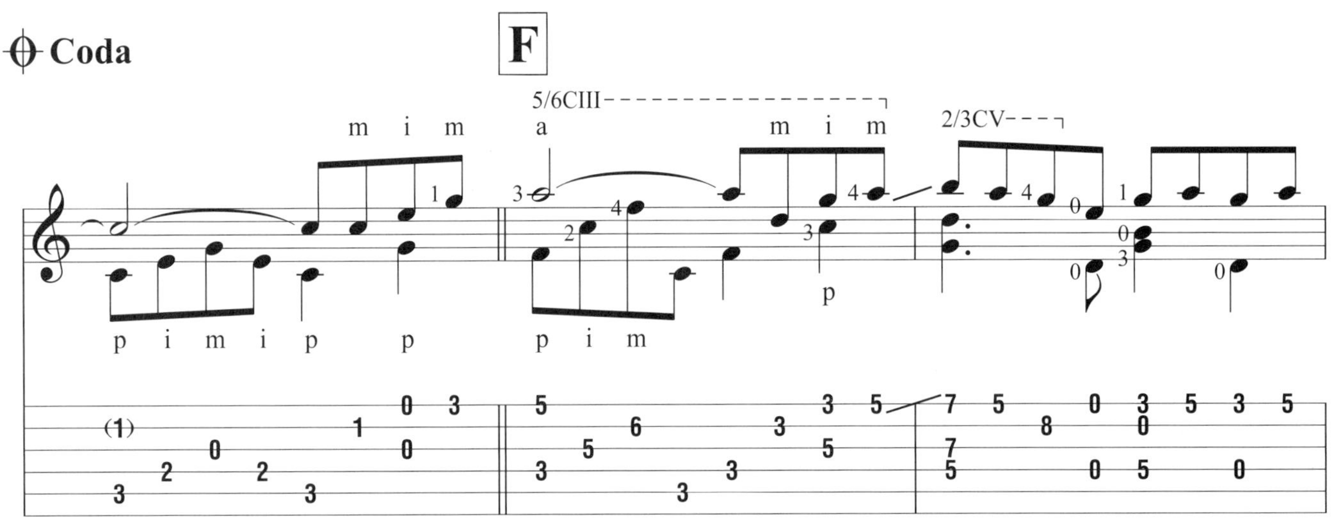
5/6CIII
2/3CV
m i m
a
m i m
p i m i p p
p i m
p

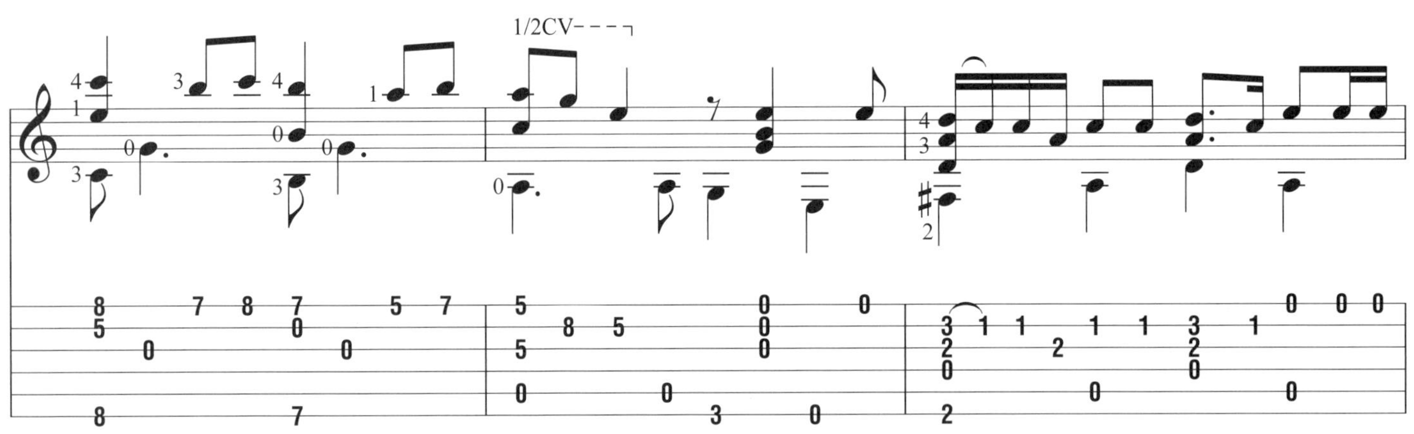
1/2CV

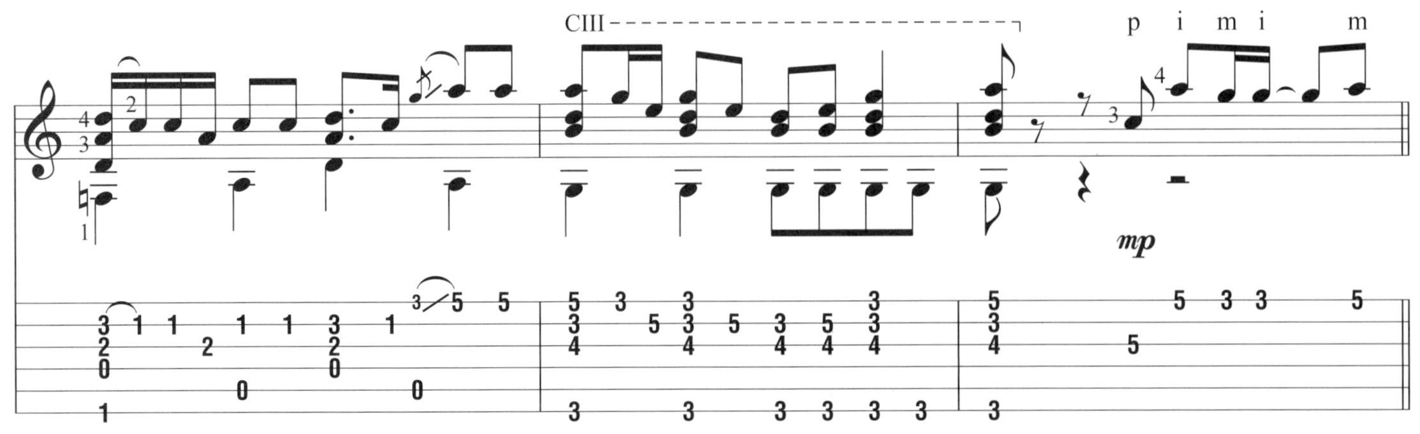
CIII
p i m i m
mp

G

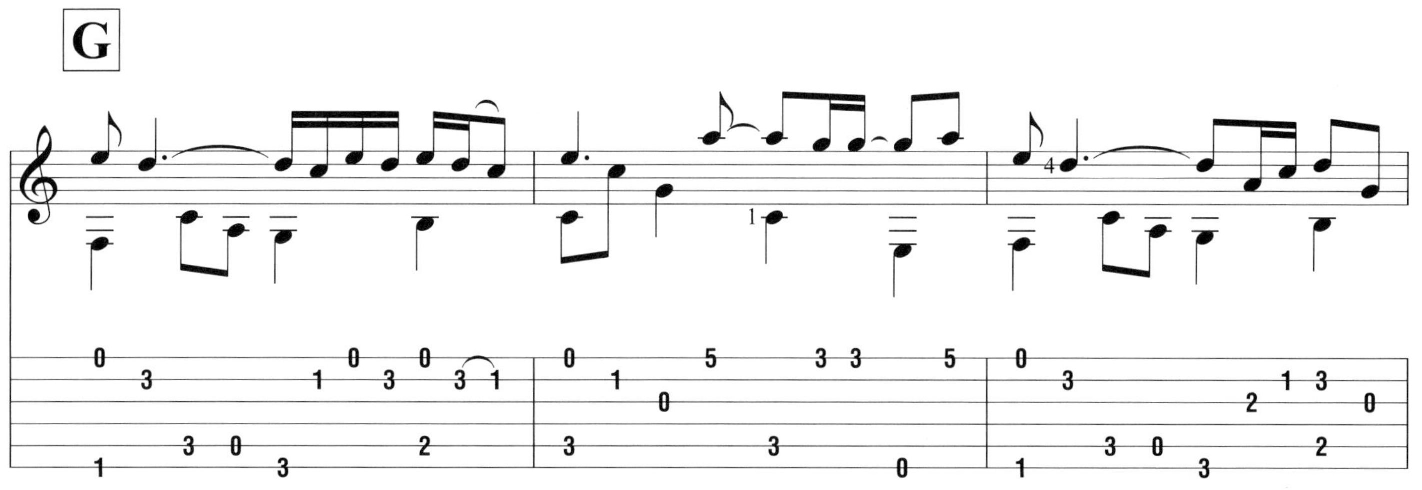

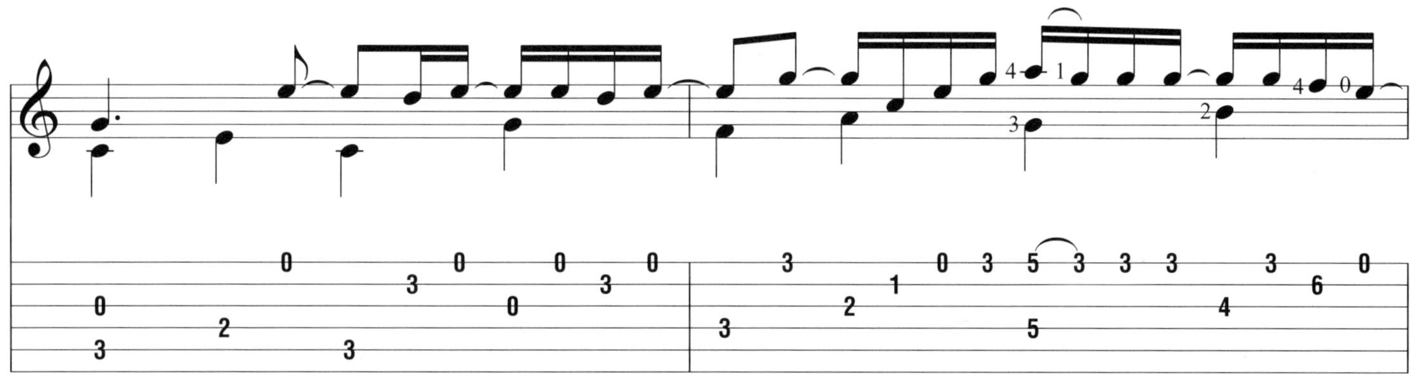

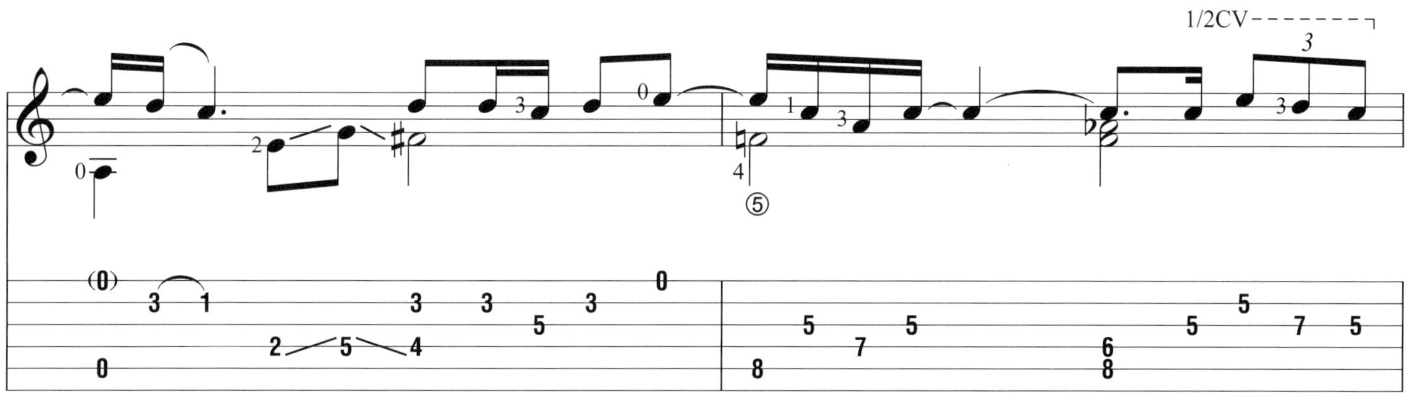

You Say

Words and Music by Lauren Daigle, Jason Ingram and Paul Mabury

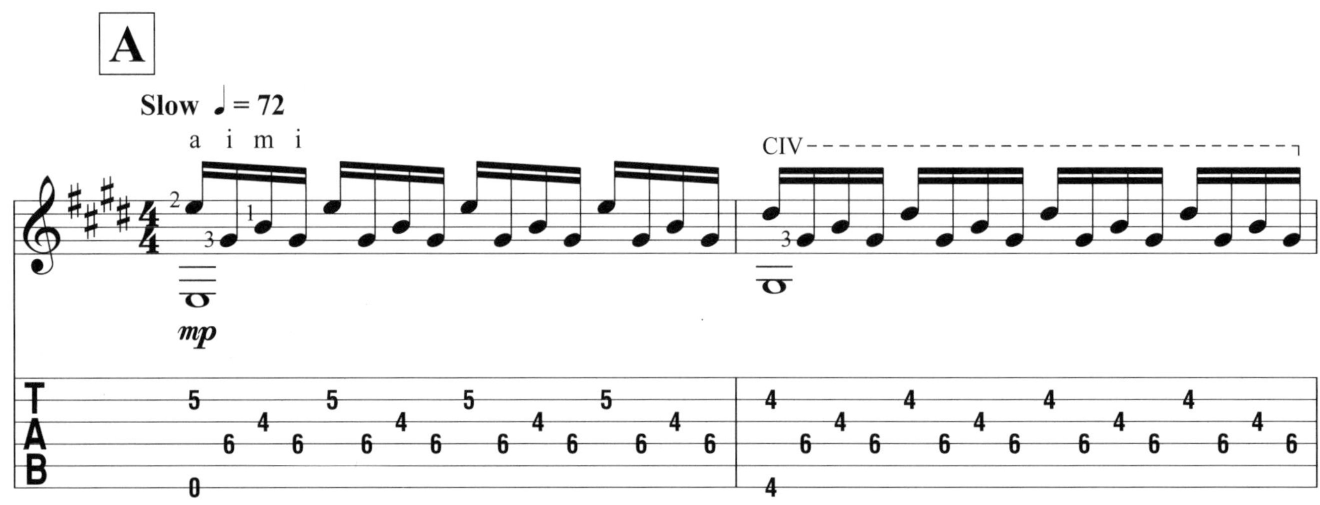

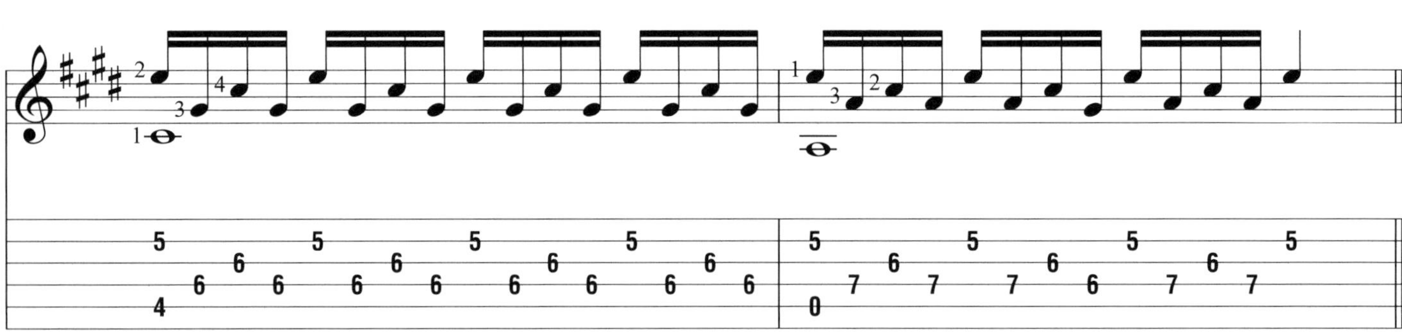

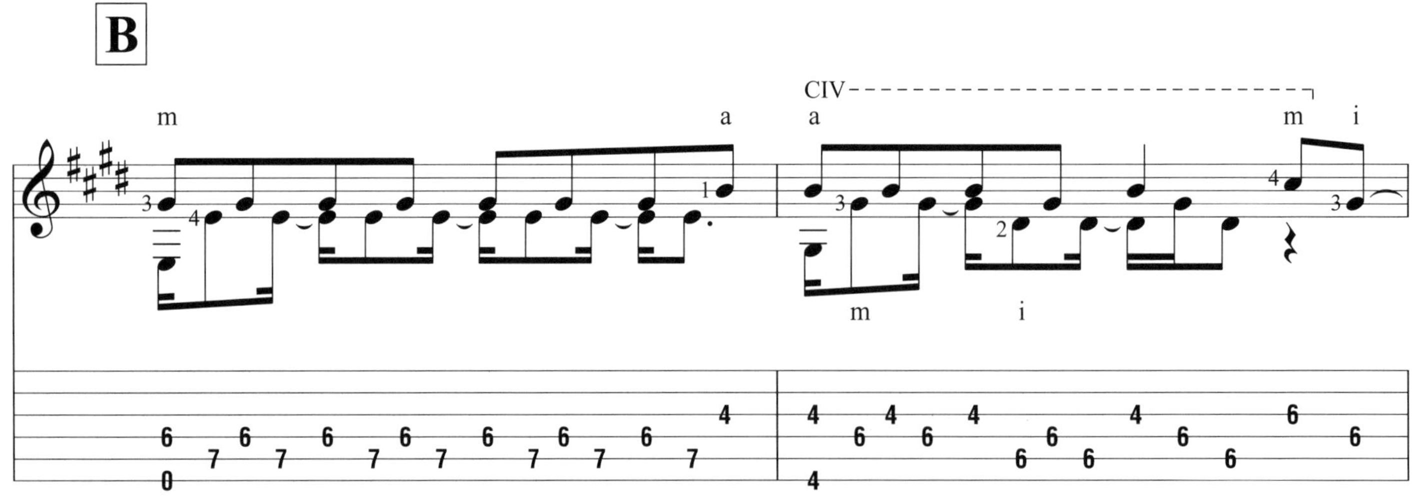

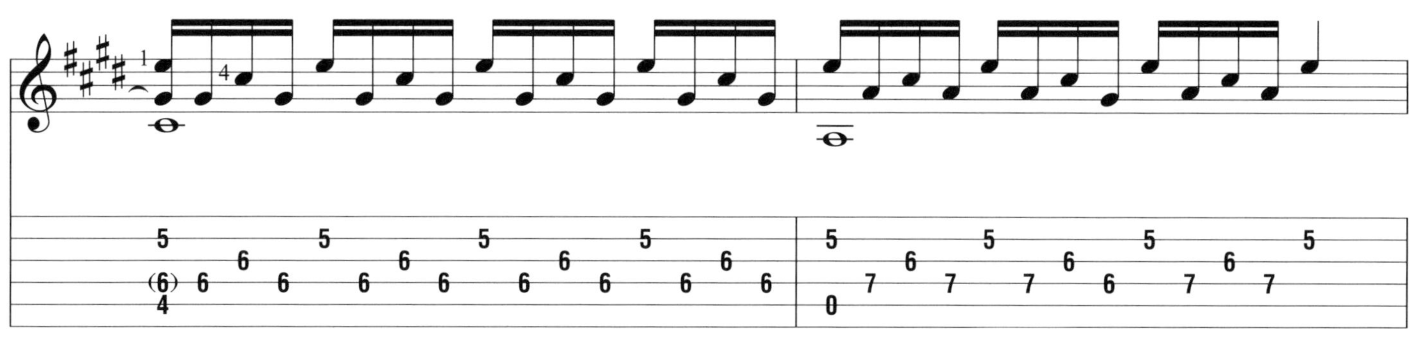

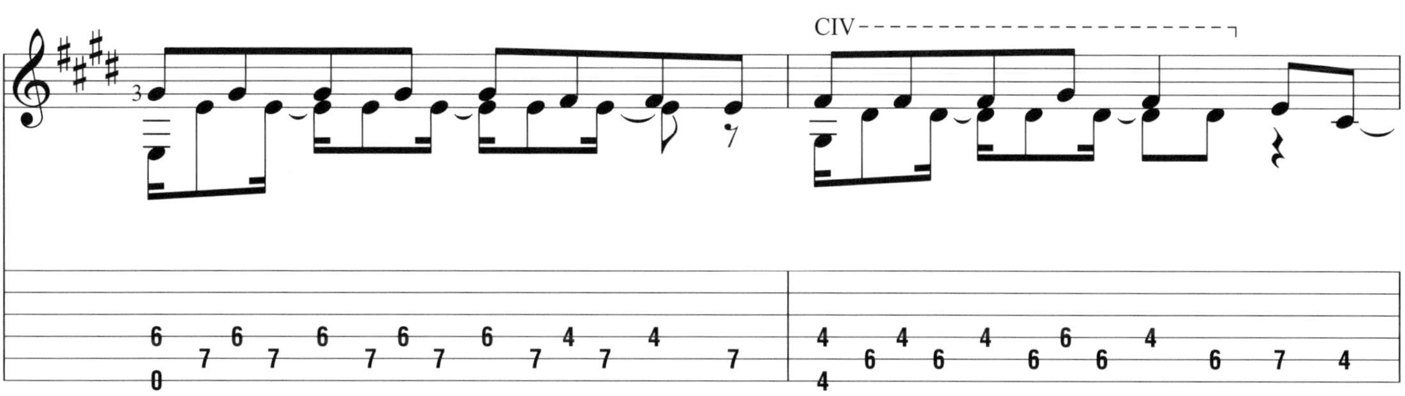

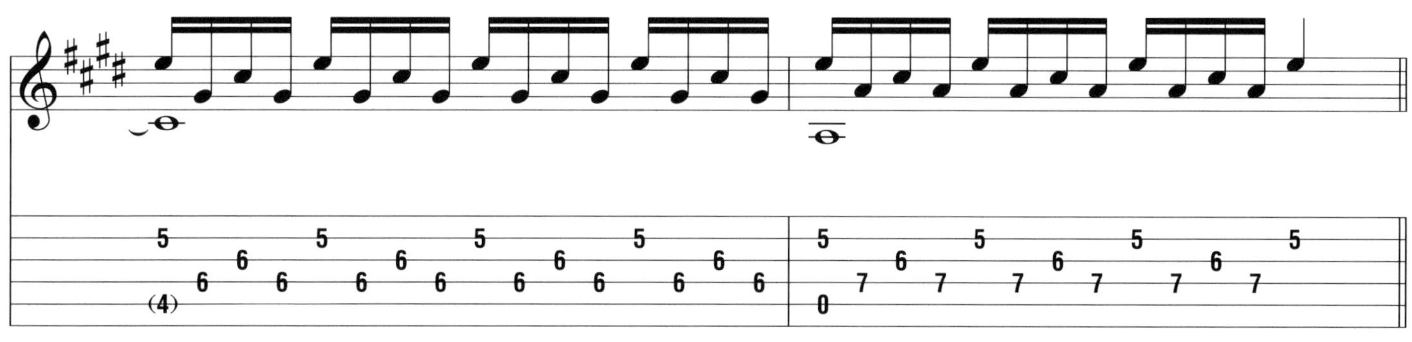

C

2nd time, a tempo

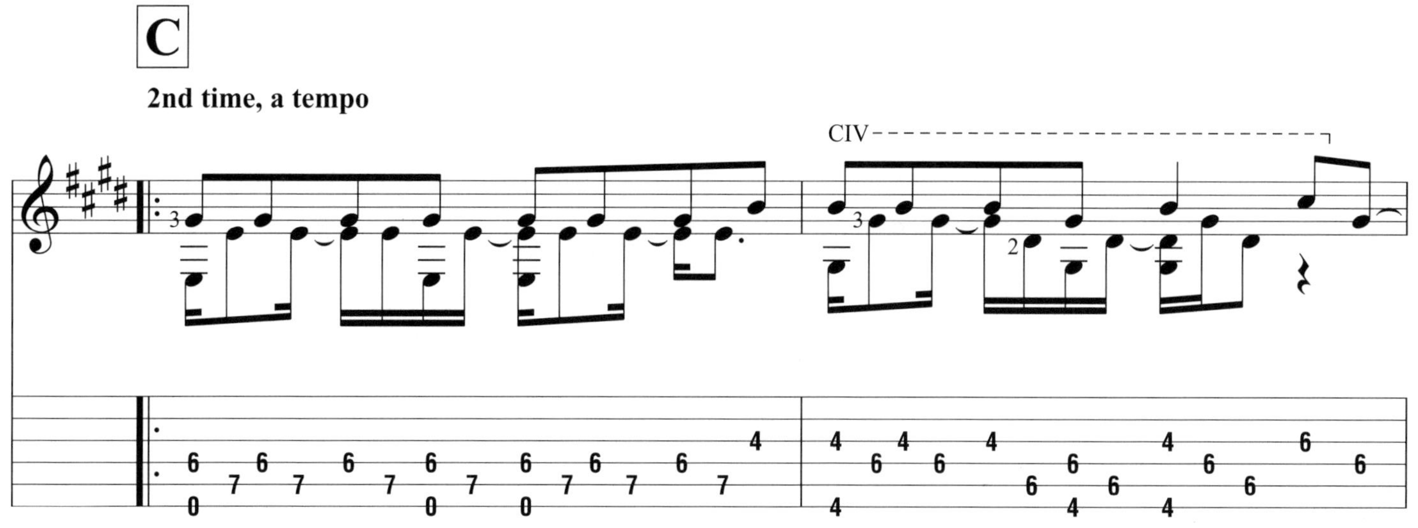

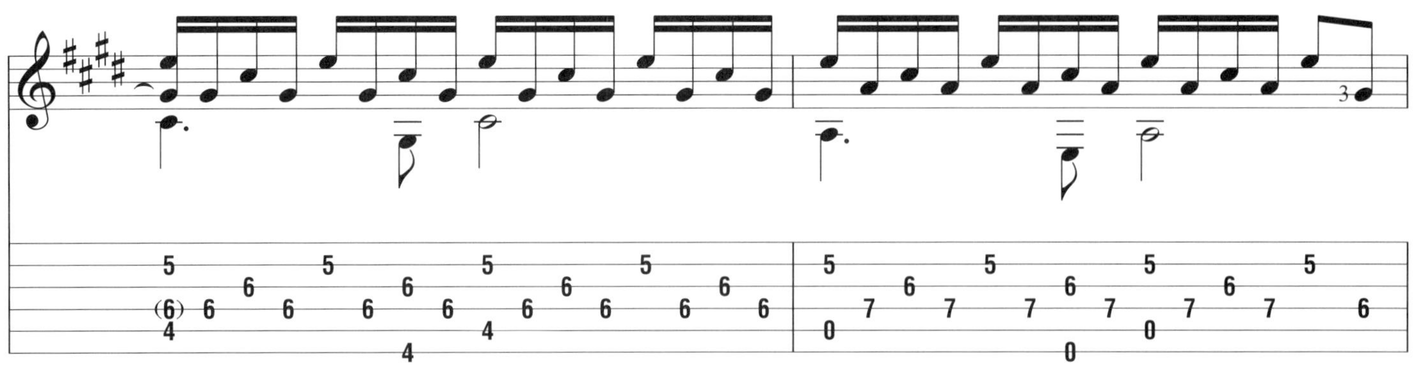

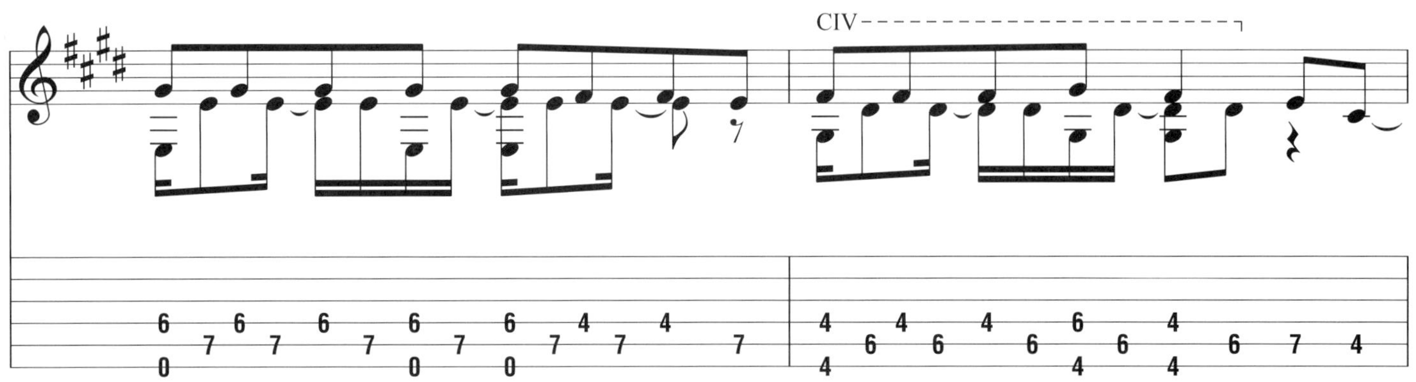
CIV

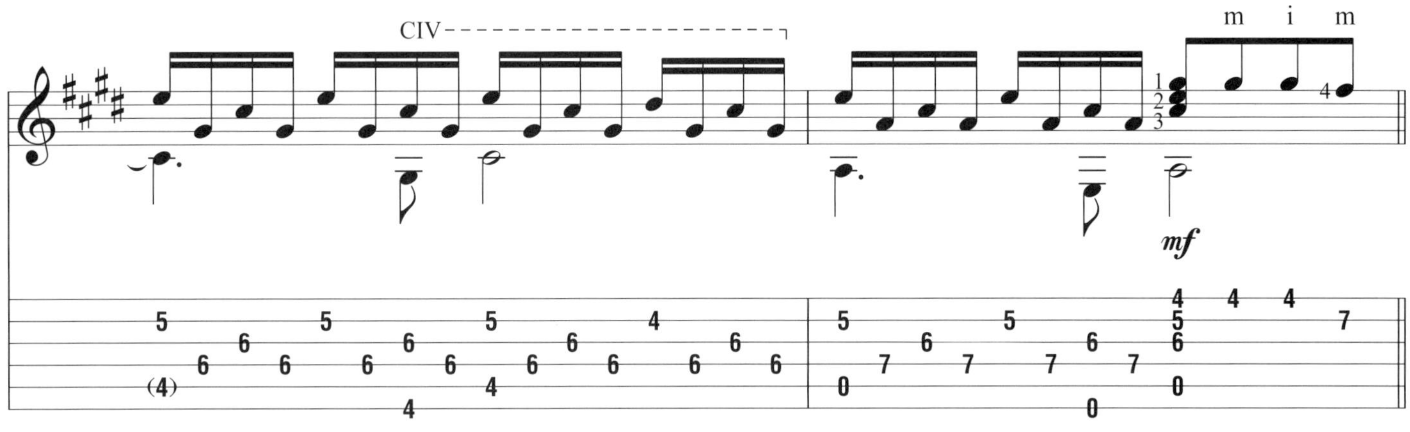
CIV
m i m
mf

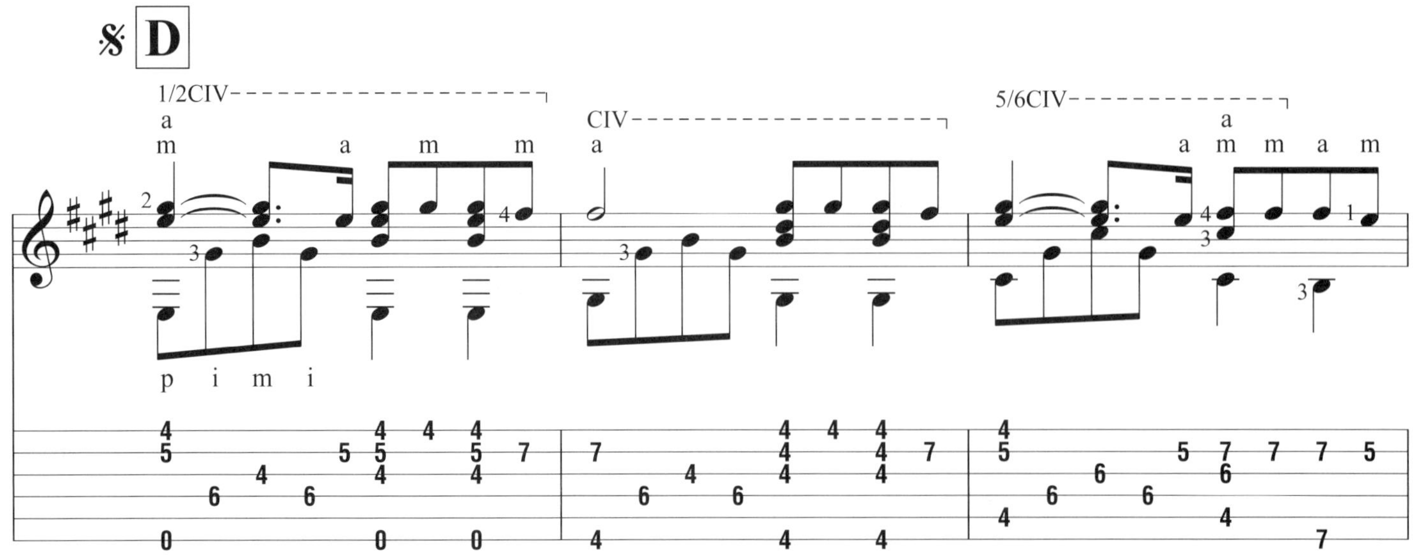
D
1/2CIV
a
m a m m
p i m i
CIV
a
5/6CIV
a
a m m a m

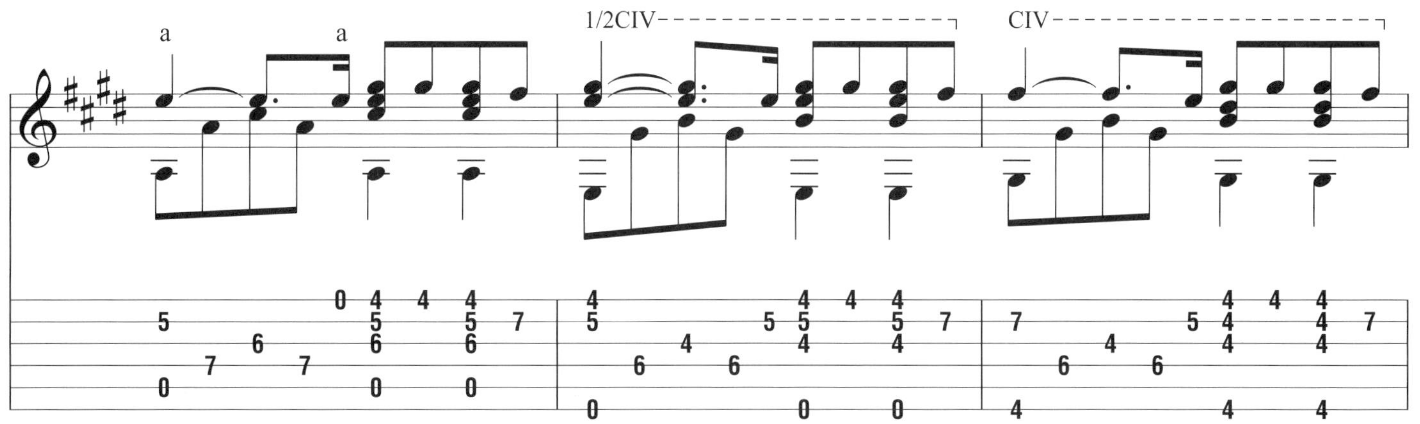
a
a
1/2CIV
CIV

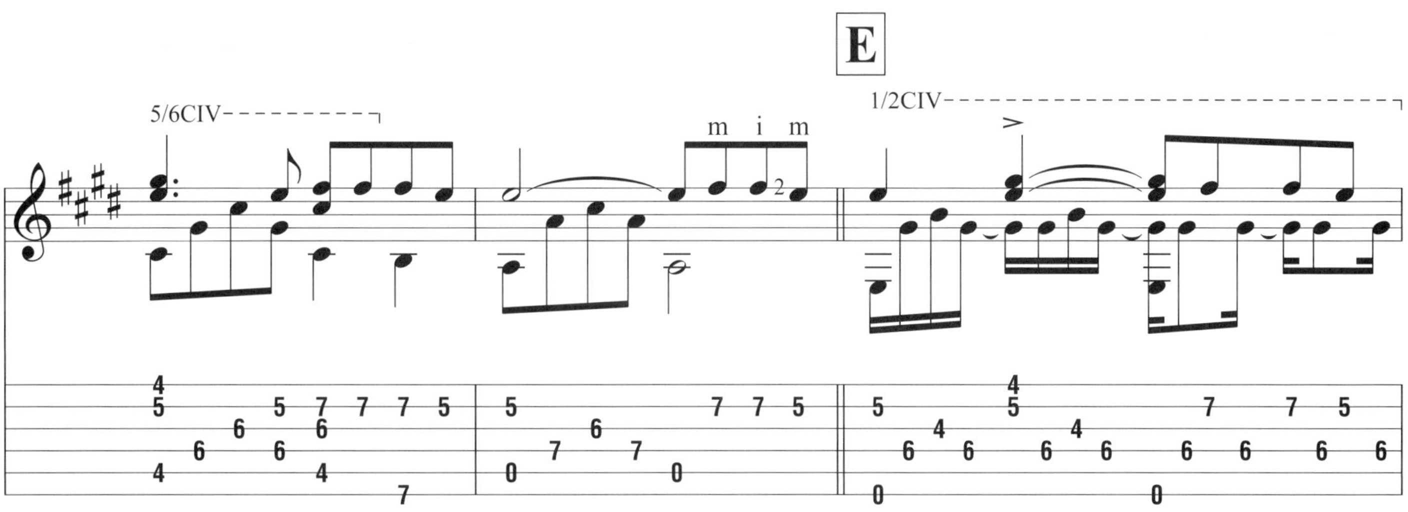
E
5/6CIV
m i m
1/2CIV

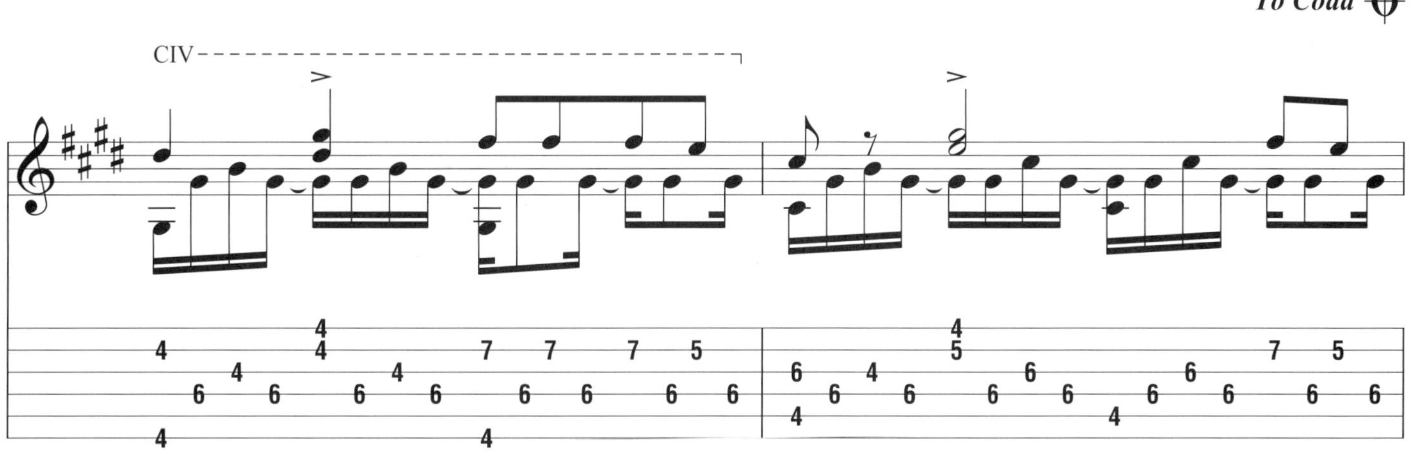
To Coda
CIV

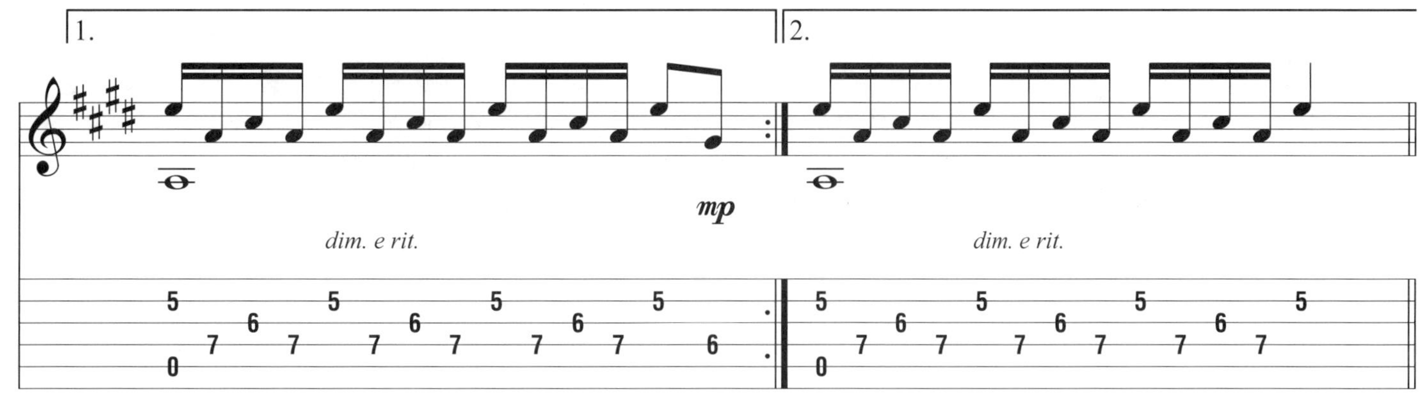
1.
2.
mp
dim. e rit.
dim. e rit.

F

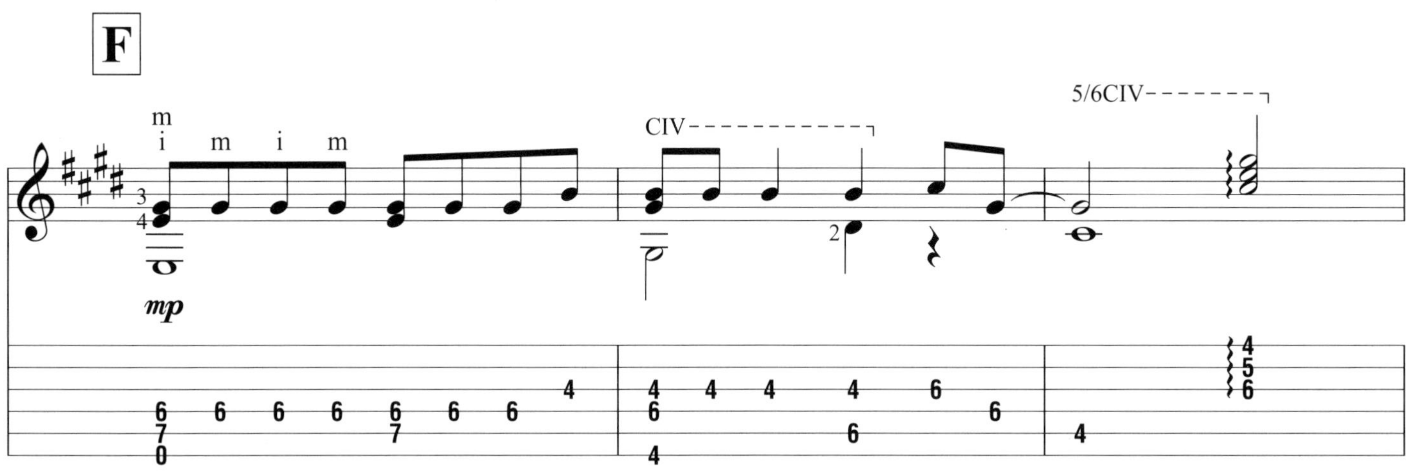

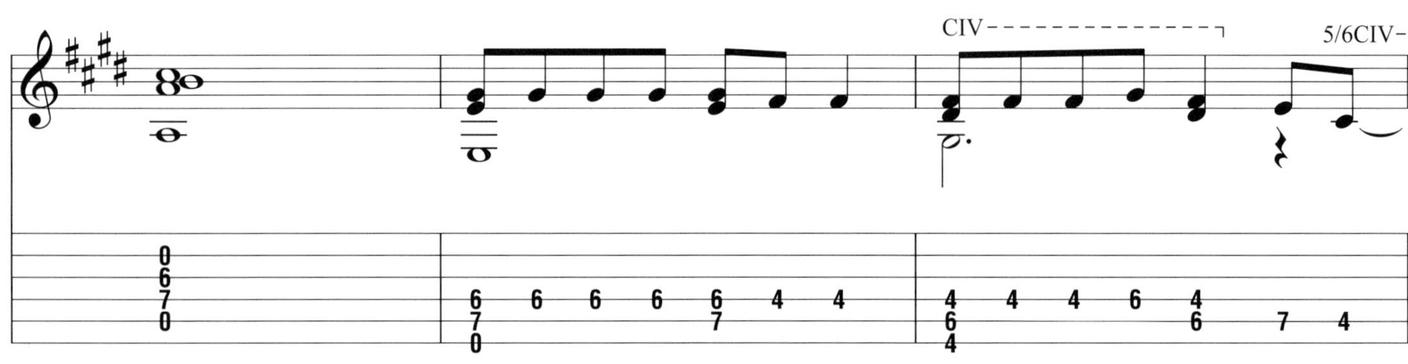

D.S. al Coda

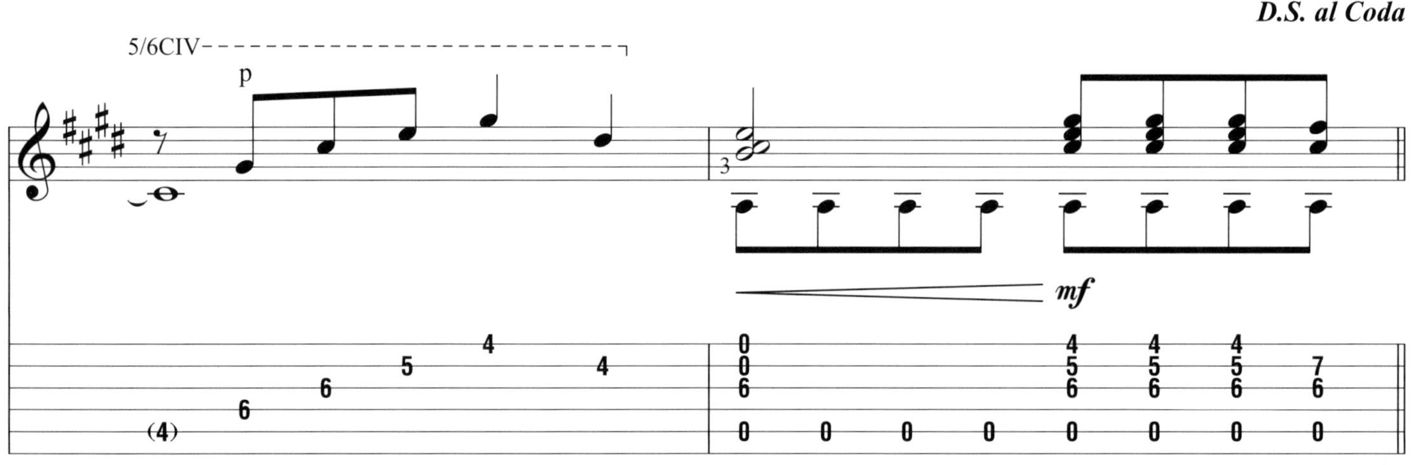

Coda

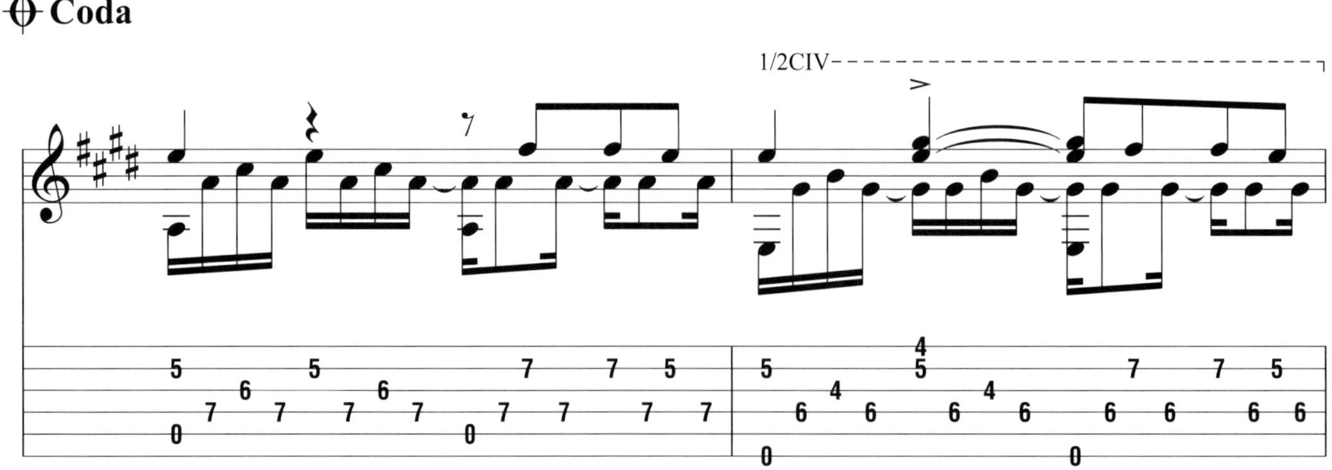

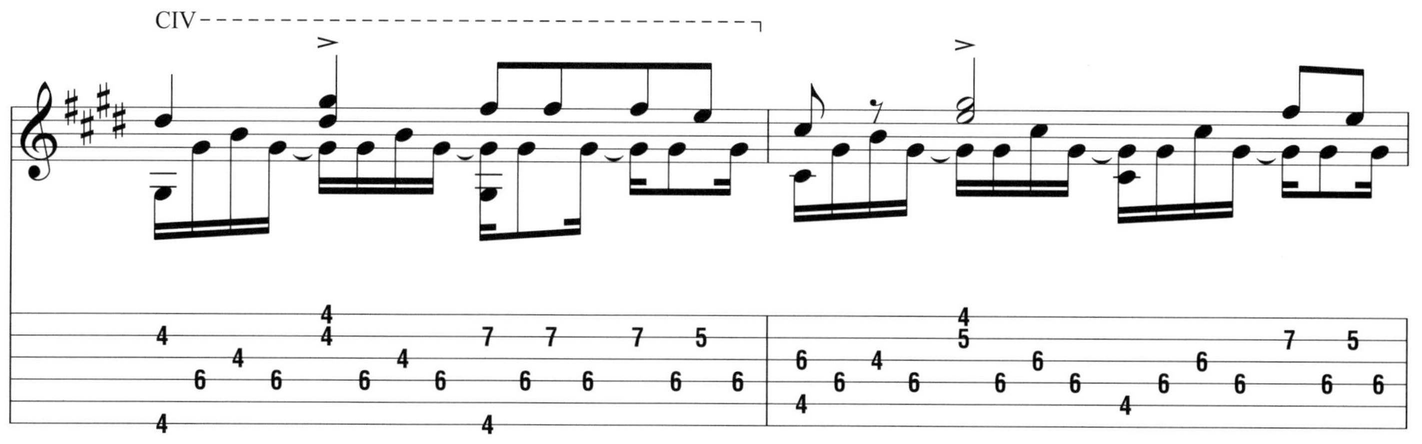
CIV

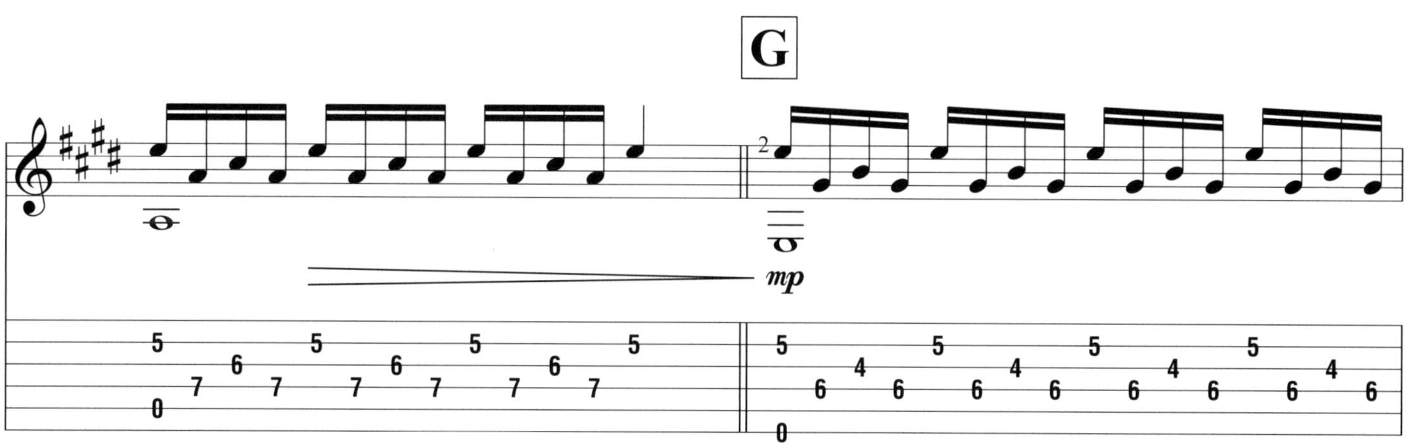
G
mp

CIV

rit.

CLASSICAL GUITAR

PUBLICATIONS FROM HAL LEONARD

THE BEATLES FOR CLASSICAL GUITAR

Includes 20 solos from big Beatles hits arranged for classical guitar, complete with left-hand and right-hand fingering. Songs include: All My Loving • And I Love Her • Can't Buy Me Love • Fool on the Hill • From a Window • Hey Jude • If I Fell • Let It Be • Michelle • Norwegian Wood • Obla Di • Ticket to Ride • Yesterday • and more. Features arrangements and an introduction by Joe Washington, as well as his helpful hints on classical technique and detailed notes on how to play each song. The book also covers parts and specifications of the classical guitar, tuning, and Joe's "Strata System" – an easy-reading system applied to chord diagrams.

00699237 Classical Guitar $19.99

CZERNY FOR GUITAR

INCLUDES TAB

12 Scale Studies for Classical Guitar

by David Patterson

Adapted from Carl Czerny's *School of Velocity, Op. 299* for piano, this lesson book explores 12 keys with 12 different approaches or "treatments." You will explore a variety of articulations, ranges and technical perspectives as you learn each key. These arrangements will not only improve your ability to play scales fluently, but will also develop your ears, knowledge of the fingerboard, reading abilities, strength and endurance. In standard notation and tablature.

00701248 ....$9.99

MATTEO CARCASSI – 25 MELODIC AND PROGRESSIVE STUDIES, OP. 60

arr. Paul Henry

One of Carcassi's (1792-1853) most famous collections of classical guitar music – indispensable for the modern guitarist's musical and technical development. Performed by Paul Henry. 49-minute audio accompaniment.

00696506 Book/Online Audio $17.99

CLASSICAL & FINGERSTYLE GUITAR TECHNIQUES

by David Oakes • Musicians Institute

This Master Class is aimed at any electric or acoustic guitarist who wants a quick, thorough grounding in the essentials of classical and fingerstyle technique. Topics covered include: arpeggios and scales, free stroke and rest stroke, P-i scale technique, three-to-a-string patterns, natural and artificial harmonics, tremolo and rasgueado, and more. The book includes 12 intensive lessons for right and left hand in standard notation & tab, and the audio features 92 solo acoustic tracks.

00695171 Book/Online Audio $17.99

CLASSICAL GUITAR CHRISTMAS COLLECTION

INCLUDES TAB

Includes classical guitar arrangements in standard notation and tablature for more than two dozen beloved carols: Angels We Have Heard on High • Auld Lang Syne • Ave Maria • Away in a Manger • Canon in D • The First Noel • God Rest Ye Merry, Gentlemen • Hark! the Herald Angels Sing • I Saw Three Ships • Jesu, Joy of Man's Desiring • Joy to the World • O Christmas Tree • O Holy Night • Silent Night • What Child Is This? • and more.

00699493 Guitar Solo..$10.99

CLASSICAL GUITAR WEDDING

INCLUDES TAB

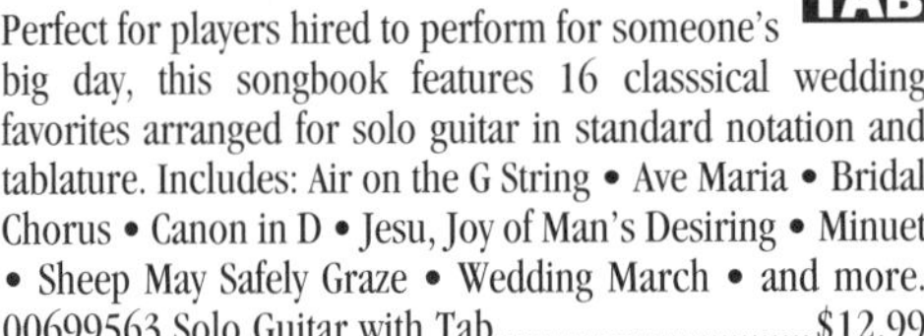

Perfect for players hired to perform for someone's big day, this songbook features 16 classsical wedding favorites arranged for solo guitar in standard notation and tablature. Includes: Air on the G String • Ave Maria • Bridal Chorus • Canon in D • Jesu, Joy of Man's Desiring • Minuet • Sheep May Safely Graze • Wedding March • and more.

00699563 Solo Guitar with Tab..............................$12.99

CLASSICAL MASTERPIECES FOR GUITAR

27 works by Bach, Beethoven, Handel, Mendelssohn, Mozart and more transcribed with standard notation and tablature. Now anyone can enjoy classical material regardless of their guitar background. Also features stay-open binding.

00699312 ....$14.99

MASTERWORKS FOR GUITAR

Over 60 Favorites from Four Centuries
World's Great Classical Music

Dozens of classical masterpieces: Allemande • Bourree • Canon in D • Jesu, Joy of Man's Desiring • Lagrima • Malaguena • Mazurka • Piano Sonata No. 14 in C# Minor (Moonlight) Op. 27 No. 2 First Movement Theme • Ode to Joy • Prelude No. I (Well-Tempered Clavier).

00699503 ....$19.99

HAL•LEONARD®

Visit Hal Leonard Online at **www.halleonard.com**

A MODERN APPROACH TO CLASSICAL GUITAR

by Charles Duncan

This multi-volume method was developed to allow students to study the art of classical guitar within a new, more contemporary framework. For private, class or self-instruction. Book One incorporates chord frames and symbols, as well as a recording to assist in tuning and to provide accompaniments for at-home practice. Book One also introduces beginning fingerboard technique and music theory. Book Two and Three build upon the techniques learned in Book One.

00695114 Book 1 – Book Only.............................$6.99
00695113 Book 1 – Book/Online Audio...............$10.99
00695116 Book 2 – Book Only.............................$6.99
00695115 Book 2 – Book/Online Audio...............$10.99
00699202 Book 3 – Book Only.............................$9.99
00695117 Book 3 – Book/Online Audio...............$12.99
00695119 Composite Book/CD Pack $29.99

ANDRES SEGOVIA – 20 STUDIES FOR GUITAR

Sor/Segovia

20 studies for the classical guitar written by Beethoven's contemporary, Fernando Sor, revised, edited and fingered by the great classical guitarist Andres Segovia. These essential repertoire pieces continue to be used by teachers and students to build solid classical technique. Features 50-minute demonstration audio.

00695012 Book/Online Audio $19.99
00006363 Book Only..$7.99

THE FRANCISCO TÁRREGA COLLECTION

edited and performed by Paul Henry

Considered the father of modern classical guitar, Francisco Tárrega revolutionized guitar technique and composed a wealth of music that will be a cornerstone of classical guitar repertoire for centuries to come. This unique book/audio pack features 14 of his most outstanding pieces in standard notation and tab, edited and performed by virtuoso Paul Henry. Includes: Adelita • Capricho Árabe • Estudio Brillante • Grand Jota • Lágrima • Malagueña • María • Recuerdos de la Alhambra • Tango • and more, plus bios of Tárrega and Henry.

00698993 Book/Online Audio $19.99

0719
005